THE NEW
ORNAMENTAL GARDEN

Dedication

For Clive, who taught me to garden.

THE NEW
ORNAMENTAL
GARDEN

SIMON RICKARD

CSIRO
PUBLISHING

CSIRO PUBLISHING GARDENING GUIDES

National Library of Australia Cataloguing-in-Publication entry

Rickard, Simon.

The new ornamental garden/by Simon Rickard.

9780643095960 (pbk.)
9780643101760 (epdf)
9780643102293 (epub)

Includes bibliographical references and index.

Gardening – Australia.
Plants – Australia.

635.90994

CSIRO PUBLISHING
150 Oxford Street (PO Box 1139)
Collingwood VIC 3066
Australia

Telephone: +61 3 9662 7666
Local call: 1300 788 000 (Australia only)
Fax: +61 3 9662 7555
Email: publishing.sales@csiro.au
Web site: www.publish.csiro.au

All photographs are by the author.

Set in 10.5/14 Adobe ITC New Baskerville
Edited by Janet Walker
Cover and text design by James Kelly
Typeset by Desktop Concepts Pty Ltd, Melbourne
Printed in China by 1010 Printing International Limited

CSIRO PUBLISHING publishes and distributes scientific, technical and health science books, magazines and journals from Australia to a worldwide audience and conducts these activities autonomously from the research activities of the Commonwealth Scientific and Industrial Research Organisation (CSIRO).

The views expressed in this publication are those of the author(s) and do not necessarily represent those of, and should not be attributed to, the publisher or CSIRO.

Original print edition:
The paper this book is printed on is certified against the Forest Stewardship Council® (FSC®) 1996 FSC® A.C Standards. The FSC® promotes environmentally responsible, socially beneficial and economically viable management of the world's forests.

CONTENTS

FOREWORD

It is well and truly time that an experienced Australian gardener produced a book that not only says it as it is but is willing to question all those old chestnuts and one-liners that have been pumped out by successive garden writers.

Here, joy of joys, this is all done successfully in an entertaining and beautifully written way that is sure to engage the reader as soon as the cover is opened.

The questions posed (both big and small) and the answers given in Simon's book will, no doubt, have some people reeling, but I found myself cheering, thinking that I wished I'd got it all down on paper first!

As if all this isn't enough, the pictures are a delight and genuinely enhance the whole book, demonstrating the points being made perfectly. They aren't used to hide any deficiencies in the written word, as so many titles seem to do these days. The text sparkles every bit as brilliantly as the images.

Stephen Ryan
Host of ABC TV's *Gardening Australia*

ABOUT THE AUTHOR

Simon Rickard is a passionate gardener and plantsman. He is best known as the former head gardener of the Digger's Club, in which role he oversaw two of Australia's best-known public gardens, Heronswood and the Garden of St Erth, until 2009. More recently Simon has been a kitchen gardener, growing bespoke produce for Annie Smithers' Bistrot in Kyneton, Victoria. Simon is a botanical guide for Botanica World Discoveries, helping to bring alive the world's most beautiful and influential gardens for Australian gardeners abroad. Simon has lectured and held masterclasses for the Stephanie Alexander Kitchen Garden Foundation, the University of Melbourne and many local horticultural societies. As a garden writer he has contributed to *Your Garden* and *ABC Organic Gardener* magazines and *The Digger's Club* notes. He has made several appearances on gardening radio and television, most notably on ABC television's much-loved *Gardening Australia*.

ACKNOWLEDGEMENTS

I am indebted to many generous souls who have given freely of their time, knowledge, encouragement and opinion over the years. In particular I would like to thank Clive and Penny Blazey, founders of the Diggers Club, for giving me the opportunity to hone my gardening skills while living at Heronswood for the best part of four years; David Glenn, Marcus Ryan and Sue Rattray of Lambley Nursery for sharing their considerable expertise; Stephen Ryan of Dicksonia Rare Plants for his encouragement and for feeding my rare plant habit; Bernard and Lucy Chow of the Peony Garden for their unstinting kindness; the inimitable Dave Pomare for sharing his encyclopaedic knowledge and unbridled enthusiasm for all things horticultural, and my former colleague Andrew Carpenter for teaching me how to love plants with spikes. Last, but not least, I am indebted to my parents who made innumerable personal sacrifices to nurture a young boy's love of plants.

Many of the photographs in this book were taken in Lambley Nursery's inspirational dry climate garden, thanks to David Glenn and Criss Canning. The gardens at Heronswood and the Garden of St Erth also feature frequently, for which my thanks to the Diggers Club.

INTRODUCTION

A new mood is emerging in Australian gardening. Climate change, water restrictions and a shortage of time in our busy lives have combined to make us rethink the way we garden. Gone are the days when we had the water, the time and the inclination to keep immaculate, emerald-green lawns bordered with lush rhododendrons, perfectly clipped standard roses and bedding annuals. Today we want different things from our gardens. We want our gardens to enhance our lifestyle without enslaving us and we want our gardens to reduce our environmental footprint, not increase it.

Years of prolonged drought have seen water resources dwindle across many parts of Australia. Tough water restrictions have been in place in our towns and cities for many consecutive years. Gardeners and the horticultural industry have been the hardest hit. Public and private gardens have turned brown, large trees have died and sports grounds have been reduced to dust. There was a mood of despondency and despair among gardeners in the early years of the 21st century. You could be forgiven for thinking that many would simply give up gardening altogether. But gardening is one of the oldest expressions of human culture and the urge to do it is not cast off so easily. Gardeners all around Australia have continued to create places of beauty despite the drought, re-imagining how they can use water in their gardens and what plants might flourish without a constant need for the sprinkler.

This task hasn't been made easy for them. The overwhelming majority of nurseries continue to present the same plants they always have, regardless of their appropriateness to our climate. A visit to almost any retail nursery will almost always reveal birch trees, better suited to Scandinavia than Sydney, and a selection of rhododendrons native to the cool monsoonal forests of the Himalayas. Few of us have conditions even approaching 'cool monsoonal forest' in our backyards, yet these plants continue to be offered to us!

The law of supply and demand dictates that if nurseries are continuing to sell rampantly inappropriate plants then somebody must be buying them. The fact is that Australian garden tastes are *still* being driven by the British. The overwhelming majority of glossy gardening books and sexy coffee table magazines in Australia come from Great

The fabled Tibetan blue poppy has broken many a gardener's heart.

Britain – even some of those with 'Australian guide to …' in the title. These books entice us with tantalising images of crisp white birch trees, billowing pink rhododendrons, electric blue Tibetan poppies and dainty snowdrops. Naturally enough we long to grow these treasures in our gardens, too. But where such plants thrive in green and pleasant England, they struggle under the brutal Australian sun. Australian gardeners pine over photos of dreamy British gardens and despair that we will ever have gardens their equal.

Of course it *is* possible for us to have gardens of a standard equal to those of the British but we must be prepared to *change*. We need to change our tastes, change our assumptions of what makes a garden beautiful, and above all change the plants we grow. We must face up to the fact that Australia's climate is nothing like Britain's and for that reason we cannot expect to grow the same plants as them. This is not to say we have to relinquish our dream of having gardens which are abundant and colourful, or condemn ourselves to gardens which are all prickly cacti and sticky grevilleas. It simply means that we have to learn to find beauty in plants other than birches and rhododendrons, and in looks other than the 'woodland', 'bog garden' and 'herbaceous border' which are at the heart of English garden style.

If the recent prolonged drought has had one positive effect, it is that we are finally beginning to come to terms with the true nature of our climate and let go of our long-held aspiration for an English garden. Emancipated from this unattainable dream, we are at last ready to find our own creative direction with planting and landscaping styles.

This book presents a range of plants which, in my own experience as a gardener, have the potential to transform Australian gardens from tired, heat-stunned places into havens of beauty and abundance. The plant range presented here is by no means exhaustive but it can be used as a starting point for those who have the enthusiasm and desire to create a garden regardless of what the weather throws at them. Some of the plants in this book will be new and unfamiliar to readers. Others have been around for a long time but have been forgotten, underestimated or maligned and deserve a second look. This book also aims to help the gardener look at his or her climate afresh and choose plants based on this understanding. Gardeners in the tropics were forced to accept their climate and adapt their gardens to it long ago. In many ways they are already decades ahead of those of us in the south of the country. The scope of this book is mainly appropriate to gardens in the southern half of our continent, in an arc from Brisbane around to Perth.

I believe Australians are entering a new phase of maturity on our garden journey. We are ready to forge a new path for ourselves in which our gardens work *with* our climate and our lifestyle, not fight against them. We are leaving the confusion and despondency of drought behind us and looking towards the future with excitement and optimism. It is an exciting time for Australian gardeners – time to completely rethink what we want from our gardens, how we design them and how we manage them. Above all it is a time to discover a whole new palette of beautiful plants.

1
UNDERSTANDING CLIMATE

What is climate?

Climate is the term used to describe patterns of interrelated meteorological events, taken together, over time. More simply, climate is the average of weather conditions taken over time. Or as writer Robert Heinlein put it even more succinctly, 'climate is what you expect, weather is what you get'.

Our picture of climate has been built up over many years by observing meteorological phenomena such as precipitation, maximum and minimum temperature, wind speed and direction, atmospheric pressure, humidity, evaporation, ocean currents and sea temperatures. By looking back at past observations we are able to make predictions about what might happen in the future. The more observations we make over time, the more finely tuned our predictions become.

We tend to think of climate in terms of how hot or cold, wet or dry the weather is at a particular location. We think of Brisbane as hot and humid, London as cold and damp. But climate is also concerned with how meteorological events are distributed over time. For example, let us imagine that three hypothetical towns receive the same annual rainfall. Town A receives most of its rainfall during the summer months, Town B receives most of its rainfall during the winter and

Town C's rain is spread evenly throughout the year. Although the three towns' total *annual* rainfall is identical, each location would experience very different weather patterns over the course of the year. In other words, they have different climates (see Figure 1.1).

Understanding climate is also about observing the ways in which meteorological phenomena *interact* with one another and with local geography. Let us suppose that two hypothetical towns five kilometres apart have the same average rainfall spread evenly throughout the year. But Town A is high up on a mountain and Town B is down in the valley. Town B experiences higher average temperatures (22°C) than Town A (12°C) because of its lower altitude. The higher temperatures at Town B cause it to have a higher evaporation rate than Town A and therefore a 'drier' climate than the annual rainfall taken on its own might suggest (see Figure 1.2). This would be vital information for gardeners in the two towns.

Let's look at a real example of how meteorological and geographical factors interact to create climate, and how it might affect gardening.

Australians think of London as a rainy, foggy, drizzly place. Yet London's average rainfall is just 583 mm – only 37 mm more than

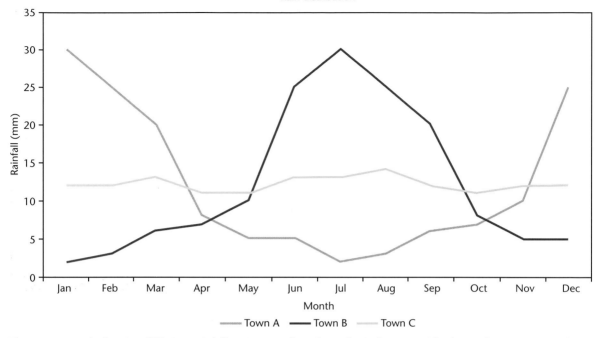

Figure 1.1 Graph showing differing rainfall regimes at three hypothetical towns with identical average annual rainfall.

Australia's driest capital city, Adelaide (546 mm) and *less* than that of Canberra and Hobart (each around 616 mm). If London's rainfall is practically the same as Adelaide's, why are London's gardens so green, soft and luxuriant when Adelaide's are so dry and dusty? Clearly, absolute rainfall is not the only climatic factor which affects a garden. There must be other phenomena at play.

By examining how the geography of the two cities differs we can see why their gardens are so different from one another. London is situated on a relatively flat, narrow island. No point of the island is much further than 100 km from the coast. England's climate is influenced by both the Atlantic Ocean to its west and the English Channel to its east.

These large bodies of water keep temperatures mild throughout the year. The warm Gulf Stream which travels up Europe's west coast gives Britain a milder climate than similar latitudes in North America. The prevailing winds across England are warm, moist south-westerlies off the Atlantic Ocean. London's annual average rainfall is spread evenly throughout the year. Because the sea has such a strong influence, London's evaporation rates are about the same as its precipitation. London lies at a latitude of around 51°N – closer to the North Pole than the equator, so its summers tend to be short and mild.

In sharp contrast, Adelaide is sandwiched in a narrow strip of land between the vast, hot

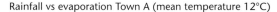

Rainfall vs evaporation Town A (mean temperature 12°C)

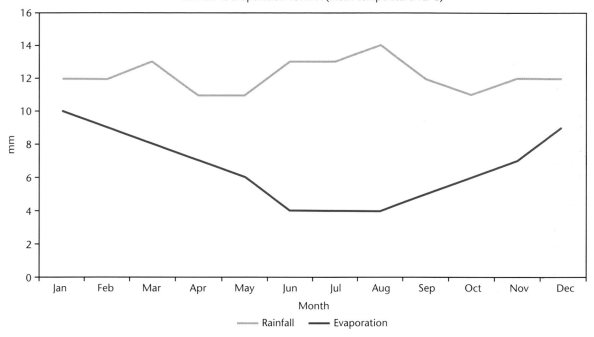

Rainfall vs evaporation Town B (mean temperature 22°C)

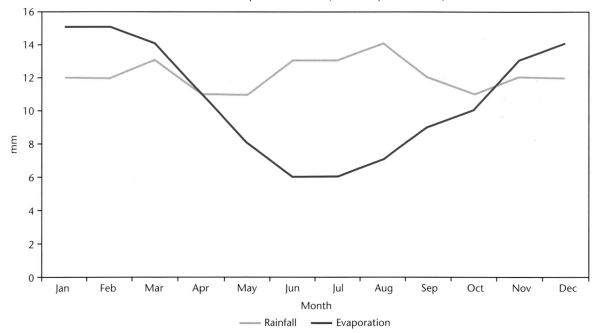

Figure 1.2 Graphs showing monthly rainfall and evaporation at two hypothetical towns five kilometres apart but differing in altitude.

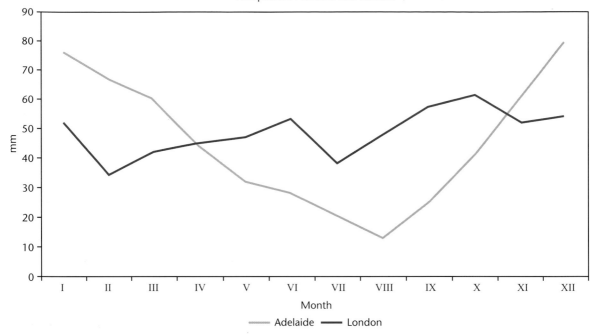

Figure 1.3 Graph showing rainfall distribution in Adelaide and London. The southern hemisphere months have been shifted by six months so that the seasons align.

deserts of central Australia and the cold waters of the Southern Ocean. A permanent band of high pressure called the *subtropical ridge* sits over southern Australia. During the summer months, high pressure cells tend to lie right over South Australia, producing fiercely hot, sunny days and pushing rain-bearing low pressure systems southward. Melbourne and Hobart benefit from occasional summer rains but Adelaide rarely does because it lies further north, closer to the subtropical ridge. In winter the subtropical ridge migrates north allowing cold, moist air from the Southern Ocean to bring rain to Adelaide. Consequently rainfall in Adelaide is confined to the cooler months (see Figure 1.3).

Adelaide's latitude is around 34°S – closer to the equator than to the South Pole. Its summers are long and punishing. Adelaide and London's temperature regimes follow the same seasonal pattern but there is a difference of around 8°C between their average temperatures (see Figure 1.4).

Adelaide's annual evaporation rates are nearly three times its annual precipitation. During the rain-free summer months evaporation rates can be 10 times that of precipitation (see Figure 1.5).

Although Adelaide receives almost identical annual rainfall to London, the two cities experience very different climates due to a suite of other climatic factors.

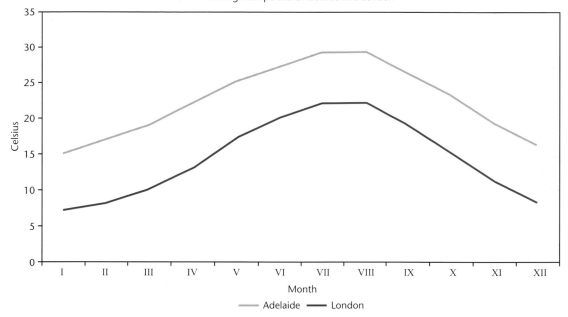

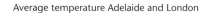

Figure 1.4 Graph showing average temperature in Adelaide and London. The southern hemisphere months have been shifted by six months so that the seasons align.

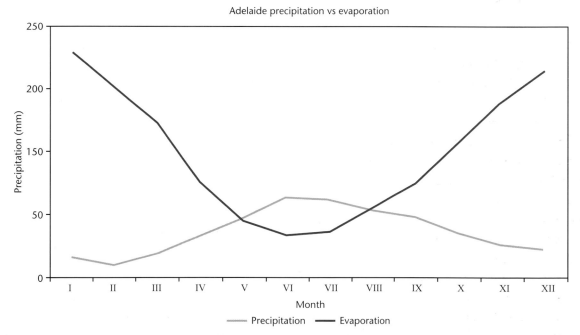

Figure 1.5 Graph showing Adelaide's monthly precipitation and evaporation. There are only two months of the year when precipitation exceeds evaporation.

Getting a handle on climate

To try to make sense of climate with all its interdependent variables, scientists look for patterns in different parts of the world and classify climatic types according to their similarities. There are many different approaches to classifying climate. Each approach aims to describe the relationship between two or more meteorological or geographical phenomena. Some approaches are very simple, comparing obvious weather features like precipitation and temperature. Others are more nuanced, incorporating phenomena such as air pressure, evapo-transpiration and sea currents. No single approach gives us a perfect understanding of climate, but each is a useful tool in building up a better picture of the world around us.

Climate classification is a useful tool for gardeners which allows us to compare our own climate with that of other regions. It can tell us a lot about what kind of plants might do well in our gardens and what kind of 'look' we can hope to achieve.

The *Köppen* (or *Köppen-Geiger*) system of climate classification is one of the most widely used approaches to understanding climate. It classifies world climates into five major classes based on vegetation types – equatorial, arid, temperate, continental and polar. Each of these five major classes is assigned two minor classes, one based on rainfall distribution (e.g. dry summer, dry winter) and the other on temperature regime (e.g. hot summer, cool summer). This basic approach has been extrapolated into around 30 different climate classifications, each of which is given a three-letter code (see Figure 1.6). For example the central Australian desert is assigned the code BWh. The 'B' means that the climate belongs

to the 'Arid' vegetation class, the 'W' means that it experiences 'desert'-type precipitation ('W' stands for *Wüste*, German for desert) and the 'h' means that it is a 'hot' desert (as opposed to 'k' for a cold desert like the Gobi Desert in northern Asia). From the map below we can see that the BWh climate also prevails in the Sahara in North Africa and the Sonoran Desert in North America.

There are many different variations on the Köppen system of climate classification. None of them is perfect, but from a gardener's point of view they are a useful springboard for thinking about our own climate afresh.

Broadly speaking Australia has about a dozen climate types under the Köppen system. Most of our capital cities fall into just a few of those classifications (see Figure 1.7).

The Mediterranean climate (Csa and Csb)

Perth and Adelaide experience what is known as a Mediterranean climate. The main feature of the Mediterranean climate is that it has two well-defined seasons; a hot, dry summer and a mild, wet winter. Its name derives from the fact that the lands surrounding the Mediterranean Sea – those of southern Europe, North Africa and the western Middle East – experience this seasonal pattern. Besides the countries of the Mediterranean basin, several other parts of the world experience a Mediterranean climate. They tend to lie on west coasts of continents at latitudes of around 30–40°N and S, adjoining some of the world's driest deserts (see Figure 1.6). California, central Chile and the western Cape of South Africa experience a classic Mediterranean climate and so, of course, do the south-west of Western Australia around

World map of Köppen-Geiger climate classification

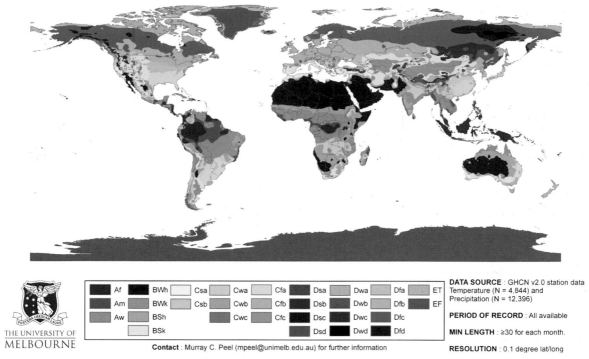

Af	BWh	Csa	Cwa	Cfa	Dsa	Dwa	Dfa	ET
Am	BWk	Csb	Cwb	Cfb	Dsb	Dwb	Dfb	EF
Aw	BSh		Cwc	Cfc	Dsc	Dwc	Dfc	
	BSk				Dsd	Dwd	Dfd	

DATA SOURCE : GHCN v2.0 station data Temperature (N = 4,844) and Precipitation (N = 12,396)

PERIOD OF RECORD : All available

MIN LENGTH : ≥30 for each month.

RESOLUTION : 0.1 degree lat/long

Contact : Murray C. Peel (mpeel@unimelb.edu.au) for further information

Figure 1.6 Köppen climate world map. Source: Peel MC, Finlayson BL and McMahon TA (2007) Updated world map of the Köppen-Geiger climate classification. *Hydrology and Earth System Sciences* 11: 1633–1644.

Perth and eastern South Australia around Adelaide. The dry east coast of New Zealand experiences a climate with many features in common with the Mediterranean climate.

The dry-summer/wet-winter rainfall pattern characteristic of the Mediterranean climate is controlled by permanent subtropical high-pressure systems over adjoining ocean areas. The Mediterranean climate is also known as the 'dry-summer subtropical climate' because it shares certain features with subtropical climates, but its defining characteristic is its dry summer and wet winter.

By comparing the average monthly precipitation and temperature for some cities which experience Mediterranean climates

(Perth, Adelaide, Cape Town in South Africa, Santiago in Chile, Rome in Italy and Los Angeles in California) it becomes clear how sharply defined this climate classification is. Temperature regimes are remarkably uniform across these cities (see Figure 1.8). Precipitation varies in absolute terms but it follows a very clear seasonal pattern (see Figure 1.9).

The Mediterranean climate, although drought stricken for the hottest part of each year, has given rise to some of the richest floras in the world, notably in south-west WA, the Western Cape of South Africa and the Canary Islands. The Western Cape is a tiny area, only a third the size of Great

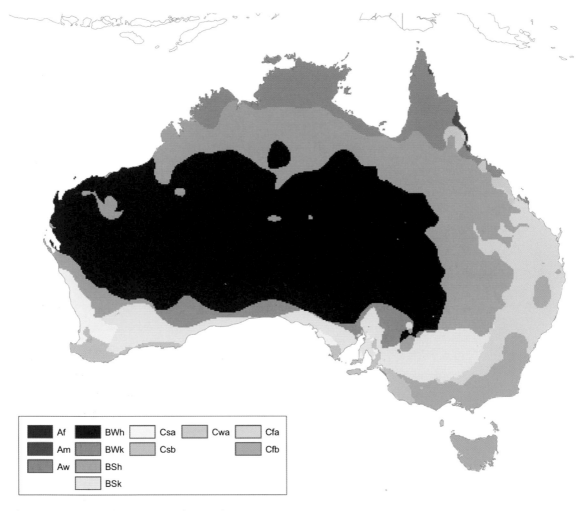

Figure 1.7 Köppen climate map of Australia.

Af		BWh		Csa		Cwa	Cfa
Am		BWk		Csb			Cfb
Aw		BSh					
		BSk					

Britain, but it contains 9000 plant species. That is around 4% of all the plant life on earth. Of those species, 70% are endemic, growing nowhere else. The Mediterranean basin is home to about 25 000 plant species – around 15% of the earth's total plant species. Compare this with Britain's rather impoverished 1500 species. Gardening in a Mediterranean climate is *not* the restriction many Australian gardeners feel it to be. Rather, it is an incredible bonus. There is a huge palette of plants for Mediterranean climate gardeners to choose from although, perversely, the hardest Mediterranean climate plants to grow outside their home range are those endemic to south-west Western Australia. Many plants from this biome, while incredibly beautiful, are also incredibly finicky in their cultural requirements. Most Australian gardeners have more success with plants from California, Chile, South Africa and the Mediterranean basin than with plants from WA.

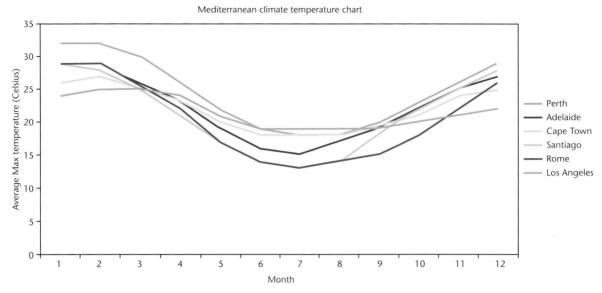

Figure 1.8 Temperature in six Mediterranean climate cities. Southern hemisphere calendar shifted by six months to align seasons.

The Mediterranean climate is a versatile climate to garden in. There is enough winter chill to grow some temperate climate plants and if you can irrigate during the summer months subtropical plants are happy to grow in Mediterranean climates, too. Subtropical citrus trees are an essential feature of Mediterranean climate gardens from Spain to

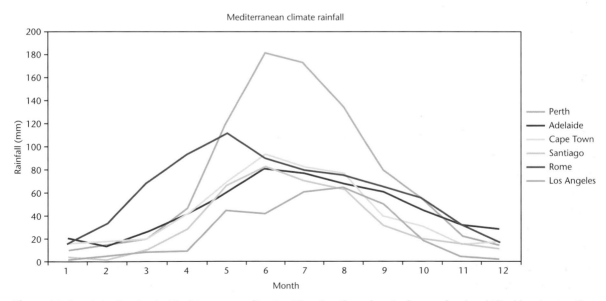

Figure 1.9 Precipitation in six Mediterranean climate cities. Southern hemisphere calendar shifted by six months to align seasons.

The Mediterranean climate has nurtured some of the world's most influential garden traditions such as the Renaissance gardens of Italy (Villa Gamberaia).

Israel and California. Perhaps because of its versatility the Mediterranean climate has nurtured some of the world's most influential gardening cultures such as the Islamic garden tradition of the Middle East and Spain, the renaissance gardens of Italy and in more recent times the modernist and post-modernist gardens of California. These serve as great sources of inspiration to gardeners in similar climates.

The humid subtropical climate (Cfa and Cwa)

Sydney and Brisbane experience a humid subtropical climate. This climate is typified by warm (but not too hot), humid summers and cooler (but not cold) winters. Rainfall is plentiful, in the range of 1000–2000 mm annually, either spread evenly throughout the year or with a dry season during the cooler months. The geographical distribution of this climate is the opposite of the Mediterranean climate, situated mostly on the south-eastern coasts of continents around 25–40°N and S. The humid subtropical climate covers much bigger areas than the more restricted Mediterranean climate, including large tracts of southern Brazil, Uruguay and northern Argentina, the southern states of the USA from Virginia to Texas, the east coast of South Africa, eastern China, Korea, Japan and, oddly, parts of Eastern Europe including the Balkans, Romania, the Caucasus and northern Turkey (see Figure 1.6). Many Australians would not think of Eastern Europe – or indeed Washington DC or Tokyo – as having a 'subtropical' climate, which to most of us suggests swaying palm trees rather than snowmen. But under the Köppen system they are defined as having a 'subtropical climate' because of their rainfall, humid summers and an average winter minimum within the rather wide range of −3° to 18°C.

In Australia the humid subtropical climate type is much less well defined than the Mediterranean climate and scientists apply different variations of it to quite a big chunk of eastern Australia. In its broadest sense, the humid subtropical climate in Australia covers an area from around Atherton in Queensland to around Shepparton in Victoria, extending inland to Roma and Moree, straddling the Great Dividing Range in northern NSW, as far south as Bega along the eastern coast fringe and extending as far west as Dubbo and Narrandera in the west of the range. Not many gardeners would liken the experience of gardening in Dubbo to gardening in Sydney or Brisbane, however. In its most restricted sense the humid subtropical climate covers an area from around Townsville in the north, through south-eastern Queensland and coastal NSW south to around Sydney.

The humid subtropical climate is one of the most generous climates to garden in, in Australia. Normally, gardeners in humid subtropical climates have merely to *control* plant growth rather than encourage it. Humid subtropical regions of the world are a

The humid subtropical regions of the world have been a rich source of garden plants including many beautiful bamboos.

rich source of garden plants. Eastern China, Japan and the Americas have given us such beauties as gardenias, camellias, jacarandas and the bull bay Magnolia (*Magnolia grandiflora*). Our own humid subtropical areas have given the world the stunning Illawarra flame tree (*Brachychiton acerifolius*), the handsome bangalow palm (*Archontophoenix cunninghamiana*) and the Moreton Bay fig (*Ficus macrophylla*). It is possible to grow tropical plants in suitable microclimates in the humid subtropical climate, like the frangipani (*Plumeria rubra*) from Central America.

Although the humid subtropical climate is blessed with plentiful rain, on the Australian continent this precipitation is tempered with periods of acute drought – an overriding feature of our continent's climate. Sydney and Brisbane have just experienced many consecutive years of punishing drought. Drought is something that Australian gardeners in this otherwise generous climate must plan for in the future.

The humid subtropical climate nurtured the ancient and venerable southern Chinese and Japanese gardening traditions. Many elements of these traditions translate easily into modern contexts and, indeed, Japanese gardening culture has exerted enormous influence on modern garden design. In more recent times the Brazilian landscape architect and garden designer Roberto Burle Marx created bold, beautiful gardens in Brazil, Argentina and Florida, showing another approach to gardening in the humid subtropical climate. There is no shortage of inspiration for gardeners in this climate type to draw on.

The temperate maritime or oceanic climate (Cfb)

The temperate maritime climate is related to the humid subtropical climate but features milder summers, colder winters and usually four more or less distinct seasons. Under this classification precipitation is described rather nebulously as 'adequate and reliable'. This climate type is generally found on the west coast of continents at around 45–55°N and S, poleward of Mediterranean climate areas (see Figure 1.6). The exception to this rule is in Australia and Africa, where it is found on the south-eastern corner of those continents, and in New Zealand where it covers much of both islands.

In temperate maritime climates oceanic influence keeps both summers and winters relatively mild compared with surrounding areas. The most extensive temperate maritime climate area in the world is western and central Europe. The temperate maritime climate is therefore the benign

'English' climate that Australian gardeners dream about.

Under the Köppen system Melbourne, Hobart and Canberra experience a temperate maritime climate – the same as London, Aberdeen, Vancouver and Gothenburg in Sweden. This will come as a great surprise to anyone who has ever gardened in the grinding drought and scorching hot winds of south-eastern Australia. Canberra, Melbourne and Hobart's climates may well share similarities with southern Sweden and British Colombia on paper, but in real life gardening in our region is a completely different experience.

South-eastern Australia's rainfall and temperature regimes resemble those of temperate maritime climates in Europe but there are several important differences from a gardener's point of view. Great Britain lies unusually close to the pole for this climate type, between the latitudes of 50 and 60°N. It experiences a mild, protracted spring giving way to a mild, short summer. Because of its northerly latitude, Britain's summer days are very long. In mid-summer the sun rises at four in the morning and does not set until 10 at night. Anyone who has experienced a northern European summer knows that the quality of the sunlight is quite different from what we are used to. It is soft and gentle in comparison with our harsh sun. Evaporation rates in northern Europe are fairly low. In Britain, they rarely exceed the rate of precipitation. Water deficit is almost unknown.

Plants respond to these conditions by growing in a particular way. In the soft, long days of a fleeting British summer plants are able to

England's mild, protracted spring gives way to a mild, short summer, resulting in soft, luxuriant plant growth.

photosynthesise for up to 18 hours per day. They have to grow quickly before autumn's shortening days and crisp nights close in. The summer growing season is short but very intense. This is the key to the lush softness of British gardens.

By contrast, south-eastern Australia's temperate maritime zone lies much closer to the equator than Britain, between 30 and 42°S. It experiences a short spring – just a few weeks – before giving way to a long, hot summer. Evaporation rates are high under our bright southern sun. Canberra's annual average evaporation is 1677 mm, 1072 mm *more* than its annual rainfall of 615 mm. In other words, Canberra experiences a permanent water deficit even in an average year, let alone during the periodic droughts that are a feature of south-east Australia's overarching climate. Plants respond very differently in the climate of south-eastern Australia to that of Britain. In south-eastern Australia new growth begun during our short spring is quickly checked by summer heat and dry. The lushness maintained by the English garden throughout summer here stops with the first hot winds of late spring and quickly gives way to brown lawns, crispy-edged foliage on trees and plants which look hard and wizened.

From a gardener's point of view the climates experienced by Canberra, Melbourne and, to a lesser degree, Hobart have much more in common with the Mediterranean climate than with the temperate maritime. Mediterranean climate plants are perfectly adapted to our long, dry summers in which evaporation exceeds precipitation. They are perfectly happy in our bright sunshine, poor soils and cope much better with the periodic drought of south-eastern Australia than 'English' style plants. Perhaps the only part of Australia that parallels the UK's temperate maritime climate is remote south-western Tasmania.

Semi-arid climates (BSk and BSh)

Semi-arid climates are intermediate between the humid climates (temperate maritime *Cfb* and humid subtropical *Cfa*) and the arid desert climates (the BW climates). They are defined by annual rainfall in the range of 250–500 mm annually, whereas true desert climates are defined as having less than 250 mm annually.

Semi-arid climates are found on the fringes of the world's largest deserts, notably a vast tract of central Asia (the S in the climate code stands for *Steppe* – a vegetation type particularly associated with central Asia). Central and southern Argentina, central-western USA and Mexico, the southern fringe of the Sahara and the areas adjacent to the Kalahari Desert in southern Africa also experience this climate (see Figure 1.6).

The Köppen system recognises two kinds of semi-arid climate – the hot semi-arid climate (BSh) and the cold semi-arid climate (BSk). In Australia the hot semi-arid climate forms an arc of country from central inland NSW around Ivanhoe and Condobolin, north through outback Queensland across the NT to north-east WA near Broome. The cold semi-arid climate covers an arc from central inland NSW from Lake Cargelligo south through the Riverina and Sunraysia, across to Port Augusta and Ceduna in SA and then tracing a coastal strip around to southern inland WA around Kalgoorlie.

Semi-arid climates have given us some of the most elegant of all garden plants, like this agave.

Semi-arid climates are by no means impossible to garden in. Gardeners living in these climates simply need to banish any thought of ever having an 'English' style garden. Vegetation from semi-arid climates is dominated by grasses, low scrubby trees and shrubs and cacti and succulents. Many of these are perfectly worthy garden subjects. In fact, some of the most elegant and spectacular of all garden plants come from semi-arid climates. English gardeners are particularly enamoured with semi-arid yuccas and agaves, cosseting them in pots which are moved outside in summer and brought into conservatories in winter. In Australia we can grow yuccas and agaves just about anywhere yet we take them completely for granted. We see yuccas and agaves as second-class plants, not 'proper' (i.e. 'English') garden plants like roses or rhododendrons. Gardeners in the American desert states, including the denizens of glamorous Hollywood, faced up to the reality of their climate long ago and have created some of the most distinctive and beautiful gardens in the world using their native yuccas and agaves. Semi-arid gardens don't have to be ugly gardens!

Water deficit and drought

Highly variable annual rainfall is a feature of the climate in many parts of Australia. Such variability naturally leads to drought. Drought is generally defined as an 'acute water shortage' caused by deficient rainfall. In recent years drought has been a problem for gardeners in places which normally experience plentiful rainfall like Brisbane and Sydney. But Melbourne, Perth, Adelaide and Darwin experience seasonal water deficit as a feature of their 'normal' climate.

In normal years the climate of Australia is heavily influenced by the subtropical ridge. The subtropical ridge is a band of high pressure lying over central Australia. It brings hot, sunny weather and suppresses rain in southern Australia during the summer months, which is why Perth and Adelaide, and to a lesser degree Canberra and Melbourne, experience such dry summers. In winter the subtropical ridge migrates north, suppressing rain in northern Australia as the monsoon trough which brings Darwin its summer rain simultaneously migrates north.

The term *El Niño* has entered public awareness in recent years. El Niño events are associated with the longer droughts which Australia experiences fairly regularly. The Spanish name 'El Niño' was coined by Peruvian fishermen who noticed a warm sea current which appeared every few years around about Christmas time (El Niño means 'the baby boy' referring to baby Jesus). El Niño events occur when there is a shift in the prevailing patterns of sea temperature, air pressure, winds, convection and cloudiness in the tropical Pacific Ocean between Australia–Indonesia and South America. This disturbs the normal weather patterns. During an El Niño event South America experiences a warm sea current but the Australia–Indonesia region experiences cooler than normal sea temperatures, causing less water to be fed into the atmosphere from the sea. Eastern Australia can experience below average rainfall and above average temperatures during the winter/spring of an El Niño event. As a consequence evaporation rates are

higher and drought may follow. Our worst droughts have all coincided with El Niño events, but not all El Niño events automatically cause a drought. El Niño events affect all of eastern Australia except for western Tasmania which is rarely affected.

The opposite of an El Niño event is a *La Niña* ('baby girl') event. La Niña events are more powerful than El Niños, bringing an increased risk of above average rain to nearly all of the continent and lower than normal temperatures in the spring to autumn period. Our worst historic floods have occurred during La Niña years. Dorothea Mackellar was right when she described Australia as a land 'of droughts and flooding rains'.

El Niño events are a *normal*, regular feature of the Australian climate, occurring about every three to eight years. Yet for some reason we still seem surprised when Australia experiences a drought. It is almost as if we expect our weather to follow the reliable spring-summer-autumn-winter regime that our predominantly European cultural heritage has taught us to expect. Even after 200 years of European settlement we are still shocked when it doesn't. If we look carefully at our flora and fauna we can see that they are adapted to the boom and bust cycles brought by drought and flood. River red gums (*Eucalyptus camaldulensis*) are adapted to extended periods of drought (under their 'normal' climatic regime) but rely on occasional periods of inundation to survive and reproduce. Many marsupials and birds have population explosions during flood years, dwindling back to very low numbers during droughts. They have reproductive mechanisms which cope with the variability in rainfall and resources. Both short and long dry seasons are an ever-present feature of Australian climate. Gardeners should stand prepared.

Seasonal dryness

A tool used by climatologists for assessing the duration and severity of a dry season is the *ombrothermic diagram*. Ombrothermic diagrams show the mean monthly precipitation for a location on one axis and its mean maximum temperature on the other, traditionally beginning with the mid-winter month (July in the southern hemisphere, January in the northern). A location is said to experience a dry season if the line created by temperature rises above the line created by precipitation. The difference between the two lines gives an indication of the severity of the dry season and its length can be seen in the horizontal axis. Comparing ombrothermic diagrams for our capital cities is an interesting way of seeing just how much their climates differ from one another (see Figure 1.10).

The ombrothermic diagrams for Perth (Figure 1.10g) and Adelaide (Figure 1.10f) show very clearly the severe summer dry season associated with the Mediterranean climate. At the other extreme Darwin (Figure 1.10h) shows the classic monsoonal pattern of a *very* wet summer and a very dry winter. Sydney (Figure 1.10d) and Brisbane (Figure 1.10e) demonstrate clearly the two variations on the humid subtropical climate; Sydney experiences no dry season at all while Brisbane experiences a winter dry season.

It is interesting to note that, just as in the Köppen classifications, Canberra's ombrothermic diagram (Figure 1.10a) suggests that it does not experience a 'dry season' at all. Try telling that to anyone who has ever actually had a garden in our national capital! Canberra is the second driest city after Adelaide in terms of absolute rainfall. Its rainfall is almost identical to Hobart which, according to its ombrothermic diagram (Figure 1.10c), *does* experience a brief dry season in February. Why, then, does Canberra 'feel' so much drier than Hobart from a gardener's point of view?

There are many other meteorological and geographical factors at play which the ombrothermic diagram, comparing only two variables, cannot take into account. Canberra is at a much higher elevation than Hobart; around 580 m above sea level compared with Hobart's 30 m. Although Canberra's *average* temperatures are about the same as Hobart's, its daily maximum and minimum temperatures are in fact more extreme. Canberra can be very hot during the day in summer but night-time temperatures are considerably cooler so its mean temperatures are similar to Hobart, which actually experiences much less temperature fluctuation. Canberra is closer to the equator at latitude 35°S (Hobart is at 42°S) so it experiences a longer summer season and greater influence from the subtropical ridge. It is also much further from the coast than Hobart so its climate is not moderated by the sea. Canberra's inland location, together with its local topography and prevailing winds combine to make the experience of gardening in Canberra feel very different to gardening in Hobart even though their average annual rainfall is identical.

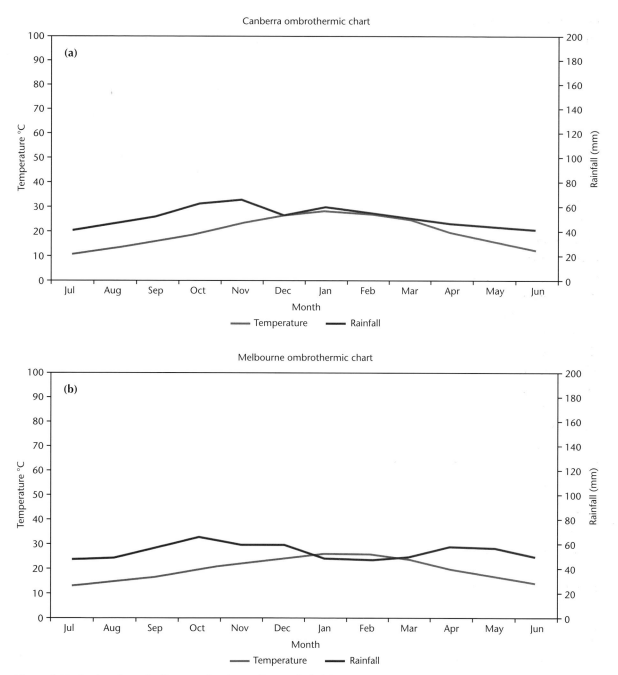

Figure 1.10 Ombrothermic diagrams for Australian capital cities.

Melbourne's ombrothermic diagram (Figure 1.10b) suggests something which its 'temperate maritime' Köppen classification does not hint at. It shows that Melbourne experiences a dry season in January and February. Not a very long or intense dry

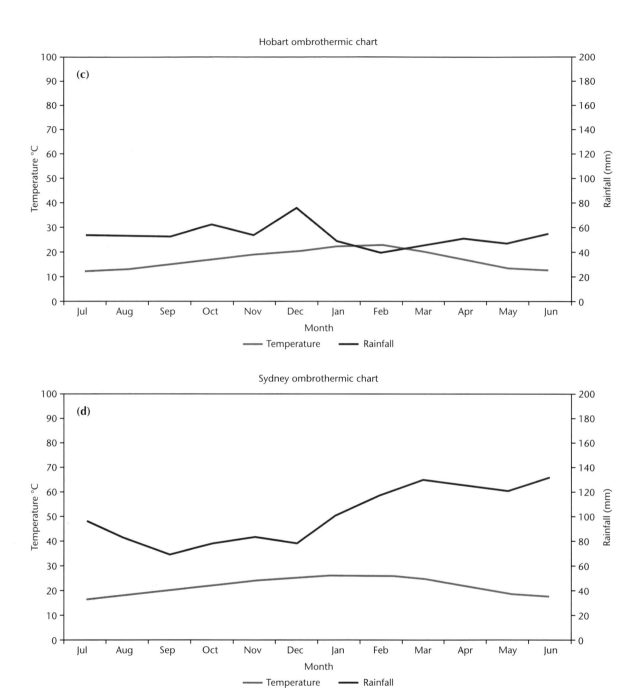

Figure 1.10 (continued) Ombrothermic diagrams for Australian capital cities.

season compared with Adelaide, but much more than London which does not experience a 'dry season' at all.

Melbourne is the butt of many jokes about weather. The jokes about the city having four seasons in one day are actually very close to

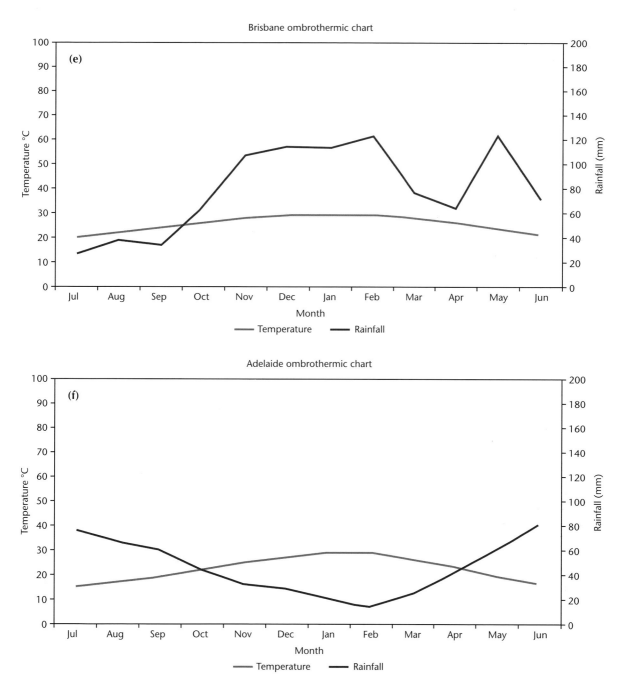

Figure 1.10 (continued) Ombrothermic diagrams for Australian capital cities.

the mark due to Melbourne's unique combination of geography and wind patterns. To its north-west lies desert country. To its south-west lie the cold waters of the Southern Ocean. Melbourne's prevailing winds come from the south-west bringing moist, cool

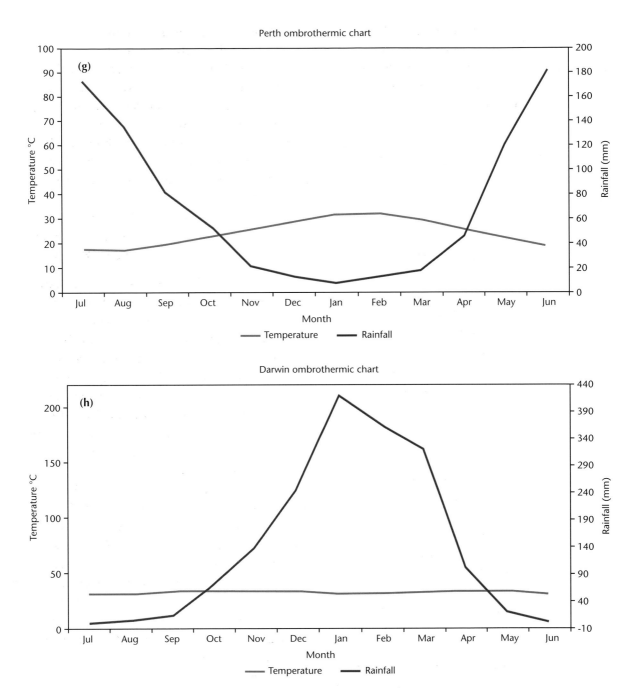

Figure 1.10 (continued) Ombrothermic diagrams for Australian capital cities.

(Sydneysiders might say 'drab') weather from the Southern Ocean. But when the wind shifts to the north-west – as it does on a few days every summer – it blasts hot, dry weather down from the inland deserts. During summer Melbourne can be a drizzly 18°C one day and a desiccating 40°C the next. The Mediterranean basin experiences similar hot winds blowing in from the Sahara, depositing red sand from the desert dunes over Morocco, the Canary Islands and southern Europe. Victoria's fierce northerly winds coupled with dry summers bring not only dust storms but bushfires. Victoria is one of the most fire-prone regions in the world, along with California, South Africa and the Mediterranean basin. This supports the view that Melbourne's climate has more in common with the Mediterranean climate than with Britain's benign temperate maritime climate, at least from a gardener's perspective. British gardeners rarely have to endure 40°C days, dust storms, bushfires or months of water deficiency. Melburnian gardeners, like Californians, South Africans and Greeks, must do so each and every year.

Climate zones and plant hardiness

There are several approaches to classifying Australia's various climates into practical gardening climate zones. We often see zoned climate maps of Australia in gardening books, but how useful are they really? Some gardening climate maps simply divide up the country along the lines of the major Köppen classes, i.e. a 'tropical' zone, an 'arid' zone, and a 'temperate' zone. This simple system has the benefit of telling the gardener something about the basic *qualitative* features of their climate and leaving the rest up to the judgement of the gardener. Under this system 'temperate' meant just that – not too hot and not too cold. Unfortunately it doesn't tell the gardener much about seasonal rainfall patterns or temperature regimes, or any of the other climatic features which are important in the cultivation of plants (like frost or lack thereof). As a result, Adelaide, with its brutally hot, rainless summer, tended to get lumped into the 'temperate zone' along with Melbourne, with its typically mild, drizzly summers, and Sydney with its humid, wet summers. This zoning system probably worked adequately in the days when it was possible to have a sprinkler running on the garden all summer long. Under such conditions a garden in Adelaide could indeed have a climate equivalent to one in Sydney.

The majority of climate maps for Australian gardeners take their lead from UK and USA garden books and are based on *winter hardiness*. This means the amount of cold a plant can withstand before it dies. British gardeners talk about a plant being 'hardy to 5°C', 'frost hardy' or 'fully hardy' meaning that it can take any weather the British Isles can dish out. For British gardeners cold is the most important limiting factor on plant growth. This system works well for the restricted range of climates found in Britain but not for Australia's greater variety of climates. The difference between a London winter (minimum –5°C) and an Edinburgh winter (minimum –7.5°C) is not as great as the difference between a Canberra winter (min –5°C) and a Darwin winter (min +18°C). Therefore books which tell us that a plant is 'frost hardy' as opposed to 'fully hardy' do not really help Australian gardeners that much.

Other gardening climate maps are based on plant hardiness zones developed by the United States Department of Agriculture (USDA) to encompass the much wider range of climates experienced by the USA.

Figure 1.11 USDA plant hardiness zones superimposed on a map of Australia. Source: After USDA plant hardiness map.

Thirteen zones from 0–12 are recognised under this system. Each of these zones is divided into two sub-zones to give 26 different hardiness zones; however, like the British system, the USDA hardiness zones use winter minimum temperature as their defining parameter. For example, if a plant is said to be 'hardy to Zone 10' it means that it can survive a winter minimum within the range of −1° to 4°C. The corresponding hardiness map shows areas which experience average minimum temperatures in the −1° to

4°C range as 'Zone 10' (see Figure 1.11). What this system does not show is how many times the minimum temperature occurs at any location or how much of that temperature a plant can endure before it is damaged. A place classed as Zone 10 location might fall to −1°C on just one night every year, or it might fall to −1°C every night for three months of every year. Similarly, a 'Zone 10 plant' like a banana might grow happily at the first location but die outright at the second. USDA hardiness zones don't give any indication about other climatic features apart from winter minimum. For example, Brisbane, Melbourne and Broken Hill are all classified as Zone 10 because they experience a similar average winter minimum temperature, yet in every other way they experience very different climates. Knowing that a plant is 'hardy to −1°C' is not much help to a Broken Hill gardener if that plant also needs 1000 mm of rain annually or to a Brisbane gardener if the plant cannot withstand summer humidity.

A USDA hardiness map modified for Australia is sometimes seen in gardening books. It has hardiness zones from 1 to 7 corresponding to USDA zones 7 to 12 (and a bit beyond to cover the equatorial climate of our far north). Like the full USDA system, the only climatic feature this modified system informs us about is winter minimum. On that basis Albany, Mt Isa and Sydney are all lumped into the same zone (Zone 4) despite having very different climates in every other way.

Where winter cold is seen as the main limiting factor on plant growth in Britain and the east coast of America, gardeners in California realised decades ago that summer heat is just as important to the success or failure of gardens in their climate. The 'Sunset zones' were developed in Sunset Books' garden guides to help gardeners in America's west understand their wildly differing climates better. The Sunset zones

GOING WITH THE SEASONS

The best way to understand climate is to spend time in your garden and feel the changing seasons. Learn to recognise and predict the growth cycles of plants, the comings and goings of birds and insects, note the direction of winds and rain. Notice dewy mornings when water is drawn into the earth, lengthening or shortening days. Look for patterns of growth and decay. Talk to elderly gardeners, farmers and folk with indigenous backgrounds. They have the benefit of hindsight. In this way you develop your intuition about gardening and the workings of nature, one of the great joys of gardening.

Aboriginal weather traditions are based on generations of observation, not only of temperature and rainfall but the behaviour of animals and plants. Indigenous traditions recognise seasons differently from the spring-summer-autumn-winter model superimposed on Australia from Europe. In the southern part of the country Aboriginal people traditionally recognise up to six seasons per year while those in the north recognise only two or three. Once you begin to develop your own seasonal intuition you come to realise how obvious and logical the indigenous seasonal calendars are and how ill-fitting the four European seasons are to the actuality of our climate.

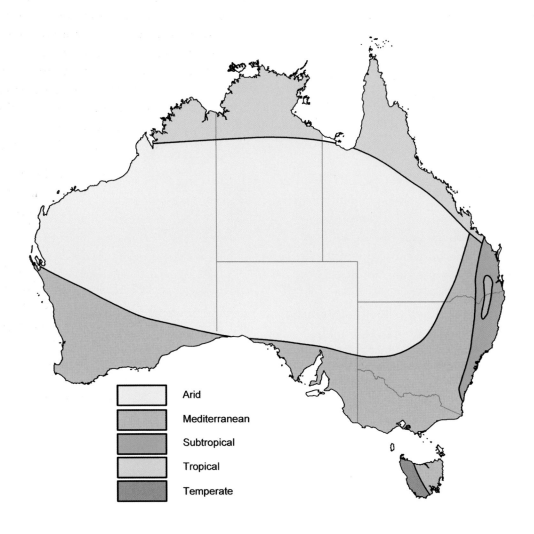

	Arid
	Mediterranean
	Subtropical
	Tropical
	Temperate

Figure 1.12 Modified Köppen map from an Australian gardener's point of view – enlarged Mediterranean climate zone, temperate maritime climate reduced to areas unaffected by regular drought and humid subtropical climate confined to areas with strong coastal influence.

are a great guide for Australian gardeners as they take into account not only winter cold but summer heat, length of growing season, latitude, influence from moist oceanic or dry continental air and microclimates created by

geography: a major achievement on the part of its developers. Forty-five different climate zones are recognised, covering all of the western states of the USA including Hawaii and Alaska. Many of the Sunset zones are applicable to Australia, it just takes a bit of homework to work out which zone corresponds to your local climate.

Australia's gardening climate zones

Taking a fresh look at Australia's range of climates through a gardener's eyes we could say there are five main gardening climate zones in Australia (see Figure 1.12). The 'Mediterranean zone' incorporates most of southern and inland Australia including Geraldton, Perth and the south-west corner of WA, Adelaide and southern coastal parts of SA, all of Victoria including Melbourne north through Canberra and up the Great Dividing Range as far as north as Toowoomba, and south to the eastern part of Tasmania. The 'subtropical zone' incorporates the area from Bundaberg south through Brisbane, south-east Queensland and northern NSW south along coastal NSW to Bega. The 'tropical zone' incorporates coastal areas of Queensland north from Bundaberg, through the Gulf country, northern NT and across to Broome. The 'arid zone' incorporates the very dry, central parts of the country. The west coast of Tasmania is cool, wet and unaffected by El Niño and has a climate all its own. It is possibly the only part of the country where gardeners should even entertain the thought of having the British ideal of emerald-green lawns and lupin-filled borders!

This map (Figure 1.12) is designed to use as a basic tool for deciding what will grow in your area without too much mollycoddling and fuss. It is, of course, a massive oversimplification of the many subtle variations on regional climates. It takes into account some of the broad climatic features which limit plant growth under Australian conditions as discussed above and attempts to smooth out some of the inconsistencies (from a gardener's point of view) inherent in climate maps based on plant hardiness alone. Even so it is far from telling the whole story.

2
HOW PLANTS ADAPT TO CLIMATE

At the time of writing an astounding 400 000 species of plant have been described to science. Plants grow almost everywhere on Earth from the steamy wet tropics to the open ocean and the driest deserts. Plants even live *inside* the rocks and ice on the frozen continent of Antarctica. Each species of plant is closely adapted to its habitat. Over many millions of years and thousands of successive generations, each plant's physiology and behaviour has been fine-tuned by natural selection through disease, predation, climate and geology. Climate and geology exert the most significant pressures on plant evolution because they form the backdrop against which a plant's life is played out. Plants are literally shaped by their climate. Indeed, one could say that every plant species is a living expression of its climate – an awe-inspiring demonstration of the subtlety and richness of our planet.

Every gardener knows that plants have particular cultural needs. We know that growing a tropical plant in a frosty area or an alpine plant in the tropics is a sure death sentence. Intuitively, we understand that each plant is adapted to specific climatic conditions which cannot be compromised. Learning how plants adapt to different climates helps us understand *why* plants are suited to certain garden conditions and not to others.

Every plant is a living expression of its habitat, shaped by forces of climate and geology.

Limiting factors on plant growth

Each species of plant has a specific set of climatic parameters in which it can survive. The correct balance of temperature, water, sunlight and other factors is necessary for a plant to grow, complete its life cycle and pass its genes into the next generation. Outside these parameters the plant cannot function normally and it dies. Climatic variables work

Plants have specific climatic parameters in which they can survive. Waterlilies need to be fully immersed in fresh water.

in combination. Changing just one variable may render conditions unsuitable for a plant to grow. Gardeners are all too familiar with the results of not catering to a plant's specific water needs, namely death by desiccation or by drowning. It seems obvious to us that a waterlily will not grow in the same garden bed as a cactus since their water requirements are so completely different. But there are many other climatic factors which limit plant growth, even if they are less well recognised by gardeners.

Water

Like all forms of life, plants depend on water to sustain life. Water is one of the raw products needed for *photosynthesis*. Photosynthesis is the chemical process whereby plants use solar energy to turn water and carbon dioxide into sugars to feed and build the plant. Oxygen is given off as a by-product of this process, so water is vital not only to plant life but to oxygen-dependent animal life, too.

Structurally, vascular plants are essentially bundles of capillary tubes, like a bunch of drinking straws standing in a glass of water. The bottom ends of the straws represent the root system of the plant through which water is taken up. It travels up special tubes called *xylem* to the leaves. Leaves have specialised pores in them called *stomata* which are used for collecting CO_2 from the air for photosynthesis. Stomata are like the tops of the straws through which water can be sucked out of the system. When a plant's stomata are opened for gas exchange, water is simultaneously lost in a process called *evapotranspiration*, in the same way that we lose water through sweating. Plants can lose more than 90% of the water they collect with their roots through evapotranspiration. The air sucks water out of the leaves almost as quickly as the roots take it up. When a plant loses water more quickly than it can absorb it, it suffers *hydric deficit*. Its cells lose turgidity, the plant wilts, burns and can ultimately die. Different plants have evolved different thresholds at which they suffer hydric deficit and in fact there are plants adapted to life in the driest of deserts as well as permanently submerged in water.

Plants which are adapted to life in water are collectively called *hydrophytes* (from the Greek for 'water plants'). Hydrophytes lack many of the normal adaptations of land plants. Hydrophytes do not have the protective cuticle which land plants need to prevent their cells from dehydrating. They have no need for structural rigidity as water supports their mass and because they need a high degree of flexibility so as not to be damaged by the movement of water around them. Hydrophytes

Hydrophytes are adapted to life permanently surrounded by water.

lack xylem and stomata as they are able to absorb water and dissolved CO_2 directly from their surroundings. Consequently their leaf shapes have evolved into forms which maximise surface area such as very finely dissected, feathery leaves or broad, flat, thin leaves (think of aquarium plants). Hydrophytes' roots have lost the nutrient-collecting ability of land plants' roots. They are used simply to anchor the plant in its substrate or as food storage organs.

Marine plants face a very special problem. They live in a salty environment that would kill normal plants. In normal plants the salt water would suck the fresh water out of the plant's cells by osmosis, causing them to dehydrate. Marine plants are adapted so that the water inside their cells has the same salt concentration as the water surrounding them. Thus their cells remain turgid and hydrated. Plants which are adapted to salty conditions on both land and water are called *halophytes*. Mangroves are halophytes. They have evolved several adaptations to living with their roots submerged in salt water. Some mangrove species concentrate salt in their leaves and excrete it through the leaf surface as crystals. Others have filtration systems in their roots which allow them to exclude salt ions.

Plants which are adapted to life in arid places are collectively termed *xerophytes* (from the Greek for 'dry plants'). They have an amazing array of defences against desiccation which we will examine in detail later. Cacti are the ultimate xerophytes. Their characteristic blocky shape reduces their surface area while maximising their volume. This minimises the effects of heat and evapotranspiration while allowing more storage space for water. In many ways, a cactus is no more than a bag of moisture covered by a watertight, photosynthetic skin. The core of a cactus is over 90% water, stored in the form of a thick mucilage which cannot evaporate quickly if the plant is wounded. Interestingly, several genera of cacti from wet climates have different adaptations to their desert cousins. The well-known orchid cactus (*Epiphyllum*) has broad, flat, thin stems which function essentially as leaves. *Pereskia* cacti from tropical South America actually *have* leaves and woody stems. They are deciduous during

Cacti from arid climates are leafless and squat in order to conserve water.

Pereskia are cacti which are adapted to monsoonal climates. They have leaves like any other shrub.

Succulent plants avoid losing water from their leaves by opening their stomata at night when temperatures are lower.

the winter dry season and grow leaves again during the wet summer, just like a normal deciduous shrub.

Water loss through evapotranspiration is a problem for all plants because it leads to hydric deficit. When its stomata are opened to collect CO_2 a plant simultaneously loses moisture. Most plants fix atmospheric carbon by what is known as the C3 pathway. The C3 pathway requires them to have their stomata open during the daytime so that CO_2 can be immediately converted into sugars while sunlight is available. This pathway works well in climates where moisture is abundant but C3 plants do not cope well with moisture stress – they wilt easily. Plants from dry climates tend to open their stomata only at night when temperatures are cooler, thereby reducing the amount of water lost through

evapotranspiration. Opening stomata at night creates its own problems because there is no sunlight available to drive photosynthesis. Plants which open their stomata at night have evolved a different pathway for fixing carbon dioxide called CAM photosynthesis, short for Crassulacean Acid Metabolism after the succulent Crassulaceae family in which it was first observed. In CAM photosynthesis, CO_2 is able to be stored overnight until sunlight is once again available to drive photosynthesis. A small percentage of plants employ a third photosynthetic pathway called C4 carbon fixation which allows them to photosynthesise in hot, sunny climates without suffering water loss.

Temperature

Like all chemical processes photosynthesis works best within an optimum temperature range, in this case between 15 and 35°C. Outside this range photosynthesis is slower and less efficient. Yet plants have adapted to live in conditions of both extreme heat and extreme cold.

Cacti from arid climates have a globular shape to minimise their surface area while maximising their volume.

Cacti are the ultimate survivors in very hot areas. Their most important adaptation to heat is their characteristic globular shape, which minimises their surface-area-to-volume ratio. They have no leaves or appendages through which they might lose water. The globular shape of cacti means that half of the plant is always shaded from the sun, helping to keep its core cooler. Cacti's spines and dense hairs are not only for defence but to shade their surface, lowering their temperature. Even so, desert cacti are able to

Plants from cold alpine regions hug the ground for protection.

withstand very high internal temperatures which would be fatal to animals.

Plants from cold alpine and polar regions grow very low and tight to the ground where they can benefit from the soil's radiant heat and they can get some shelter from freezing winds. Plants from very cold climates have chemicals in their cells which prevents the water inside from freezing and rupturing the cell wall. Their specialised metabolisms allow them to undergo frequent freezing and thawing without harm. The mosses, Antarctic pearlwort and Antarctic hairgrass which grow on the continent of Antarctica are able to continue to photosynthesise at temperatures approaching freezing. Photosynthetic processes cannot happen as quickly as they can at warmer temperatures so the growth of these plants is very slow. The same is true for plants living in very hot deserts like cacti. They photosynthesise very slowly in extreme heat so their growth is proportionately very slow.

Humidity and evaporation

Plants have adapted to extremes of atmospheric humidity. They are found growing in cloud forests where everything is permanently bathed in clouds and fog, and also in deserts where evaporation rates exceed precipitation by many times. Interestingly, it is in these very dry environments that atmospheric humidity plays its most important role for plant growth.

The Atacama Desert in Chile is the driest place on earth. Incredibly, parts of it have received *no rainfall whatsoever* since records began in the late 16th century! The sun beats

By condensing fog on their woolly hairs cacti are able to collect enough water to live in rainless deserts.

Plants from very humid places are adapted to having so much water available in the atmosphere that they would frizzle up in seconds in the dry air of the Atacama Desert. Filmy ferns are tiny, delicate ferns of the family Hymenophyllaceae (literally, 'membrane leaf'). They live in places which are extremely humid or permanently wet. They are often found growing on rocks under waterfalls where they receive a constant mist of water. Filmy ferns' fronds are only one cell thick and have no need for stomata. Because they live in such permanently humid surroundings gas exchange and water absorption occurs directly through the cell walls of the leaf, as if they were water plants.

Abundant humidity has allowed plants to leave the soil and colonise ecological niches *en plein air*. *Epiphytes* live upon the trunks and limbs of trees (epiphyte means 'upon plants'). They are a common sight in humid biomes, especially in rainforests. Life in the canopy allows them to collect more light than they could on the forest floor. But having no contact with the soil means epiphytes had to evolve strategies for gathering water.

down from the cloudless sky every single day of the year creating a landscape of permanent water deficit. Yet even in this most extreme of environments specially adapted plants can grow. Coastal regions of the Atacama Desert are subject to a sea fog known as the *camanchaca*. This fog condenses on the woolly, white hairs of the cactus *Copiapoa columna-alba*, providing not only enough moisture for the cactus itself to grow but for lichens to colonise its trunk.

The bizarre and ancient *Welwitschia mirabilis* grows in the hostile Namib Desert in Africa. It also survives on night-time sea fogs which it collects not with hairs but on its enormous, curling, strap-shaped leaves which can be up to three metres in length. These leaves have channels in them to help condense the water and funnel it to the roots of the plant.

Welwitschia mirabilis survives in the Namib Desert by condensing sea fog on its long, strap-shaped leaves.

High humidity has enabled plants to leave the ground and colonise ecological niches in the air. Epiphytic ferns thrive in rainforest treetops in humid rainforest in northern NSW.

Epiphytic orchids have very thick, spongy roots which absorb humidity directly from the air to keep the plant hydrated. Epiphytic bromeliads do things differently. They have rather rudimentary roots, used only for support. They use their leaves to collect water. Their leaves grow in a rosette shape with a deep well in the centre which collects rainwater – sometimes even enough water to support colonies of normally aquatic animals like frogs and crabs.

Epiphytic bromeliads live life far above the ground where their roots cannot absorb water from the soil. They collect rainwater in a well formed by their leaf rosette.

Seasonality

Seasons are caused by the Earth's tilted axis. One hemisphere of the Earth is always closer to the sun than the other. The hemisphere closer to the sun experiences warmer weather and longer days while the hemisphere further from the sun experiences colder weather and shorter days. Equatorial areas experience little seasonal variation because they are always turned more or less directly towards the sun. The further you travel toward the poles, the more pronounced the seasons become because the Earth's tilt toward and away from the sun over the course of the year is more pronounced at higher latitudes. Hence the poles experience winters where the sun never rises and summers where the sun never sets.

Plants respond to variations in seasonal day length and temperature over the course of the year, relying on them to cue different stages of growth such as bud set, fruit formation and dormancy. The importance of seasonality on growth cycles rarely rates a mention in books on ornamental plants though it sometimes does in books on food plants. We often read about the number of 'chilling hours' required by stone fruits to initiate flowering, or the number of 'growing days' a pumpkin vine needs to produce fully ripe fruit. This is an important concept to keep in mind as the length and intensity of a growing season or dormant season can mean the difference between success and disappointment.

'Seasons' are as much a function of day length as temperature. In Britain the average daily temperatures in spring and autumn might not be that different but the day length pattern varies considerably. Plants from higher latitudes are extremely sensitive to the lengthening of days in spring or the shortening days of autumn. The closer such plants are grown towards the equator, the more their growth patterns are disrupted. Onions, for example, are dependent on the rapidly lengthening days of spring to tell them to grow and the long days of mid-summer to tell them to form a bulb and become dormant (at which point they can be harvested). Onions do not perform well in the tropics where day length does not vary so much through the year.

Most deciduous trees and shrubs come from higher latitudes of the northern hemisphere or from high altitude areas which experience a climate with four distinct seasons. They are adapted to a long, mild spring with dramatically increasing day length to initiate vigorous growth; a mild summer with very long days and short nights during which growth can continue unchecked; a distinct autumn with crisp nights and rapidly decreasing day length to halt growth and ripen the new season's wood; and finally a cold, dark winter to induce full dormancy. Under such conditions northern hemisphere deciduous trees grow beautifully, exhibiting vigour, disease resistance, tidy symmetrical growth, durable wood which is unlikely to split or shed limbs, and stunning autumn colour. In climates which lack distinct seasons they never achieve their full potential. The widely planted Bradford pear (*Pyrus calleryana*) is a case in point. In warm, humid climates, like Sydney's, Bradford pears grow rank and their wood is soft. They are prone to fungal attack and shedding branches. They do not flower or colour as

Northern hemisphere deciduous trees (here *Nyssa sylvatica*) are adapted to climates with four distinct seasons. In humid coastal areas they rarely perform as well as they do in cold mountain districts.

convincingly as they do in places with distinct, cold autumns and winters. The Blue Mountains, just a few kilometres to Sydney's west but much higher in altitude, have more clearly defined seasons including a crisp autumn and cold winter. Here, where the climate suits them better, Bradford pears are shapely, sound, floriferous in spring and magnificently coloured in autumn.

Seasonality also affects subtropical and tropical plants. Melbourne, with its frost-free climate, ought to grow frangipanis as well as Sydney and Brisbane. Yet it is rare to see well-grown frangipanis in Melbourne because Melbourne's climate does not deliver enough *consistent* heat over summer to ripen the frangipani's new wood, which tends to collapse and rot off in Melbourne's wet, cool winters. Mangoes grow and flower well in Sydney's summer warmth and humidity but in the absence of a distinct winter dry season they rarely set fruit. Darwin's classic monsoonal regime of a very wet and a very dry season suits mangoes perfectly.

It is difficult to be prescriptive about what seasonal regime each plant needs to thrive but it is something for the gardener to be aware of and try to develop some intuition about. Signs of seasonal incompatibility to watch out for are, in climates with cold winters, new growth of woody plants that remains green, sappy and not fully ripened as the cold season begins. This can lead to frost damage resulting in stunted, unhappy plants which never achieve their full potential. Sometimes young trees can be protected from frost for the first few years until they grow up above the ground frost zone. But if this problem manifests itself year after year it is time to rethink the suitability of the plant to your climate. In warm, humid climates, keep an eye out for herbaceous and woody plants which grow throughout the winter when they should have a dormant period. Failure to become dormant often results in loss of vigour, predisposition to disease and early decline.

How do plants adapt to dry climates?

Plants from the world's Mediterranean and semi-arid climates have developed an impressive array of adaptations for coping with drought. Surprisingly, plants from completely unrelated families in far-flung corners of the globe have evolved strikingly similar adaptations. Broadly speaking there are three main strategies for coping with a dry climate: toughing out the dry times, beating a temporary retreat and what could be described as the 'kamikaze strategy'.

1. Toughing it out

Plants whose strategy is to tough out dry seasons are primarily concerned with conserving water. The better they are able to conserve water, the better they can continue to grow and function through the dry times.

One adaptation for conserving water is to have a *thick, waxy cuticle* on the surface of the foliage. This prevents moisture from being lost from the leaf surface. Eucalypts have made this adaptation a specialty. The Mediterranean relative of the eucalypts, the myrtle (*Myrtus communis*) uses exactly the same strategy, as do strawberry trees (*Arbutus* spp.) and dry-climate oaks (*Quercus* spp.). Oak trees from wet climates have large, soft, deciduous leaves but those native to dry climates, like the Mediterranean holm oak, have hard, small, evergreen foliage. Plants with waxy, hard, evergreen leaves are called *sclerophyllous* plants, from the Greek for 'hard leaf', hence Australia's eucalypt-dominated *sclerophyll forests*.

A dense *coating of down or hair* on one or both surfaces of the leaf blade creates a humid microclimate at the leaf's surface, whereby loss of moisture through transpiration is slowed. Hairy leaves are efficient at collecting moisture from light rainfall or even dew. Downy or hairy leaves are particularly

Sclerophyllous plants have a thick, waxy cuticle on their foliage to prevent desiccation in dry climates. Australian eucalyptus, Mediterranean arbutus and cork oak (*Quercus suber*) have similar hard, waxy foliage.

common among Mediterranean plants, well-known examples being lamb's ears (*Stachys byzantina*) and sage (*Salvia officinalis*). But this adaptation is also seen in plants from other parts of the world, for example in cacti from the Americas.

Plants with hairy foliage often have *silver-coloured foliage*. The pale colour helps to reflect the heat of the sun, thereby reducing transpiration. Again, this is very commonly encountered among Mediterranean plants like wormwoods (*Artemisia* spp.) and is partly responsible for the characteristic look of

Mediterranean gardens. Plants from other parts of the world which have evolved this adaptation include the cushion bush (*Leucophyta brownii*) from coastal southern Australia and the spectacularly metallic silver tree (*Leucadendron argenteum*) from South Africa.

Some plants have evolved *specialised leaf pores* (or stomata) to limit the loss of water through transpiration. Oleanders' stomata are contained in tiny chambers on the underside of the leaf called *stomatal crypts*. The entrance to the crypts is covered with tiny hairs. This

Hairy foliage slows water loss through transpiration and helps to collect moisture from rain and dew. Here lamb's ears (*Stachys byzantina*) from the Mediterranean, *Echium wildpretii* from the Canary Islands and the old man of the Andes cactus (*Oreocereus celsianus*) display varying degrees of this adaptation.

adaptation is thought to retain humidity around the stomata, reducing moisture loss through transpiration. Some Australian banksias have evolved a similar adaptation.

The overwhelming majority of plants from dry climates have *small leaves*. Small leaves minimise surface area through which water can be lost. Lavender and rosemary are familiar examples of small-leaved Mediterranean plants. Australian grevilleas have made a specialty of this adaptation and in fact there are grevilleas named after

lavender and rosemary (*Grevillea lavandulacea* and *G. rosmarinifolia*) due to the similarity of their foliage. These plants' leaves appear 'smaller' than they actually are. Looking closely, you can see that the edges of the leaf are rolled under so that a smaller surface area is exposed to direct sun but a larger surface area is available for photosynthesis. Many grasses and other plants roll their leaves into a tube during dry weather, creating a humid microclimate within the leaf tube and reducing the area of leaf blade exposed to the sun.

Many small-leaved, hairy-leaved and sclerophyllous plants have *high concentrations of volatile oils* in their foliage. It is not entirely clear what purpose this serves but the fact that so many Mediterranean and semi-arid

The stomata on the underside of an oleander leaf are sheltered in stomatal crypts.

climate plants display it suggests that it is an adaptation to dry conditions. It is thought that the volatile oils cool the surface of the leaf as they evaporate from it. This adaptation

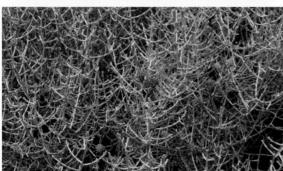

Silver foliage reflects the sun's heat. Here *Convolvulus cneorum* from Mediterranean Europe, cushion bush from Australia and the South African silver tree have all evolved this adaptation.

Grevillea lanigera from Australia and lavender from Mediterranean Europe both have very small leaves with rolled margins.

Euphorbia stygiana from the Azores rolls its foliage into a tube during dry weather.

Mediterranean rosemary and oregano and the Australian *Eriostemons* have high oil concentrations in their foliage.

is so prevalent in certain parts of the world that it gives them their characteristic scent. The Australian bush gets its unmistakable smell from the oils in the foliage of our ubiquitous gum trees, as well as *Prostanthera*, *Eriostemon* and other native shrubs. The south of France is scented with *garrigue* herbs – sage, rosemary, thyme and lavender. Greek hillsides are fragrant with oregano in the summer heat. Unfortunately these oils make dry-climate plants, which are adapted to bushfires, highly flammable. Keep this in mind when designing a garden in a fire-prone area.

Brooms from dry climates have vestigial or no foliage at all (*Genista lydia*).

Some plants have taken reducing foliage size a step further, having only *vestigial foliage* or none at all. Brooms, some euphorbias and of course cacti all display this adaptation. Plants devoid of foliage must compensate by having special photosynthetic stems to do the job normally done by leaves. Many Australian wattles have no true leaves but conduct photosynthesis in specialised leaf petioles called *phyllodes*. Ruscus are leafless but have modified stems called *cladodes* which conduct photosynthesis. Stems, phyllodes and cladodes have fewer stomata than true leaves and consequently lose less water.

Succulent plants store water in specialised cells in the stems, leaves and roots, often in the form of a mucilage which does not evaporate quickly. When gardeners refer to 'succulents' we are referring collectively to plants from many different families such as the Crassulaceae (houseleeks), Euphorbiaceae (euphorbias), Aizoaceae (pigfaces), Apocynaceae (*Stapelia* or starfish flowers) and even the daisy family Asteraceae (*Senecios*). The fact that so many unrelated plants have evolved succulence as an adaptation to dry climates is an indication of how closely climate shapes plant physiology.

It may seem insignificant but even a plant's *leaf orientation* can help to keep it cool and conserve water. The Australian eucalypts use this adaptation to their advantage. They hold their leaves perpendicular to the ground so

Some plants photosynthesise through modified, leaf-like stems called cladodes (*Ruscus aculeatus*).

Many wattles lack true leaves, photosynthesising through modified leaf petioles called phyllodes (*Acacia glaucoptera*).

Houseleeks, euphorbias, pigfaces and *Senecios* have all evolved succulence as a means of surviving drought.

that the greater part of their surface area is out of the sun's glare during the hottest part of the day. This is the reason eucalypts cast such meagre shade. The perpendicular orientation of eucalypt leaves also means that any precipitation will drip immediately off the leaves onto the tree's root zone before it evaporates. Even fog and dew can be utilised by gum trees in this way. On foggy mornings in Victoria's highlands it can seem like it is raining under the canopies of giant mountain ash trees (*Eucalyptus regnans*) as the fog condenses on their leaves and drips onto their roots. Although they are unrelated to one another, *Yucca, Agave, Dasylirion, Beaucarnea* and our native grass trees

(*Xanthorrhoea*) look strikingly similar. Each of them bears many long, narrow leaves arranged in a perfect sphere around the central growing point. Only a small proportion of the foliage is exposed to the hot sun at any time and the growing point is kept shaded.

Many semi-arid and coastal regions are rocky and exposed, subject to hot, dry winds from the desert or to salty sea winds. Plants in these places have evolved a *compact growth habit* to help them survive. In the Mediterranean basin there is a whole community of plants, called garrigue, which is characterised by this hummocky, ground-

They exhibit a similar low, hummocky habit of growth with small, hairy leaves loaded with strongly scented oils which is, of course, why they feature in the cuisine of that region. There are similarly adapted plant communities in other dry, exposed regions of the world such as the *fynbos* of South Africa, the *matorral* in Chile and of course Australia has its own heathland communities such as the incredibly biodiverse *kwongan* heathlands of south-west WA. California has its own version of this type of vegetation known as *chaparral*. Many people have seen chaparral, without realising it, in photographs – it is the low, scrubby vegetation covering the hillside around the famous 'HOLLYWOOD' sign. Indeed the Hollywood Hills may derive their name from a chaparral plant, the California holly (*Heteromeles arbutifolia*), which commonly grows there.

It is easy to observe plants' above-ground adaptations for toughing out drought. But there can be a lot going on underground, too. Many dry-climate plants have some kind of *specialised root system* to help them survive drought. Agapanthus have thick, *succulent roots* which store water. Some plants have a

Agave stricta, Yucca rostrata and *Xanthorrhoea semiplana* have their foliage arranged in a perfect sphere around the growing point, minimising exposure to the sun.

Hummocky garrigue vegetation covers the dry rocky slopes leading down to the Mediterranean Sea.

hugging growth habit. Many of our most familiar garden plants have come from garrigue plant communities. Lavender, sage, rosemary and thyme are all garrigue plants.

Coastal heath vegetation in southern Australia looks similar to garrigue, featuring low, hummocky plants adapted to exposure and salt spray.

specialised *tap root* for water storage, such as cacti and baobab trees (*Adansonia* spp.). One of the most interesting underground adaptations is a *dual root system* whereby a plant sends down a very deep tap root to search for ground water as well as growing a secondary, fibrous root system close to the surface to allow it to benefit from precipitation. Carob trees and cistus are two plants which use this strategy. The tap root of a carob tree may be up to 40 m deep – four times the height of the tree itself – and the surface root system may extend for many metres beyond the canopy of the tree to collect rainfall.

The carob tree has a dual root system. Its long tap root is able to search for ground water while its fibrous surface roots collect rainfall when it is available.

2. Beating a retreat

Summers are harsh in Mediterranean and semi-arid climates. Rather than toughing out the heat some plants simply stop photosynthesising, switch off their metabolisms and wait until times are good again. Just as deciduous trees from northerly latitudes drop their leaves and go to sleep during the cold, dark winters, so many Mediterranean and arid climate plants drop their leaves and undergo a *summer dormancy* during the hottest, driest part of the year. They cannot photosynthesise without foliage, but they cannot become desiccated either.

The most familiar group of plants to undergo summer dormancy are the *geophytes*, better known to gardeners as 'bulbs'. Geophytes (meaning 'ground plant' in Greek) belong to many unrelated plant families but they share the adaptation of having modified leaf bases, stems or rhizomes which allow them to spend part of each year dormant underground. In many cases bulbs are actually dormant for a much greater part of the year than they are in active growth, growing for just a few weeks

Geophytes survive dry times as a dormant bulb. *Urginea maritima* from the Mediterranean basin has bulbs nearly the size of soccer balls.

during the cooler, damper months and retreating underground for the remainder of the year.

Geophytes belong to such diverse families as the Amaryllidaceae (which includes daffodils), Liliaceae (lilies), Primulaceae (cyclamen) and Iridaceae (iris and crocus).

We tend to associate tulips with the Netherlands but in reality they are native to Mediterranean and cold semi-arid climates in

Dioscorea elephantipes is a dry climate relative of the sweet potato from South Africa. It is an extreme geophyte, forming a huge, trunk-like storage organ called a caudex.

southern Europe, North Africa, Iran, Turkey, north-western China and particularly Kazakhstan and Uzbekistan. Wordsworth's famous 'host of golden daffodils' must have referred to the single *Narcissus* species native to the UK (*N. pseudonarcissus*) as most *Narcissus* are natives of southern Europe (especially Spain), North Africa, Turkey and central Asia. Crocus and bulbous iris share a similar distribution. The Mediterranean basin and central Asia are not the only places where geophytes have evolved. South Africa is another hot spot for them, particularly the western Cape. From this part of the world come nerines, gladiolus and naked ladies. California is home to the genus *Brodiaea* and the exquisite but little known *Calochortus*.

Bulbous plants are not the only group of dry-climate plants to have evolved summer dormancy. Some perennials like bear's breeches or oyster plant (*Acanthus mollis*) become dormant in times of severe drought, surviving as an underground rootstock with thick, succulent roots. Even some woody plants have evolved summer dormancy in response to a dry climate. Clematis is a genus of creepers featured in many British garden books for their colourful flowers. Clematis species from summer rainfall climates of China and Europe grow and flower during the summer and become dormant in winter. Their Mediterranean cousin *Clematis cirrhosa* var. *balearica* from Majorca and Minorca does things the other way around. Just like a daffodil, it grows and flowers during the winter but drops its leaves and becomes dormant during the summer. Similarly the lush horse chestnuts associated with English gardens (but native to the Balkans) are

Summer-dormant bulbs are adapted to summer-dry climates. Tulips grow wild in the Mediterranean and central Asia, naked ladies are native to South Africa and *Calochortus* to California.

dormant in the winter whereas their Californian relative *Aesculus californica* enters dormancy during the hot, dry summer months.

Bulbs are not the only plants which undergo summer dormancy. Bear's breeches, California horse chestnuts and succulent aeoniums also shed their leaves during summer drought.

3. The kamikazes

Some plants do not even attempt to survive drought. Their strategy is simply to turn their toes up and die as soon as the going gets tough. But these kamikaze plants with their *annual life cycle* have a trick up their sleeves: they produce prodigious quantities of seed. Each seed is a package of genetic information capable of lying dormant for months, years or even decades until conditions are once again right for growth. In this way plants from unpredictable climates travel through time, waiting for another opportunity to flourish.

The mass flowering of West Australian desert wildflowers is one of the most spectacular examples of this. Winter rains turn the desert sands into a lurid tapestry of colour as seeds which have lain dormant in the sand since the last rains germinate, grow, flower and reproduce in a matter of a few weeks. In some parts of the world there can be years or decades between rain events. In many ways it is the seed of these desert annuals which is the main phase of their life cycle. The flowering adult phase seems like a brief interlude necessary only for the creation of more seeds.

Some of the best-known spring garden flowers are descended from Mediterranean and semi-arid climate annuals. Flanders poppies, opium poppies, cornflowers, corncockles, snapdragons, stocks and sweet peas all originate in southern Europe and the Middle East. California poppies come from the deserts of California and everlasting daisies from Australia.

A variation on the annual life cycle exists in which a plant grows through *two* growing seasons before it seeds and dies. Such plants

Echium simplex and *Geranium maderense* are giant biennials from the Canary Islands and Madeira respectively.

Corn poppies die during the Mediterranean's summer drought but they set prodigious quantities of seed to ensure that a new generation will grow with the first autumn rains.

are said to have a *biennial life cycle*. Many of our food crops are biennials such as carrots, beetroot and cabbage, as well as flowers like foxgloves and hollyhocks. These biennials

Mediterranean gardens derive their classic 'look' from the drought adaptations of the plants grown in them.

grow over the warmer months, become dormant in winter and flower the following spring. But biennials from summer-dry climates germinate in the autumn and grow through the winter, toughing out just one summer dry season to grow through another winter then flower and die the following spring. This adaptation is relatively common in Mediterranean climates, especially in the Canary Islands and Madeira where some jaw-dropping super-sized biennials have evolved, like the stunning *Echium simplex* and *Geranium maderense*.

These many different adaptations to surviving dry seasons give Mediterranean and semi-arid gardens their characteristic look. There is always plenty of silver foliage, an abundance of bun-shaped, small-leaved plants, lots of fragrant foliage and the trees are pre-dominantly evergreen. Growth is mainly in the autumn and winter with flowering peaking in the springtime.

How do plants adapt to wet climates?

Plants from very rainy, humid climates have different adaptations to those from dry climates. Sometimes these adaptations have more to do with *shedding* water than with retaining it.

The abundance of water and humidity characteristic of the humid subtropical climate, coupled with its warm, but not too hot, temperatures, allows plants to photosynthesise under optimum conditions, resulting in rampant growth. In Australia this climatic type is home to many of our rainforests, especially around the NSW–Queensland border. Rainforests are characterised by very dense canopy cover. Plants growing on the rainforest floor must have special adaptations to enable them to photosynthesise in low light conditions. Their leaves tend to be very large, maximising the surface area available to catch sunlight and enabling them to outcompete plants growing around them. To make full use of the weak rays of sunlight which penetrate to the rainforest floor, their leaves are very rich in chlorophyll, giving them a rich, dark green colour. Their leaves are held horizontally to collect as much light as possible; the opposite to gum leaves, which are held vertically to minimise it.

To help shed water from heavy rain, rainforest plants' leaves are designed like umbrellas. They have a waxy, waterproof cuticle on the upper surface so that water beads on them rather than soaking in. The leaves of rainforest plants tend to be convex in profile so that water rolls off rather than collecting on them, which could lead to branches snapping off during torrential downpours. Like the small, pointy extensions on the ribs of an umbrella, the leaves of rainforest plants often terminate in a drawn-out 'drip-tip' which guides water off the leaf surface away

The foliage of the umbrella plant is adapted to life under the rainforest canopy.

The shade and generous rainfall of the rainforest floor shaped the lush, glossy appearance of many indoor plants.

from the centre of the plant. One example of a rainforest plant displaying these adaptations is, perhaps unsurprisingly, the umbrella plant (*Schefflera* spp.).

In the same way that harsh sun, drought and exposure have sculpted the hummocky, grey, small-leaved plants of the Mediterranean garden, the deep shade and generous rainfall of the rainforest floor have shaped the lush, glossy plants which give subtropical gardens, not to mention house plants, their characteristic look throughout the world.

Far up in the rainforest canopy epiphytic orchids, ferns, mosses, bromeliads and other

plants cling to the branches and trunks of the trees. These plants are able to thrive here without any contact with the soil due to the high rainfall and humidity. Some variations of the humid subtropical and equatorial climates have a dry season in winter. Epiphytes living under these conditions have evolved differently to their cousins in areas which are wet all year round. Epiphytic orchids native to regions with a dry season, like soft-cane *Dendrobiums* from northern India and the *Cattleyas* from South America have developed specialised succulent stems called *pseudobulbs*. These enable the orchid to

Dogwoods are native to China and the eastern USA. These regions experience a variation of the humid subtropical climate with a very cold winter; a climate which has no analogue in Australia.

Summer flowering bulbs like lilies are adapted to grow during the wet summer months and become dormant during the cold, dry winter months.

store water during the wet season and survive on it during the dry. Many such species enter dormancy during the dry season. By contrast, orchids from tropical climates which do not experience a dry season, like the *Phalaenopsis* and *Vandas* from South-East Asia, have not evolved these specialised storage organs and never become dormant.

Rainforest is not the only vegetation type found in humid subtropical climates. The eastern part of North America experiences a variation of the humid subtropical climate with a bitterly cold winter. Here, deciduous broadleaf forests are the norm, just as in temperate Europe. In many ways these deciduous forests resemble subtropical rainforests during the warm, humid summer months but in winter they are bare and snow covered like the temperate forests of Europe. The forests of the south-eastern states of the USA are home to lush, large-leaved plants, rich green in colour and adapted to high humidity and rainfall. Eastern China has a similar humid subtropical climate with a

cold winter and, interestingly, the two regions share many genera of plants – dogwoods, magnolias and wisteria to name but a few.

China and North America are both home to summer-flowering bulbs such as *Liliums* and *Arisaemas*. Unlike the Mediterranean climate bulbs which become dormant to escape the heat and dry of summer, bulbs from humid subtropical climates are adapted to grow during the summer when there is plenty of rainfall and undergo dormancy during the winter, when it is very cold and dry.

Plants have adaptations which allow them to fill every conceivable ecological niche, including many in climates much drier and harsher than our own. Sometimes Australian gardeners feel it is impossible to get anything at all to grow in our gardens, burdened with water restrictions and poor soils. In fact there is a huge palette of plants just waiting to be discovered. Understanding how plants adapt to climate allows us to learn to identify plants which will thrive in our own gardens.

3
GARDEN MICROCLIMATES

A *microclimate* is a set of localised climatic conditions which exists within a broader regional climate. Put more simply, a small climate within a big climate. We all recognise microclimates intuitively. We know that standing under a shady tree on a summer day feels cooler than standing in the middle of an exposed asphalt carpark. We know that sheltering under the eaves of a building when it is raining will prevent us from getting wet. We know that there is likely to be a cool breeze at the beach on a hot day. We automatically seek out microclimates where we feel comfortable. Unlike humans, plants can't move to a more favourable microclimate if they don't feel comfortable so it is important to learn to recognise the microclimates in your garden and site plants appropriately. Even the smallest city garden contains a few different microclimates. Some spots in the garden are sunny, others are shady. Some spots are windy, others more sheltered. Some spots will be frosty in winter, others might never experience frost. You can use this knowledge to choose plants most likely to succeed within your garden spaces.

Gardeners need to think about microclimate on a couple of different levels. One is the level of your local region, where microclimates are shaped by proximity to the sea or to mountains. The other level is within your own garden where different microclimates are created by buildings and trees.

Local area microclimates can be noticeably different from the broader climate of an area due to the influence of geography and human activity. Mountains strongly influence the weather conditions in their vicinity due to their sheer physical size. Mountains attract cloud and bring down rain. Areas at the top of a mountain experience cooler microclimates than those at the bottom. The top of the mountain might receive snow in winter. Frost, which tends to run down slopes, will accumulate at the foot of mountain. The area at the bottom of the

Mountains and large bodies of water influence weather conditions around themselves, creating localised microclimates.

mountain, with its hotter summers and frostier winters might be considered a 'harsher' microclimate than the area at the top from a gardening point of view.

The northern slopes of mountains, exposed to sun for the greater part of the day, tend to have warmer microclimates than southern slopes which are constantly in shade (in the southern hemisphere). The side of the mountain exposed to prevailing wind will have a windier microclimate than the side protected by the mountain; however, rain clouds are blown in on prevailing winds so the exposed side of a mountain might also receive the majority of rainfall, giving it a wetter microclimate than the lee side of the mountain which is said to be in a 'rain shadow'. Combinations of these different variables result in a range of different microclimates within a relatively small area, sometimes just a few hundred metres from each other. The effect of geography on microclimate, and therefore vegetation, is

It is easy to 'see' the microclimates in New Zealand's Southern Alps by the change in vegetation. Tussocky alpine plants cling to the snowy peaks, dense beech forests blanket the sheltered lower slopes and swamp plants inhabit the wet valley floors.

easily seen from the air. Flying over the Royal National Park south of Sydney, it is easy to see fingers of emerald-green rainforest, with its emergent palm trees, snaking up the sheltered south- and east-facing creek gullies. Higher up the slopes are the drier, more open eucalypt forests. On the hot, exposed tops of the plateau the low, scrubby coastal heathland vegetation dominates, sometimes blackened by fire.

The sea and large bodies of water exert a significant influence on their local microclimate. Large bodies of water act as both a heat sink and a source of atmospheric moisture. It takes a lot of heat energy to change the temperature of a large body of water so its temperature tends to remain constant. Water absorbs heat energy during hot weather and radiates it in cold weather, acting as a buffer against fluctuations in air temperature. Seaside areas tend to remain warmer than inland areas during winter and cooler than inland areas in summer. Air passing over large bodies of water picks up moisture, humidifying the air, resulting in lower evapotranspiration levels in plants.

Sydney city and Sydney's western suburbs are just a few kilometres apart yet they have very different microclimates because of the sea's influence. A summer day in the western suburbs might reach 37°C while in Sydney city the temperature might only get to 28°C due to the cooling effect of the sea. In winter, the night-time temperature in the western suburbs might drop to freezing while the city itself might only fall to 5°C, once again due to the sea's ameliorating influence. Although these temperature differences are small in absolute terms they make a big difference to the plants that can be grown in each area. Plants preferring a cold dormant season (like stone fruits) do better in the western suburbs whereas subtropical and tropical plants which dislike the cold (like bananas) are more likely to thrive nearer the coast.

The sea isn't the only factor affecting Sydney's microclimate. Human activity has changed local conditions significantly. Cities like Sydney contain an enormous amount of thermal mass in the form of buildings, roads and paved areas. This thermal mass acts as a heat sink, soaking up the sun's warmth during the day and radiating it slowly back at night. For this reason cities around the world tend to have warmer microclimates than their immediate surroundings. Cities behave as 'heat islands'. Sydney city experiences a warmer climate than coastal towns immediately to its north and south. Similarly, London is a huge conurbation of heat-absorbing buildings and concrete. Not surprisingly its climate is quite distinct from the surrounding home counties. London gardeners lament the fact that their gardens are too warm to grow cold-loving Tibetan

Large cities act as heat islands. Buildings have high thermal mass, creating a warmer microclimate.

blue poppies (*Meconopsis* spp.) while gardeners in other parts of Britain envy Londoners their ability to grow an increasing range of Mediterranean and subtropical plants, such as echiums and ornamental bananas (*Musa* spp.). It really doesn't matter what microclimate you are blessed or cursed with; there is always something that will grow well in your garden. You just have to find out what it is.

Microclimates in the backyard

Microclimates don't only exist on the scale of mountains, oceans and cities but also on a much smaller scale within backyard gardens. The main influences on backyard microclimates are buildings and large trees. Buildings and trees define areas of sun and shade in the garden. Sun and shade are, of course, the basic starting points for working out what to plant where.

Sun and shade

In the southern hemisphere the sun travels from east to west via the north. A north-facing aspect is typically the sunniest position in any southern hemisphere garden unless it is shaded by neighbouring trees or buildings. Be aware that gardening books from the northern hemisphere talk about *southerly* aspects as being the sunniest. British books frequently tell us that certain plants 'thrive at the base of a south-facing wall' which, for a northern hemisphere gardener, is the warmest spot in the garden but for a southern hemisphere gardener is actually the coldest. Areas on the south side of a house have a shadow cast over them by the house for some or all of the day. The shadow will be longer in winter when the

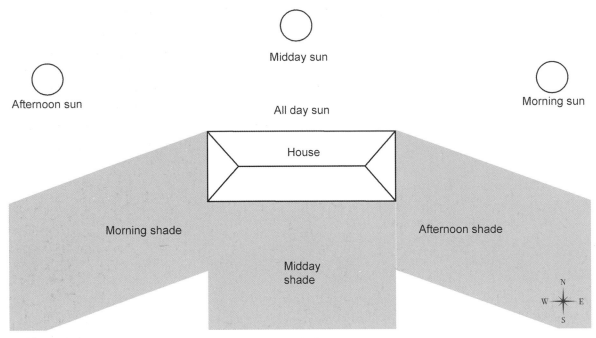

Figure 3.1 Diagram of sunny/shady microclimates around a house.

sun is lower in the sky and shorter in the summer when the sun is higher. But on the whole, the south side of the house will be shady most of the time. This is a good thing if you want to grow shade-loving tree ferns but no good at all if you want to grow sun-loving tomatoes. A northern aspect is the perfect spot for a vegetable garden but would be a bit bright for tree ferns. The eastern side of a house tends to receive morning sun until midday when the sun begins to set on the other side of the house after which it will be in shade from the rest of the day. Many plants thrive in this position – gentle morning sun followed by shade during the hottest part of the day. The western side of the house is just the opposite. It is typically quite cold and shady until midday, after which time it is baked by the punishing afternoon sun. It is one of the most difficult aspects in the garden.

Exposure and shelter

Buildings and vegetation create some areas which are especially sheltered from prevailing winds and others which are particularly exposed to it. Plants from enclosed

Forest plants like *Cordyline fruticosa* prefer sheltered garden microclimates. In exposed positions their leaves become tatty.

environments like forests and gorges prefer shelter from wind which can burn and fray their foliage. Plants from open environments like grassland and heath prefer to have a good stiff breeze going through them, tending to grow soft and disease-prone in sheltered positions.

Heat sinks

Just as large bodies of water and the thermal mass of cities create warm microclimates on a regional level, some common features of our backyards can create warm microclimates on a smaller scale. Swimming pools, water tanks, hard landscaping like paving and gravel, and of course buildings themselves act as heat sinks. They keep the microclimate of your garden warmer than it would otherwise be. Pools keep gardens cooler in summer by increasing air humidity, whereas hard surfaces reflect heat and actually make the garden hotter. The last thing most of us want in summer is extra heat in our lives, so planting a garden is the best way to ameliorate the extra heat generated by lots of hard landscaping. By keeping the sun off hard surfaces, we reduce the amount of heat they reflect back at us. On the other hand the reflected heat from hot, hard surfaces makes a great microclimate for growing plants from slightly warmer climates than our own. Citrus trees will often flourish in frosty parts of the country if grown in the warm, sheltered microclimate of a paved courtyard. By using deciduous plants near hard landscaping we can have the best of both worlds; reflected heat in winter and cooling shade in summer.

Gardening in dry shade

Gardening in dry shade presents a considerable – but not insurmountable – challenge to the gardener. British gardening books are full of advice for gardening in damp shade, damp woodland and even shady bog gardens but rarely have much to say on dry shade, which is much more common in Australian gardens.

It is important in the first instance to recognise what is making the area shady and what is making it dry. If the answer to both questions is a gum tree then the situation is fraught with its own special challenges, discussed in detail below.

In nature, dry-shade plants are found in forests under evergreen or deciduous trees, around the bases of boulders or in steep gullies and ravines cut by watercourses. Each of these situations tends to accumulate fallen leaves and other organic matter and they often have quite humusy soils. That doesn't mean to say that they are permanently 'moist', but the plants which grow in them are adapted to growing in leafy, cool soils. In the garden this is easily approximated by adding compost, leaf mould, manures or deep organic mulches to the soil. Increasing the humus content of soils in dry shade radically increases the range of plants that can be grown.

If your shady area is created by a tree (particularly a deciduous tree), you have the advantage that the tree will constantly improve the soil with its fallen leaves over the years, creating the cool, leafy soils preferred by shade-loving plants. But bear in mind that trees also take water from the soil. Some trees

Bold, massed plantings work well under trees.

Fatsias are usually sold as indoor plants but they thrive in shady, sheltered microclimates in the open garden.

are more rapacious than others in this regard. Likewise some shade plants are better adapted to cope with root competition than others. It is worth experimenting to find out what performs best under your particular tree. When you find something that thrives, plant it *en masse*. Bold, massed plantings work very well with the grand scale of trees, certainly much better than 'bitsy' plantings with one of this and one of that.

If your shade is cast by a building the situation is much easier to manage. Buildings do not take water out of the soil in the way that trees do. In fact, their footings can provide a cool, damp root run for plants in the way that boulders do in nature. Buildings act as heat sinks, tempering the climate in their immediate vicinity, so they make a good sheltered microclimate for plants native to sheltered forests and rocky ravines which appreciate such a position – many palm species for example.

Many shade plants have broad, glossy, dark green foliage as an adaptation to collecting light in deep shade. This type of foliage has a generous, lush, rainforesty feeling to it. You

can use shady microclimates to create a cooling, oasis-like feeling in your garden. Many plants we think of as indoor plants thrive in the open garden and are remarkably tough when grown in the ground. Fatsias, aspidistras, rhapis palms and mother-in-law's-tongue are classic examples, growing outdoors in a range of climates so long as they have some shelter and a modicum of humidity in the air.

There is no shortage of plants to grow in shady situations but the stumbling block most gardeners have is that they fail to recognise degrees of shade. All shade is not equal. There are degrees of shade from light, dappled shade created by high trees, to full, dark shade created by dense evergreen trees and buildings. There is also 'part shade'. This means that a position is in full sun for at least part of the day and shade for the remainder. Different plants have different shade requirements. Clivias turn yellow and burn in part shade but look beautiful in full shade. Spring bulbs like daffodils need full sun when in full growth during the winter but don't care one way or the other when they are

Daffodils need sunlight in winter and spring but tolerate shade in summer when they are dormant.

dormant in summer. For this reason they thrive under deciduous trees but flower poorly under evergreen trees. The winter rose-type hellebores are a similar story. When planted in dense shade, hellebores get smaller year by year, stop flowering and eventually die out. Hellebores are native to grassland and the edges of deciduous forest. They like *dappled* shade in summer but need plenty of sunlight during their growing season in winter. They are not happy growing in dense shade all year round. It is important to recognise what kind of microclimate a shade plant comes from in nature before choosing a spot for it in the garden.

The key to designing a beautiful garden in dry shade is to base it on *foliage*, not flowers.

Shade plants have beautiful foliage shapes and textures. *Mahonia lomariifolia, Tetrapanax papyrifer, Arthropodium cirratum* and *Rhapis excelsa*.

Foliage shapes and textures can be just as interesting as flowers even if the range of colours is not as wide. Cordylines, bromeliads and palms give a fantastic variety of shapes and colours in frost-free areas. For colder climates, *Mahonia* and *Aucuba* are good genera to start with. Coastal Mediterranean climates are lucky enough to be able to grow both temperate and subtropical plants thanks to the sea's humid microclimate (although some supplementary irrigation may be necessary in summer). Incorporating flowers into dry shade is possible but it should be thought of as a seasonal bonus, not the main focus. Clivias, lily turf (*Liriope*), rengarenga lilies, cyclamen and *Geranium maderense* all have foliage which is at least as beautiful as their flowers and it has the benefit of lasting for a much longer season.

Plants from rocky areas thrive in hot spots near gravel, paving or brickwork. Here kalanchoes from southern Africa mingle with euphorbias and sea squill from southern Europe and flannel flowers from the Hawkesbury sandstone country around Sydney.

Gardening in hot spots

Urban situations can be difficult places to garden in because of reflected heat from concrete and masonry and large areas of soil paved with concrete or asphalt. Aspects on the western side of brick buildings or adjacent to concreted or paved areas can become baking hot in summer. These conditions approximate the microclimates of rocky areas in nature and plants from such microclimates – such as garrigue, stony deserts, rocky outcrops and volcanic lava flows – thrive in hot spots in the garden.

Gardening under gum trees

One of the most difficult microclimates to garden in is around gum trees. Gum trees are very efficient at removing moisture from soil. Their roots extend far beyond the canopy in their search for moisture. For this reason the soil around eucalypts is usually very dry. But this is not the only reason why it is so difficult to garden under eucalypts.

Many eucalypts are *allelopaths*. This means they produce chemicals to try to poison the plants growing around them. Toxic *allelochemicals* interfere with the growth of rival plants by preventing their seeds from germinating and developing properly or by inhibiting beneficial soil microbes and fungi needed for other plants to grow. Allelopathy is an adaptation to reduce competition for resources. During periods of stress, such as in a drought, allelopathic plants actually produce more allelochemicals than during normal times.

Eucalypts are not the only allelopathic plant species. Many plants are engaged in chemical warfare with their neighbours and we are only beginning to understand how and why. It used to be said that it is impossible to grow anything under a walnut tree. This is perhaps overstating things a little, but walnut trees do produce an allelochemical called *juglone* which is toxic to some plant species. Australian native blackwood wattles (*Acacia melanoxylon*) produce a substance in their leaves that inhibits the germination of seeds in their leaf litter. Pine trees are difficult to garden under because of the waterproof thatch of needles they produce. This dry, waxy thatch makes the surrounding soil very acid, making certain nutrients unavailable and generally unsuitable for rival plants to grow but ideal for the mycorrhizal fungi which help feed the pine tree itself.

Adding *copious* organic matter to the soil is one solution to gardening under gum trees. Organic matter improves water retention and helps to ameliorate the effects of the allelochemicals which leach out of gum leaves. If you are able to add lots of organic matter over many years this will greatly increase the choice of plants you can grow under your gum tree. But be prepared for a constant uphill battle. If you want a low-maintenance garden, it is better to choose plants which will prosper in these tough conditions in the first place.

It is difficult to grow plants under allelopathic trees, but not impossible. A bit of experimentation is all that is needed. While native plants *seem* to be the obvious solution to gardening under gum trees, in fact not all natives are uniformly tolerant of the allelochemicals produced by gum trees. This is not surprising when you consider that it is against other Australian native plants that gum trees have evolved their chemical

Many eucalypts are allelopaths. They produce chemicals which inhibit the growth of other plants around them.

defences. Perhaps more surprising is that some exotic plants can thrive under gum trees, especially plants from other dry, evergreen forests. Many New Zealand natives such as *Arthropodium cirratum*, *Cordyline australis*, *Anemanthele lessoniana* and *Pseudopanax* species do well under eucalypts. So do many plants from sclerophyllous communities in other parts of the world such as Californian lilacs (*Ceanothus*) and manzanitas (*Arctostaphylos*) from the chaparral and live oak forests of California.

Gardening by the sea

Seaside gardens have a microclimate all their own. They are exposed to incessant, salt-laden winds and brilliant sunshine. They often have very poor, sandy soils or are set on erosion-prone cliffs. Many plants simply cannot tolerate seaside conditions but, happily, an equal number are perfectly adapted to them and actually look their *best* by the sea. Plants from coastal regions around the world, and sometimes plants from deserts (which have similar dry, sandy, salty conditions), thrive in seaside gardens. Problems only arise in seaside gardens when we attempt to grow the soft, temperate-climate plants featured in British gardening books and magazines. Obviously, plants like rhododendrons and delphiniums, native to foggy Himalayan forests and subalpine meadows, are completely unsuited to growing in the baking sun, driving salt winds and sandy soils of seaside gardens. Nor do they suit the landscape or the spirit of the seaside, an important aesthetic consideration in designing any garden.

This is not to say that seaside gardens have to look sticky and wind-blown. In fact, many seaside plants look just the opposite. Rugosa roses come from sand dunes in Siberia and northern Japan, yet they are among the lushest and most floriferous of all roses. Frangipanis from Mexico always look cool, calm and collected even in the most punishing sunshine. Our native *Crinum pedunculatum* looks very jungly yet is perfectly happy growing in sand dunes within metres of the breaking waves. Whatever seaside climate you live in, there is a huge range of suitable plants to choose from. The extra warmth provided by the sea makes it possible to grow plants from warmer climates than you otherwise could. For example, the exquisite bangalow palm (*Archontophoenix cunninghamiana*) is often seen growing in Melbourne's bayside suburbs, well south of its natural range (Mackay to Batemans Bay).

Seaside plants are adapted to constant salt spray and exposure. *Rosa rugosa* 'Alba' from sand dunes in Japan and Siberia, *Crinum pedunculatum* grows by the sea in eastern Australia and *Salvia africana-lutea* is a beach plant from South Africa.

Gardening in salty soils

Parts of Australia's landmass have accumulated salt over many thousands of years. Some land areas were once submerged beneath the sea. In others, salt has also been deposited by rain over many centuries.

Saltbush is a halophyte. It accumulates salt in its foliage which is shed at the end of the season or eaten by browsers.

Dissolved salt travels down through the soil where it exists as salty ground water. This is usually kept far beneath the soil surface by the roots of native vegetation. In places where vegetation has been removed and the ground has been irrigated for crops, salt has been able to leach to the surface. Soil salinity causes untold damage to agriculture and the environment and is very difficult to remedy.

Salty soils are difficult to garden in but not impossible. Many arid and semi-arid regions of the world have salty soils similar to our own. Halophytes are plants which specialise in growing in very salty environments like estuaries, salt marshes and salt pans. They are able to excrete salt through their foliage or concentrate it in their cells without harm. Mangroves and saltbush (*Atriplex* spp.) are well-known halophytes. The majority of gardeners are dealing with slightly salty soils or salty bore water, not Lake Eyre. Many plants display a degree of salt *tolerance* without being classed as highly specialised halophytes. Plants from the Mediterranean cliffsides grow on pure limestone soils within the reach of salty sea winds. As a group they display remarkable salt tolerance. Plants from beachside areas and coastal sand dunes obviously have good salt tolerance although they do not necessarily appreciate the semi-arid climates where most saline soils are found in Australia. Plants from other arid and semi-arid climates in central Asia, the Middle East and the deserts of North America fare well in salt-affected gardens, too. Once again, it is simply a question of experimenting and finding what works in your particular microclimate, then planting lots of it.

4
CHOOSING PLANTS FOR AUSTRALIAN GARDENS

For decades Australians have been looking in the wrong places for garden plants. Perhaps because of our predominantly Anglo-Irish heritage or perhaps because of the enormous influence British garden culture exerts on the international gardening scene we continue to live in denial about our climate, trying desperately to mimic British gardens. In so doing we condemn ourselves to gardens dependent on reticulated water for their survival.

The gardening legacy of the British is awe-inspiring. Their gardens are among the most sophisticated in the world. We are right to hold them up as paragons of excellence and try to learn from them. Unfortunately we have been learning the wrong lessons from British gardens. We think that if we grow the same *plants* as them – rhododendrons, snowdrops, flowering cherries, lupins – then our gardens will be as sublime and glorious as theirs. In fact the opposite is true. Our gardens will never be as good as theirs *so long as* we try to grow the same plants as them: our climates are just too different. As long as we are unable to find beauty in anything but those plants expressly sanctioned by British gardeners we will continue to be

disappointed by our own gardens' ability to measure up to theirs.

Learning to change our tastes

As Australian gardeners become more mature we must learn to find beauty in plants other than those cultivated in the lush bog gardens and fragile birch woodlands of the English garden. This is not easy when we are constantly bombarded with images of these in British and Australian publications alike, held up as examples for us to measure ourselves against.

Part of the reason we still fight against the reality of our climate in the vain hope of having an 'English' garden comes down to our social pretensions. Many of us still aspire to have our own miniature version of a British stately home in the Australian suburbs. Nothing bespeaks money like an emerald-green lawn framed by a garden that looks like it jumped straight from the pages of *Country Life* magazine. Strolling around Sydney and Melbourne's leafier suburbs it is not uncommon to see gardens that do their utmost to deny our prevailing climate in the

Many of us think that if we plant the same plants as the British our gardens will be as good as theirs. In fact it condemns us to mediocre, water-dependent gardens.

brought in on trucks to keep their own patches of green up to the standard expected of them by the English lifestyle magazines. It seems some people are unwilling to efface their desire for an English baronial garden just because they happen to live on the driest continent on earth. Sadly gardens of this kind, while beautiful now, will not survive for posterity the way that Sissinghurst or Hidcote have in England. They only exist for as long as the life-support system which keeps the reality of our climate at bay continues to operate.

Collectively, we need to take a deep breath and step back from our rigidly held assumptions about what makes a garden beautiful or worthwhile. We have become too narrow in our thinking about plant selection and garden design. Looking objectively, there is beauty in many plants, not only those sanctioned by the British garden press. We need to look objectively at plants that are suited to our climate, learn to find the beauty in them and learn to use them convincingly, not continue to hanker after that which we cannot grow. The real lesson we need to learn from British (and indeed American) gardeners is how and where to look for the right plants for our gardens.

Plant collecting – sourcing plants from abroad

Despite its rich horticultural heritage, Britain only has 1500 native plants. British gardeners have been selecting plants from parts of the world with *similar climates to their own* over hundreds of years, probably without knowing it at first. Plant collecting has transformed their gardens completely. The Romans were

name of 'good taste'. During Melbourne's decade-long drought, when public gardens and sports grounds turned to dust, individuals of sufficient means had water

the first to bring exotic garden plants, like apples and lavender, to England from distant corners of their vast empire. The John Tradescants (father and son) began collecting plants during the reign of Elizabeth I, both from Europe and the new colonies in North America. In the 18th century men of science like Joseph Banks brought back plant specimens from around the globe courtesy of His Majesty's Navy. The 19th and early 20th centuries was the great age of plant hunters with intrepid explorers like Ernest Wilson, George Forrest and Frank Kingdon Ward risking life and limb to introduce dozens of the plants we associate with English gardens today. The overwhelming majority of the plants we think of as quintessentially English in fact come from abroad. The foothills of the Himalayas in northern India, China, Tibet, Bhutan and northern Burma have been a particularly rich source of plants for the British due to their cool, misty-moisty climate not unlike Britain's own. From this region alone British gardeners have garnered treasures like magnolias, lilies, crabapples, rhododendrons, delphiniums, and of course the Tibetan blue poppy.

It is interesting to compare Australian and New Zealand gardens to see what effect our different climates have had on our garden cultures. New Zealand has an amazing climate with features in common with the humid subtropical climate, 'English' temperate maritime climate and the Mediterranean climate. They can grow just about anything! Because of their special climate, New Zealand gardeners were able to adopt British models of gardening, including all of the wonderful plants the British had

Many quintessential 'English' plants were brought into British gardens from the misty-moisty foothills of the Himalayas. Here *Meconopsis betonicifolia*, *Rhododendron sinogrande* and *Delphinium elatum*.

collected, with a high degree of success, whereas Australian gardeners had rather limited success in our heat and drought. New Zealand has its own uniquely beautiful native

New Zealand's indigenous plants are culturally compatible with 'English' plants due to their similar climates. Astelias have become popular in both British and New Zealand gardens.

flora which, because it evolved in a similar climate to Britain's, is culturally compatible with 'English' plants. Thus New Zealand gardeners were able to assimilate their native plants into their transplanted British style gardens, resulting in a distinct New Zealand garden 'look', and British gardeners assimilated New Zealand plants into their gardens with gusto. Although only a tiny country of four million people (about the same population as Melbourne), New Zealand punches well above its weight on the international gardening scene. Their climate gave them a head start which ours did not.

When searching abroad for garden plants naturally you begin with climates similar to your own. A gardener from Adelaide would begin by looking for plants in other Mediterranean climates, not in the monsoonal tropics or the polar regions. But sometimes, a particular region's flora can be surprisingly tolerant of conditions different to its own. Two such floras are those of Japan and New Zealand. Although Japan displays a

classic humid subtropical climate, some of its plants are extremely tough and drought hardy – *Raphiolepis*, *Fatsia* and *Aspidistra*, to name but a few. Similarly New Zealand, in many places wetter and greener than England, has a few dry patches along the east coast with climates approaching a Mediterranean climate. Some very tough garden plants come from New Zealand, too, such as Marlborough daisies and cordylines. It is always worth experimenting with plants from less obvious parts of the world. You can be pleasantly surprised.

Gardening for climate

When we choose plants appropriate to our climate, in many ways the 'look' of our gardens will be decided for us by the climatic adaptations of the plants. Because plant physiology is sculpted by climate, plants adapted to similar climates from different parts of the world can look surprisingly similar. By choosing plants that are well adapted to our climate we also choose an aesthetic theme for our gardens.

The physical appearance of plants' climatic adaptations lends many overseas gardens their uniquely distinctive regional styles. The gardens of Provence and Tuscany derive their unmistakeable Mediterranean look from their rugged landscapes and from the fact that the plants grown in them show physical adaptations to their climate. Like most places in the world, the gardens of Provence and Tuscany rarely if ever see a hose. Their ornamental plants are expected to survive on natural rainfall alone which, as we have seen, is very low in summer. As a result the plants

PARALLEL EVOLUTION: HOW CLIMATE SHAPES PLANTS

Plants that are adapted to similar climates, but from different parts of the world, can look surprisingly similar. *Ficus macrophylla* from NSW and Queensland and *Magnolia grandiflora* from the southern states of the USA are both adapted to humid subtropical climates. Their foliage is almost identical, right down to the rusty-coloured indumentum on the underside of the leaf.

Euphorbias from dry regions of South Africa and the Canary Islands have made the same climatic adaptations as cacti from the Americas. *Euphorbia obesa*, *E. caerulescens* and *E. triangularis* could all pass for cacti although they are not related to them.

Mediterranean gardens are unmistakeable thanks to the climatic adaptations of their plants.

which thrive in their gardens display adaptations which allow them to do so – silver, hairy and sclerophyll foliage, compact bun shapes, summer dormancy and so on. The same can be said for the gardens of just about any other culture with a strong gardening tradition whether it is the tropical exuberance of Balinese gardens, the evergreen sobriety of the Japanese or indeed the luxurient softness of English gardens. It seems that it is only

The most interesting dry gardens combine plants with similar cultural requirements from around the world. This way interesting shapes, colours, textures, fragrances and seasonal highlights can be combined. Here are lilies from China, yuccas from the Americas, and *Acanthus* and *Verbascums* from southern Europe.

Australians fighting against a garden style dictated by our climate!

The characteristic look of some international garden cultures is so distinctive that you might think it is created exclusively with their own native plants, and that we should follow suit in creating our own national style. In fact, many of the plants we associate with Japanese gardens actually come from China. Provençal and Tuscan gardeners are just as fond of yuccas from California as their native lavender. Balinese gardens are as likely to contain South American frangipanis as Indonesian crotons and of course neither shrub roses nor apple trees are native to the UK, though they are instrinsic features of the English landscape.

The native myth

For some Australian gardeners, growing native plants has become a moral decision rather than simply a horticultural or aesthetic one. There is a feeling that using exclusively native plants shows a proper concern for the environment whereas planting exotics shows a wanton disregard for it. The very term 'indigenous' has become so charged with political correctness that it has almost lost its original meaning.

Unfortunately this rather earnest motivation for plant selection is based on several wrong assumptions. It presupposes that all exotic plants are terrible weeds and therefore morally reprehensible, that indigenous plants are never weeds and therefore morally blameless, that all native plants are drought tolerant and therefore better for the environment, and that only indigenous plants provide habitat and food for native birds and wildlife. Sadly not one of these assumptions is correct. Perhaps some gardeners feel deep down that if they fill their inner suburban block with fence-to-fence grevilleas then we will somehow be able to turn back the clock to 1770 and thereby absolve ourselves of the guilt we feel about the social and environmental damage done since European settlement. If only plants could do all that for us!

There is a widely held misconception that native plants are invariably drought tolerant, maintenance free and indestructible, and therefore highly garden-worthy. This misconception has been the downfall of many an Australian gardener. Some natives are indeed very tough and drought tolerant, such as those from our deserts, semi-arid and Mediterranean climates. But an equal number of Australian native plants are not all that drought tolerant – those from our rainforests, subalpine areas and coastal, summer rainfall districts for example. In any case, drought tolerance does not guarantee ease of garden culture. Native plants have other cultural requirements than simply water alone.

Waratahs (*Telopea* spp.) are native plants which are *not* easy to grow well. How many of us have fallen in love with a potted waratah in full bloom in a nursery and bought it on impulse, only to be disappointed by its substandard performance in the garden? Even the relatively robust hybrid waratahs rarely achieve their full potential outside areas with the deep, rich loamy soils and reliable summer rainfall they prefer. The Dandenong Ranges on the eastern outskirts of Melbourne enjoy such conditions and magnificent waratahs

fully three metres tall and wide can be seen growing there in abundance, covered in bright red torches every spring. Just a few kilometres down the road in Melbourne city, with its poorer soils and drier summers, waratahs struggle. In dry inland areas waratahs are very disappointing indeed.

The West Australian brown boronia (*Boronia megastigma*) is another example. Every spring nurseries and supermarkets are jam-packed with pots of brown boronia for sale. Dripping with richly scented, bell-shaped flowers in the most unusual combination of chestnut brown and lime yellow, they are quite irresistible. They sell like hot cakes. But once they are planted in the garden, brown boronias usually die within a few months, not due to anything the gardener has done wrong but because they are extremely finicky in their requirements.

The heart-stoppingly beautiful WA Christmas tree (*Nuytsia floribunda*), with its profusion of egg yolk-yellow flowers, is all but impossible to grow in gardens as it is a partial root parasite on nearby plants. Many WA natives are very difficult subjects for the average gardener, especially on the east coast of Australia where they languish in the summer humidity. They tend to be very exacting about soils, pH, nutrition, seasonal watering patterns, who they grow with and the presence of mycorrhizal fungi in the soil. In many ways they are best left to specialist collectors who can cater to their every need. If you do cater to all of their needs, it then makes it very difficult to grow plants with different cultural requirements. Cultural incompatibility with plants that do not share their specific preferences is not restricted to WA natives.

Members of the Proteaceae family (grevilleas, banksias, etc.) are highly sensitive to phosphorus which makes it difficult to mix them with phosphorus-loving exotic plants in a broader garden context. This is a shame as they are plants of great beauty.

South Australia's floral emblem, the Sturt's desert pea (*Swainsona formosa*) is yet another native plant which, although desperately beautiful, is rarely seen in gardens. It is supremely drought tolerant, adapted to life in the red sands of arid central Australia in burning heat during the day and freezing cold at night. Despite withstanding such hostile conditions in nature it cannot cope with average garden conditions at all, especially near the coast where it languishes in the humid air. If Sturt's desert peas – or waratahs, brown boronia or WA Christmas trees – were easy to grow they would be in every garden in the world, such is their beauty. But they are not easy to grow and as such cannot be considered garden-worthy plants.

Sturt's desert pea is an indigenous plant but it is far from easy to grow.

Drought tolerance and dry gardening

'Drought tolerance' is a concept which has come to be at the forefront of every Australian gardener's thoughts over the last decade or so, just as the concept of 'putting on the sprinkler' has faded into distant memory. Drought is a permanent feature of the Australian climate as we have discussed. We should not be looking for drought *tolerant* garden plants so much as plants which *thrive* in dry conditions. American gardeners use the term *xeriscaping* for dry climate gardening. This refers to landscaping in a *xeric*, or arid, climate. It is a great term as it implies the use of plants which love a dry climate rather than merely *tolerating* it. The term also encapsulates the horticultural techniques which Australians are already very good at like mulching and tanking (making a small pool) around newly planted specimens. Xeriscaping might be a useful term for Australians to use during this new phase of our gardening journey. Perhaps one day we will look back and laugh that we ever made a distinction between 'normal' gardening and 'xeriscaping', or that we ever thought sloshing megalitres of water on plants woefully unsuited to our climate was ever a good idea.

At the moment we still tend to be a bit binary in our thinking about dry gardening. We feel that, if we can't have a 'proper' English garden, there are only two options open to us: a) an Australian native garden, or b) cacti and succulents. Because our tastes are largely formed by the British gardening press, we are not particularly convinced by either choice.

Cacti and succulents have a very strong, spiky, chunky, muscular quality which doesn't appeal to everyone. This may be to do with the fact that many gardeners see cacti and succulents as an 'either-or' proposition whereby one has *either* a 100% cactus and succulent garden, *or* none at all. In reality there is absolutely no reason why you shouldn't use just a few cacti or succulents in your garden for their special qualities. Think of them as shapes and textures, or as shrubs and perennials (which happen to be succulent) rather than as *succulents*. Large cacti and succulents make fantastic structural feature plants. Smaller ones can make good mass plantings. Used sensitively, cacti and succulents combine well with other kinds of plants – grasses, perennials, shrubs and trees – to create stunning effects. Despite what we think, they *don't* have to be used exclusively with their own kind.

Selecting plants for the garden does not have to be an 'either-or' proposition. There are plenty of grey shades in between the extremes of a lush 'English' garden and a spiky cactus or native garden. It is all a question of changing our tastes and choosing the right plants.

Garden-worthiness

There are 400 000 species of plant on earth but not all are created equal from a gardener's point of view. To make a good garden subject a plant must display a combination of cultural and aesthetic features:

- First and foremost it should thrive (but not be too rampant) in the prevailing climate. If a plant merely tolerates your climate you will constantly be fighting an uphill battle. A common plant, well grown and in rude good health, is much more deserving of a place in the garden than a sickly, disease-prone or high-needs plant, however rare or beautiful it is supposed to be. Many roses would not pass this test.
- A garden-worthy plant should be adaptable to growing under a range of garden conditions. Plants with very specialised cultural requirements, like many orchids and rare bulbs, are better suited to specialist collectors than to combining with other plants in the open garden.
- The plant must contribute a function to the overall garden scheme – seasonal colour, scent, architectural form, texture, shade, or

Dry gardens don't have to look like this …

WHAT IS A 'DRY' GARDEN?

When we think of 'dry' gardens many of us immediately think of either cacti and succulents or indigenous gardens. But dry gardens don't have to be either of these things. Dry gardens in different climates will look very different from one another – sometimes it is hard to spot them. Humid subtropical climate dry gardens in Sydney or Brisbane might look quite generous and green whereas a dry garden in Adelaide or Canberra might look more rustic and earthy.

How dry is 'dry'?

A 'dry' garden could be described as a garden that receives little or no supplementary irrigation apart from its natural rainfall. Dry gardening in Sydney is a different proposition from dry gardening in Canberra, Adelaide or Hobart for reasons discussed earlier. The key to having a beautiful dry garden is to identify the main features of your climate and work with them, not against them. Do you live on the coast or inland? Is your air humid or dry? Do you live in a cool, mountain district or on the inland plains?

The gardener's art is to combine native and exotic plants to create an environment which in some way evokes an emotional response. Some people like calming, restful gardens, others prefer gardens which thrill and challenge them. Dry gardens can be all of these things and more – soft and flowery, muscular and architectural, dreamy and romantic, delicate and ethereal, vibrant and exotic, nurturing, silly, awe-inspiring, fun … dry gardens have personalities as diverse as their creators. Be inspired!

even a less tangible quality like 'nostalgia' – without detracting in other ways.

The more of these features a plant combines, the more it warrants inclusion in our gardens. Let us look at some examples. Crepe myrtles contribute not only colourful flowers in summer but also bright autumn colour, shade in summer and sun in winter, they have decorative bark and they are a useful size for small gardens. The Mexican lily (*Beschorneria yuccoides*) contributes bold architectural form throughout the year and stunning spring flowers. It never looks untidy or tired. The same can be said of clivias. These are all first-class, garden-worthy plants which deserve a place in every garden.

Too often we tolerate plants which do not deserve to be in our gardens. Roses are a prime example. It is not uncommon to see sticky, sickly rose bushes defoliated by black-spot and powdery mildew taking pride of place in someone's front garden. There may be a few large, brightly coloured flowers atop the branches but if these were removed what

This hybrid tea rose and agave both have fearsome thorns. One looks healthy and handsome, the other looks gawky and inelegant. Which plant would you rather have in your garden?

would the rose bush have to recommend it? It would be nothing more than a bunch of thorny twigs poking out of the ground with a few diseased leaves hanging on for dear life. At least a prickly agave would offer structure, elegance and good health along with its thorns! If many of the roses we grow in our gardens didn't bear a brightly coloured flower nobody would look twice at them.

Of course not all roses are quite so ugly. Many are indeed fairly healthy shrubs (in the right climate) although they can still be a bit sticky, shapeless and uninteresting when not in flower. Some of the 'wild' classes of roses stand out as more garden-worthy garden subjects than their highly bred cousins. Rugosa roses are very robust and healthy with dense, glossy green foliage down to the ground. They grow in a much wider range of climates than modern roses. They are tolerant of salt spray and sandy soils, they have good autumn colour and decorative hips. Their flowers do not have the classic 'rosebud'

Beschorneria yuccoides is spectacularly garden-worthy – robust, easy to grow in a range of climates, magnificent in flower and strongly architectural throughout the rest of the year.

shape or come in such a wide range of colours as modern classes of roses, but they are highly fragrant and borne over a very long season. Rugosas do not need regular detailed pruning, just a quick once-over with hedge shears after flowering or in winter. When not in flower, rugosa roses function just like any other garden shrub, providing a solid shape and good background foliage. The problem many modern roses have is that their huge, highly coloured flowers scream for attention. They demand the best spot in the garden when in flower but look embarrassing when the show is over. At least rugosas have the good grace to disappear into the background when their work is done.

This begs the question why *do* we continue to grow sickly roses in our gardens, spraying them with fungicides and laboriously pruning them to outward facing buds only to be repaid with a third-rate performance in the garden? Perhaps it is nothing more than familiarity. Ask any Australian to name a rose variety and they will most likely say 'Peace', 'Iceberg' or 'Blue Moon' simply because they are familiar with the names. They are very unlikely to say 'Fru Dagmar Hartopp' or 'Roseraie de l'Haÿ', two excellent, garden-worthy rugosa roses. Perhaps we persevere with poor performers because of our penchant for selecting plants based on the single criterion 'are the flowers pretty?' – almost as if the rest of the plant doesn't exist.

William Martin, creator of the magnificent dry garden 'Wigandia' on the cone of an ancient volcano in the western district of Victoria, maintains that it is important for plants in dry gardens to *stress beautifully*. That is, they should not wilt, burn or turn their

Rugosa roses are extremely garden-worthy. They are tough, healthy shrubs well clothed with glossy, disease-free foliage, fragrant flowers throughout the summer, yellow autumn foliage and bright orange hips into the winter.

toes up during periods of extreme heat and drought, but show their stress in a way which still allows them to be beautiful. For example, in extreme conditions shrubby aeoniums close up their leaf rosettes, giving an effect almost like bunches of rosebuds. In dry seasons sedums might only grow to half their normal height – not as magnificent as normal, but not ugly and half dead, either. The foliage of some agaves and yuccas turns attractive sunset shades in times of extreme water stress – much prettier than wilting or burning.

As we become more mature as gardeners we must begin to select plants on their merit and functionality, not merely on the basis of whether the picture on the nursery label appeals to us. Only then will we be on the road to having truly excellent gardens.

Responsible gardening: a word about weeds

There is a feeling in some circles that any garden plant not native to Australia is a potentially disastrous weed waiting to escape. To some people all exotic plants are presumed guilty of being weeds, even in the absence of any scientific evidence to support such a presumption. It is true that many environmental and agricultural weeds did originate as garden plants. But there is a greater number of garden plants which have been grown in Australia for many decades but have never jumped the fence and become problematic. Many people likewise presume Australian native plants to be above reproach – the 'good guys' in the environmental debate. In reality the issue of weeds is not as cut-and-dried as many would like to think. There are many complexities, grey areas and paradoxes.

To scientists, weeds are an environmental or agricultural issue. But some people treat weeds almost as a *moral* issue, projecting 'good' or 'bad' attributes onto native and exotic plants. The term 'noxious weed' is frequently misapplied to plants which, while irritating in our backyards and suburbs or in particular localities, in no way fit the proper definition of a noxious weed. 'Noxious weed' sounds more effective in conversation but not all weeds are noxious. No doubt the motivation for using such hyperbole is noble.

Good versus bad: emotion has taken over the weed debate.

There is widespread community concern about the impact weeds have on our fragile environment and naturally gardeners do not want to compound this problem. But good intentions coupled with a lack of understanding have led to an atmosphere of hysteria in certain quarters. Hysteria does not help the environment in any meaningful way. It only serves to make gardeners feel anxious and guilty.

There are a number of agencies involved with identifying, classifying and legislating for weeds. For administrative reasons weed legislation tends to be state-oriented. This has led to the bewildering situation where a plant can be completely banned in one state but not in neighbouring states. For example the French, Spanish or Italian lavender, *Lavandula stoechas*, is a declared noxious weed in Victoria and is a 'regionally controlled weed' in the north-east of Victoria … but not in neighbouring NSW. Thus we have the faintly ridiculous situation where it is illegal to grow or sell French lavender in Wodonga, Victoria, but not a stone's throw away in Wodonga's NSW sister city, Albury.

Plants do not recognise geopolitical borders. A plant does not become a weed simply because it lives in Victoria but not NSW. Plants become weeds because specific sets of climatic and environmental conditions allow their uncontrolled spread. If the right combination of seasonal temperature, seasonal rainfall, soil, aspect, pollinators, seed dispersal vectors and absence of predatory species coincide, then a plant can become a weed. If they do not coincide, a plant is unlikely to become a weed.

Verbena bonariensis, sometimes called 'purpletop', comes from Argentina and southern Brazil. It self-seeds rampantly in high summer rainfall climates and is often seen naturalised along train lines and on the edge of bushland around Sydney. In predominantly winter rainfall climates like Melbourne it self-seeds within backyards but not much further. You certainly don't see it growing along every train line as you do in Sydney. A weed in one part of the country is not necessarily a weed in another – although weeds of national significance, such as bitou bush and serrated tussock, are by definition widely distributed.

Lantana camara is a much-feared weed of national significance, having taken over large tracts of coastal areas of NSW and Queensland to the exclusion of all other plants. Coastal NSW and Queensland have climates similar to lantana's South American homeland, but they lack the natural controls which limit its spread there. Lantana has not become a weed in parts of Australia which do

Lantana camara is a declared weed of national significance yet it is not problematic everywhere in Australia. This plant is growing at the Royal Botanic Gardens, Melbourne.

not experience its preferred conditions, such as in inland areas of NSW. In Victoria it is classed as a 'restricted' noxious weed which means that it must not be sold or traded. Yet some beautiful garden varieties of *Lantana camara* can be seen growing at the Royal Botanic Gardens in Melbourne. The garden varieties are thought to have much lower fertility than the wild species and therefore their potential to spread is low.

Sometimes a whole genus will get a bad reputation because just one of its species is weedy in some localities. The genus *Agapanthus* is a case in point. *Agapanthus praecox* subsp. *orientalis* is just one subspecies of a genus of 10 or so species. It can become locally weedy in high summer rainfall areas of southern Australia. In drier climates it is not problematic. The other members of the genus *Agapanthus* are very well behaved. Many of the beautiful garden agapanthus hybrids are derived from *A. inapertus* and *A. campanulatus*. They rarely set viable seed. Although agapanthus are routinely referred to as 'noxious weeds' by concerned individuals, there are in fact *no* agapanthus species listed as noxious weeds in Australia.

Weeds are a real problem but we need to get things in perspective. There are many different degrees of 'weediness'. A plant which self-seeds under garden conditions is not in the same league as Paterson's Curse, which covers thousands upon thousands of acres of agricultural land to the exclusion of all other species.

Australia has a wide range of climates. One could argue that all foreign plants will eventually become a weed somewhere in the country. This leaves gardeners in a quandary. Should we only grow plants that are actually unsuited to our climate – rhododendrons in Adelaide, for example – so that we can be sure they will never become environmental weeds? If so, where does that leave our quest to have a sustainable garden?

Some people advocate restricting ourselves to growing Australian native plants. This seems like the obvious solution, on paper at least. In actual fact some native plants are considered weeds outside their home range for the same reason that exotic plants are – they reproduce unchecked to the exclusion of locally endemic plants. Native daphne (*Pittosporum undulatum*), Cootamundra wattle (*Acacia baileyana*), bluebell creeper (*Billardiera heterophylla*, syn. *Sollya heterophylla*) and the blackwood wattle (*Acacia melanoxylon*) are just four examples of native plants which go feral outside their normal distribution. Or could these native plants simply be said to be expanding their natural distribution? The magenta cherry lillypilly (*Syzigium paniculatum*) is considered at high risk of extinction in its historical range on the central coast of NSW. Yet at the same time it is considered to be a weed species on the south coast of NSW. Some people advocate growing only locally endemic species in our gardens, from locally collected seed. But gardening is meant to be one of life's pleasures, not an exercise in asceticism. Surely there is room for us to grow both native and exotic plants for pleasure, so long as we think about the consequences of our actions? The vast majority of us garden in suburban areas with

WHAT CAN WE AS GARDENERS DO TO HELP?

Be vigilant for plants that appear to self-propagate too readily in your climate, especially the new plants which come on the market each year (remembering that a plant which is weedy in one climate is not necessarily so in every climate). Be aware of the vectors which distribute a particular plant's seeds, such as the wind or birds like currawongs and blackbirds, and deadhead seeds before they are dispersed. Dispose of prunings and unwanted plant material thoughtfully. Don't dump it over your back fence or in bushland! If you are concerned about the spread of a plant in your area, notify the proper authorities in your state.

considerable buffer zones between our garden and any sensitive bushland. Of course the risk is much higher for those of us gardening on the urban fringes and in rural areas, near bushland. Gardeners in these areas should naturally exercise more caution.

Weeds are not as black-and-white an issue as some would have us believe. Neither the fundamentalist zeal of some weed groups nor the cavalier attitude of some segments of the horticultural industry are particularly helpful in managing weeds. Calm and moderation are called for from all interested parties. Gardeners, nurserymen, scientists and weed authorities must keep talking and working together to protect the environment and agriculture without putting unnecessary strictures on gardeners.

5

PLANT INDEX

Choosing the right plant for the right position and the right function takes skill and practice but it is also one of the most enjoyable aspects of creative gardening. This index gives you clues on where each plant comes from, what kind of climate and microclimate it enjoys and how to use each plant to its best potential.

Drought ratings: Each plant in this index is given a drought rating as a guide to the kind of dry it will endure:

Tough: plants which tolerate seasonal water deficit but may benefit from a modest amount of irrigation during very hot weather to keep them looking happy.

Very tough: plants which withstand long – but not indefinite – periods of water deficit.

Super tough: plants adapted to extended periods of water deficit such as in semi-arid climates.

Trees
Acer – maples
Origin
The maples are not a group of plants you would expect to see in a book on plants that like dry conditions. Most gardeners are familiar with the beautiful Japanese maples which come from wet, humid, woodland conditions in Japan and China. But maples are also native to a range of different northern hemisphere climate types including very cold, northerly climates and some quite dry regions, too.

Season of interest
Maples are deciduous. They excel during the autumn when they have some of the most spectacular colours of all trees.

Garden uses
Maples are a useful size for small gardens. The upright selections are particularly good for narrow spaces like driveways.

Cultivation
Unlike the more familiar Japanese maples, the species listed below are very tolerant of poor soils, including heavy clays and alkaline soils. They prefer full sun or light shade.

Varieties
A. buergerianum can grow up to 9 × 6 m but is usually seen at 4 × 3 m. It is known as the

trident maple because of its three-pronged leaves, only a few centimetres long. It tends to grow as a multi-stemmed shrub with beautiful rough bark which peels off in plates. Most trees are seedling grown and there is quite a lot of variation in autumn colour from insipid yellows to bright orange-red. If you can, select your plant when it is in its autumn colour to avoid disappointment. **Drought rating: tough**

A. campestre (7 × 6 m), commonly called the field maple, has small, glossy five-lobed leaves which turn bright butter yellow in autumn. The upright Dutch selection 'Elsrijk' is sometimes available in Australia, as is the more vigorous 'Evelyn' but most plants are seed grown and show considerable variation in shape and growth habit. **Drought rating: tough**

A. monspessulanum grows to 8 × 8 m but usually achieves half this size in gardens. The Montpellier maple grows in dry, rocky limestone hills inland from the Mediterranean in southern Europe. It has small, three-lobed, dark green leaves which turn bright yellow or orange in autumn. **Drought rating: very tough**

Acer monspessulanum.

Acer buergerianum.

A. negundo (8 × 6 m) is commonly called box elder (although it is related to neither). This is a fast growing tree with compound, rather than the usual palmate, leaves. It is much tougher than its origins on the east coast of North America would suggest. The wild form of *A. negundo* does not have much to recommend it. It is rank and ungainly, has no autumn colour to speak of and self-seeds prolifically in higher rainfall coastal and mountain areas where it can become quite weedy. Happily its named varieties rarely set viable seed and are much better garden plants, more symmetrical and compact in habit. Bear in mind that they are propagated

Acer negundo 'Sensation'.

by grafting onto seedlings of wild *A. negundo* so it is important to remove suckers from below the graft union as soon as they appear (ideally before they become woody). 'Flamingo' has variegated foliage which emerges pink and green before turning white and green over summer. 'Sensation' has leaves which emerge rusty red, turn rusty green over summer and then good orange and red in autumn. 'Variegatum' is a cool looking tree with cream-variegated foliage. **Drought rating: very tough**

Arbutus – the strawberry trees

Origin

Arbutus are small evergreen trees of the Ericaceae family – the same family as rhododendrons and blueberries. But unlike their cousins arbutus are native to much hotter, drier climates of the Mediterranean, North and Central America and the Canary Islands. The best known species is *Arbutus unedo*, the Irish strawberry tree from Mediterranean Europe. The Irish moniker comes from the fact that there is a remnant population of this tree on the west coast of Ireland. The 'strawberry' part of the name comes from the red, strawberry-like fruits. These are edible, but dry and insipid. In fact its scientific name, *unedo*, means 'I eat only one'! *Arbutus unedo* is considered a weed in some parts of Australia (although it is very well behaved compared with oxalis or Paterson's Curse). In any case it is probably the least interesting member of the genus. All arbutus bear white, bell-shaped flowers in spring or summer followed by the orange or red fruits. There is also a pink-flowered variety of *A. unedo* available called 'Pink Pearl'.

Season of interest

Arbutus look great throughout the year. The spring or summer flowers, fruits and summer peeling bark are added seasonal bonuses.

Garden uses

Arbutus are fairly compact trees so they are great for smaller gardens and courtyards. They are grown primarily for their colourful, tactile bark which makes their sinuous, curving branches look alarmingly like human thighs. The old bark sheds in summer to reveal satiny, sage-green new bark. Arbutus bark is similar in colour and texture to some of our native eucalypts. But, unlike eucalypts, arbutus have glossy, dark green foliage and cast dense shade. Bear in mind that they are evergreen so don't plant them where they will deprive your house of winter sun. Arbutus are fairly slow growing but if they do get too big for their allotted space they can be easily pollarded – in other words, cut back to a low framework of branches, from which points they will sprout and grow again.

Cultivation

Arbutus species will grow just about anywhere as long as the soil drains well and is not too wet in summer. It is important to plant them out at a small size (less than a metre tall) as they do not transplant well at larger sizes. Once established, they are indestructible.

Varieties

A. × andrachnoides (5 × 5 m) is a natural hybrid between *A. unedo* and *A. andrachne* from Greece and Turkey. *A. × andrachnoides* inherits its smouldering, red-lead-coloured bark from *A. andrachne* – an improvement over *A. unedo*'s rather boring shaggy grey bark. *A. × andrachnoides* is sterile so it is the one to grow if you are concerned about arbutus self-seeding in your area.

Arbutus glandulosa.

Arbutus × andrachnoides.

A. canariensis (5 × 5 m) from the Canary Islands has satiny, salmon-coloured bark and pinkish flowers. It has larger, thinner leaves than *A. unedo* and benefits from a slightly more humid climate than the others so is better suited to coastal areas and the ranges than very arid inland areas.

A. glandulosa (5 × 5 m) from the highlands of Mexico has smooth, cinnamon-red bark which peels off in summer to reveal satiny, sage-green young bark beneath. In many ways this is the pick of the genus for Australian gardens.

A. menziesii, the Pacific Madrone, comes from the west coast of North America. It is the king

Arbutus menziesii.

of the *Arbutus* genus but is extremely rare in Australia. It has similar bark to *A. glandulosa* and dark green, smooth-margined, paddle-shaped leaves to 15 cm long. In nature it can become a large, thick-trunked tree to 30 m but usually grows to a third of this height in gardens.

A. unedo, the strawberry tree, comes from Mediterranean Europe. It has grey, shaggy bark – not as decorative as the other species – and small, dark green leaves. It normally grows to 5 × 5 m in gardens.

Drought rating: super tough

Brachychiton – the kurrajongs

Origin

The brachychitons are native to Australia. They come from a range of microclimates including arid and semi-arid areas as well as temperate and subtropical rainforest. The rainforest species are surprisingly tough and will grow in much drier climates than you might expect.

Season of interest

Brachychitons mostly flower in summer although they may flower sporadically at other times, too.

Garden uses

Unusually for an Australian native plant, some of the brachychitons are deciduous. But don't be fooled into planting one to shade your house in summer and admit sun in winter as brachychitons usually do things the other way around from northern hemisphere trees, dropping their leaves in mid-summer.

Cultivation

Brachychitons are amazingly adaptable trees. They seem to grow quite happily far outside

Brachychiton acerifolius.

Brachychiton populneus.

receives less than half the rainfall of its native range. The Illawarra flame tree drops most or all of its leaves when in flower. A tree in full bloom is one of the most spectacular of all native plants, billowing with tiny, red, bell-shaped flowers. The flowers are followed by large, black, boat-shaped pods. These are extremely decorative in themselves but be careful of the irritating, golden hairs contained inside them.

B. discolor (30 × 10 m but usually seen one-third this size in gardens) is commonly called Lacebark. It comes from the rainforests in northern NSW and southern Queensland but is amazingly adaptable to different climates

Brachychiton rupestris.

their native ranges, in a wide variety of soils. The rainforest species prefer frost-free climates but the inland species are more cold tolerant. They prefer full sun to partial shade for the rainforest species. Brachychitons have powerful roots which can crack water pipes and paving, so site them carefully.

Varieties

B. acerifolius (30 × 10 m but usually seen one-third this size in gardens) is the well-known Illawarra flame tree. Although it is a tree of east coast rainforests it is surprisingly tough, thriving even in cities like Melbourne, which

including those which are much drier and cooler than its native range. In summer it sheds its leaves and covers itself in large, furry, pink flowers. A spectacular plant.

B. populneus (20 × 10 m but usually seen one-third this size in gardens) is the common kurrajong. A tree of both coastal and semi-arid inland areas, it has attractive green, lacy bark and glossy, heart-shaped leaves. It bears cream, bell-shaped flowers followed by its characteristic black, boat-shaped pods. There is some concern that common kurrajong has the potential to be weedy in WA.

B. rupestris (20 × 10 m but usually half this size in gardens), the Queensland bottle tree, comes from dry, inland areas of southern and central Queensland but is widely adaptable. Young trees develop a massive, bottle-shaped trunk after five or so years. They have delicate, hand-shaped leaves which are extremely ornamental. Mature specimens of *B. rupestris* are very expensive but they are extremely imposing and will lend a new garden an air of establishment. They also grow very well in pots and can be used as a feature plant in paved areas or decking.

Drought rating: very tough to super tough

Ceratonia – carob tree
Origin
Carob is an evergreen tree native to the Mediterranean region. It is the source of edible carob.

Season of interest
Carob is evergreen and looks good throughout the year.

Garden uses
Carob is a handsome, compact tree for small gardens. It casts dense shade which can be useful in our hot inland areas. Carob clips to a beautiful hedge and makes a good windbreak, although it is slow growing. It can be seen growing in this way around Adelaide.

Cultivation
Suitable for Mediterranean and semi-arid climates, carob trees are very unfussy as to soil as long as it drains well. They need a position in full sun or part shade, growing happily in the dappled shade of pine or eucalyptus trees.

Varieties
Ceratonia siliqua (12 × 12 m but usually much smaller in gardens) is an umbrella-shaped tree, usually multi-trunked, with large, dark, glossy green pinnate leaves. Male and female flowers are borne on separate trees. If pollinated by a nearby male, female trees bear black, edible pods.

Drought rating: super tough

Carob makes a beautiful hedge.

Cupressus – cypresses

Origin

A small genus of coniferous trees from the northern hemisphere; some from dry climates, others from very wet climates. Do not be fooled into thinking that all cypresses (or all conifers) are drought tolerant because of the small, waxy nature of their foliage. In many cases this is an adaptation to snow and cold rather than heat and drought. *C. cashmeriana*, the Kashmir or Bhutan cypress, is a case in point. It is routinely sold as a drought-tolerant plant even though it is native to cool monsoonal forests at very high altitudes in the Himalayas (along with rhododendrons) and hates hot, dry weather.

Season of interest

Cypresses look absolutely unchanging each and every day of the year. They are always beautiful.

Garden uses

Cypresses are useful for introducing large-scale, strong, solid forms into the garden. They are very weighty and have the ability to 'ground' a planting which contains a lot of fluffy or fine-textured plants. The fastigiate forms of *C. sempervirens* are perfect for giving height and vertical emphasis to small gardens without creating horizontal bulk.

Not all cypresses are suitable for domestic gardens. Varieties of the Monterey cypress, *C. macrocarpa*, and its progeny × *Cupressocyparis leylandii* are *not suitable* for gardens under a hectare in size – do not be talked into them under any circumstances. These cypresses are very fast growing (which is their main selling point) but they do not stop at the size you want them to – they will continue growing until they reach their allotted size of around 30 m tall. If they are not hedged twice a year for their entire life they soon outgrow their desired proportions and unfortunately old wood cannot be cut into as it will not resprout.

Cultivation

The cypresses described here prefer dry-summer climates but are reasonably adaptable to humidity. They grow in any free-draining soil in full sun.

Varieties

C. arizonica (15 × 10 m) and the closely related *C. glabra* are often confused, or the names used interchangeably. Both are desert conifers from Arizona, California and Mexico. They have billowing, blue-grey foliage. 'Blue Ice' is a beautiful, tightly upright form with icy blue foliage. These species take clipping very well and make stunning low hedges for dry climates if planted closely.

Cupressus sempervirens **is a distinctive feature of the Tuscan landscape.**

C. sempervirens (15 × 10 m) comes from the Mediterranean basin and is a characteristic feature of that landscape from France to Jordan and Libya. There are two distinct forms of this tree; one wide spreading and tree like, the other very upright and fastigiate. The fastigiate forms are most useful in gardens. 'Glauca', 'Stricta' and the topically named 'Nitschke's Needle' are similar in many ways – they grow to half to two-thirds the height of the wild species. 'Glauca' is the pick of the bunch as it does not bear cones which can cause the branches to flop out of line.

Drought rating: very tough to super tough

Elaeocarpus reticulatus – blueberry ash
Origin
Blueberry ash comes from rainforest and coastal scrub on the east coast of Australia from Queensland south to Flinders Island in Bass Strait.

Season of interest
An evergreen tree, blueberry ash is beautiful year round but there are some seasonal bonuses in addition to its narrow, glossy dark green leaves. In spring it bears pretty, fringed, bell-shaped flowers among the foliage followed by blue berries and occasionally shows the odd red leaf in autumn, prior to shedding its old foliage.

Garden uses
Despite its rainforest origins this tree is amazingly drought tolerant, at least in humid coastal areas and milder mountain areas. It is not a plant for drier inland climes. Blueberry ash is very neat and upright in form and is unworried by urban pollution. It is great for tight, shady spots where height is needed but not bulk, such as up the south side of a house. Two or three specimens together are good for giving a feeling of privacy and intimacy in urban terrace gardens without creating a gloomy, dark space. Blueberry ash grows very well in the shade of larger trees or buildings.

Cultivation
Blueberry ashes grow to 10 m in nature but usually attain 4–5 × 2–3 m in cultivation. They will grow in most soil types but benefit from the addition of plenty of organic matter

Elaeocarpus reticulatus.

prior to planting and a good mulch to keep the soil cool. They look best in half to full shade but in humid coastal areas can also be grown in full sun.

Varieties

In addition to the common white-flowered variety there is also a pale pink-flowered form called 'Prima Donna'.

Drought rating: very tough

Erythrina – coral trees

Origin

Erythrinas are a genus of perennials, shrubs and trees in the pea family. They are widespread around the world in the tropics and subtropics, including in Australia. Most of the cultivated varieties come from South Africa and South America.

Season of interest

Different *Erythrina* species bear their magnificent flowers in different seasons, mostly from late spring to autumn. Plants which have been pollarded or coppiced flower later in the season than they otherwise would.

Erythrina crista-galli.

Garden uses

The larger erythrinas are feature trees for big gardens. The smaller varieties may be pollarded or coppiced to fit into smaller gardens.

Cultivation

Erythrinas prefer hot, humid climates but are very adaptable to less ideal conditions. They do not fare well in very frosty areas with cool summers. They grow in any well-drained soil, particularly sandy soils, and they flourish by the coast. Erythrinas are fast growing. Their young wood is prone to dying back at the tips and they are prone to shedding branches. They benefit from being pollarded or coppiced every winter. This encourages fresh, new growth and keeps them neat and in bounds.

Erythrina crista-galli is currently declared a noxious weed for NSW (restricted in some areas) and WA (prohibited).

Varieties

E. crista-galli (9 × 9 m) is a corky-barked tree from Brazil. It bears large, coral-red flowers in fat spikes in summer and autumn. There is a beautiful old pollarded specimen by the herbarium at the Royal Botanic Gardens, Melbourne. It is not weedy in Melbourne's cooler climate.

E. × *bidwillii* 'Blakei' (3 × 3 m) is a sterile hybrid which appeared in NSW in the mid-19th century, at a time when Australians first took an interest in plants from the tropical and subtropical climates. It is a hybrid of *E. crista-galli* from Brazil and *E. herbacea* from Central America. It bears pillar-box red flowers in long spikes in summer and autumn.

Erythrina × *bidwillii* 'Blakei'.

This variety benefits from being cut back hard every year.

Drought rating: very tough

Lagerstroemia – crepe myrtle
Origin
Crepe myrtles are deciduous trees from subtropical areas from India, through South-East Asia to China.

Season of interest
Crepe myrtles are trees for four seasons. They are grown primarily for their ruffled summer

Lagerstroemia 'Biloxi'.

flowers but many have brilliant autumn colour and their marbled bark is beautiful in winter.

Garden uses
Crepe myrtles are among the best trees for small gardens. They can be used even in small courtyard areas.

Cultivation
Crepe myrtles are very adaptable trees. They grow happily in just about any climate, although they are faster and more vigorous in humid coastal climates. Some varieties are more frost tolerant than others. Crepe

Lagerstroemia 'Tuscarora'.

myrtles usually grow as multi-stemmed trees but the larger varieties can be trained to a single trunk. They may also be pollarded to keep them more compact and shrub like.

Varieties
Most of the cultivated crepe myrtles are varieties of *L. indica* or hybrids of *L. indica* and *L. fauriei*.

Lagerstroemia 'Zuni'.

L. 'Biloxi' (6 × 5 m) has lilac-pink flowers and good orange autumn colour.

L. 'Natchez' (8 × 6 m) is a robust variety with white flowers and yellow autumn colour. It is one of the most vigorous varieties in frosty areas.

L. 'Tuscarora (8 × 6 m) is a robust variety with coral pink flowers and orange autumn colour.

L. 'Zuni' (3 × 3 m) is a compact variety with lavender flowers and orange autumn colour.

Drought rating: very tough

Malus – crabapples
Origin
Crabapples are small trees from a wide range of habitats from Europe, Asia and North America.

Season of interest
Spring blossom and autumn foliage colour are the seasonal high points. Some cultivars like 'Golden Hornet', 'John Downie' and 'Gorgeous' produce prodigious quantities of fruit which make delicious crabapple jelly.

Garden uses
Crabapples are modestly sized trees which are great for small gardens. They have several seasons of interest.

Cultivation
Crabapples prefer a deep, well-drained soil in full sun but are actually quite adaptable. They do best in areas with cold winters to give them a proper dormancy and initiate flowering.

Malus 'Golden Hornet'.

Unlike their cousins the apples, crabapples do not benefit from regular pruning and are best left to their own devices save for removing badly placed or dead branches.

Varieties

M. 'Golden Hornet' (4 × 3 m) has shell-pink blossom in the spring and heavy crops of egg-

Malus trilobata.

yolk yellow fruits in the autumn which hang on the tree well if they are not stripped by birds.

M. 'Gorgeous' (3 × 3 m) has pink spring blossom and brilliant red fruits which hang on the tree into winter if they are not eaten by birds first.

M. 'John Downie' (4 × 3 m) has shell-pink blossom in spring with large, orange and red fruits in the autumn. The fruits look like miniature apples and are sweet enough to eat raw – children love them.

M. *trilobata* (7 × 4 m) is the most drought tolerant of all the crabapples, coming from Greece, Syria, Lebanon and Israel. Its narrow, fastigiate shape lends height to small gardens without creating much horizontal bulk. It has dainty white flowers in the spring and unusual, maple-like leaves which turn orange in the autumn.

Drought rating: very tough

Mespilus germanica – the medlar
Origin

The medlar is an unusual member of the pome fruit family which includes apples, pears and quince as well as loquats and hawthorns. It probably originated in the eastern Mediterranean or western Asia region and was certainly cultivated in Iran from very early times.

Season of interest

The medlar is a tree for all seasons with its big, white spring blossom, dark green velvety summer foliage, brilliant yellow and pink autumn foliage and knobbly brown fruits which hang on the tree into winter if the

Mespilus germanica.

birds let them. The fruits make very nice jelly or can be collected and stored in a cupboard until they are soft (in a process known as 'bletting') after which the flesh can be sucked out and eaten. It tastes something like gritty stewed apple – an acquired taste!

Garden uses

Medlars are very handy as specimen trees for small gardens. Their wide-spreading canopies look cool and generous in summer. They can also be used as foundation trees in mixed plantings and are ideal for underplanting with spring bulbs. They branch very low to the ground so they are not suitable for planting along driveways or paths unless set well back.

Cultivation

Medlars need full sun to partial shade. They are usually grafted onto quince or hawthorn rootstocks. If possible choose quince as hawthorn can sucker to form an impenetrable, spiky thicket. Medlars on quince rootstock grow well on any soil, including heavy clays. Medlars need no pruning except to remove badly placed or dead branches.

Varieties

There are several named varieties available in Australia, differing only subtly from one another. 'Nottingham' has smaller fruits and a more upright growth habit than 'Dutch', which is more spreading. Both reach around 4 × 5 m.

Drought rating: very tough

Olea – the olive

Origin

The olives are a genus of about 20 evergreen trees and shrubs from the Mediterranean, Africa, Asia and even Australia (the native olive, *O. paniculata*). Best known is 'the' olive *O. europaea* subsp. *europaea* which has been an important source of fruit and oil around the Mediterranean since time immemorial. The olive tree, along with the pencil pine, is one of the defining features of Mediterranean landscapes. In fact some people define the Mediterranean climate in Europe as the area in which olives can be grown.

Season of interest

Olive trees look beautiful year round.

Garden uses

Olives can be grown as informal trees or formally clipped standards. They make beautiful hedging and are tough enough to withstand neglect in pots.

Cultivation

Olives need an aspect in full sun or very light shade. They perform well in any soil type as long as it is well drained, including very alkaline soils. They are extremely resilient trees and can be cut back to the ground or

Olive trees are defining features of the Mediterranean landscape.

even burned in a fire and still re-shoot from beneath the ground. They move well at any size or age, even as very elderly trees hundreds of years old.

Varieties

There are many varieties of European olive available in Australia, all of them equally beautiful from an ornamental point of view. If you want to harvest fruit from your olive tree it is best to grow two different varieties of trees as cross-pollination increases yields significantly. Specialist olive nurseries can advise on suitable pollination partners; 'Frantoio' is a good all-round pollinator. All olives produce oil and edible fruit but some

varieties such as 'Frantoio' and 'Verdale' are particularly noted for their high oil production while others such as 'Kalamata' and 'Manzanillo' are grown for their exceptionally good eating fruits. All varieties grow to 10 × 10 m in the wild, more often seen at 4 × 4 m, easily pruned to almost any size.

The African olive, *O. europaea* subsp. *africana* (syn. *O. europaea* subsp. *cuspidata*), is aggressively weedy in certain areas and should not be grown.

Drought rating: very tough to super tough

Pistacia – pistachios

Origin

Pistachios are a genus of shrubs and small trees related to mangos and cashews from the Canary Islands, Mediterranean basin to Asia, also represented in North America.

Season of interest

Evergreen species look good throughout the year while deciduous species excel in summer and autumn.

Garden uses

The Chinese pistachio is one of the best small trees for autumn colour in hot, dry areas and even colours reasonably well in mild coastal areas. The edible pistachio provides nuts (in the right climate) as well as being very ornamental. The mastic tree is an excellent hedging plant and foundation shrub although it is rarely seen in Australia.

Cultivation

The pistachios are very tough plants, tolerant of extreme heat, drought and poor soils

Pistacia chinensis looks cool and soft in summer. Its autumn colour is stunning.

including saline soils. *P. chinensis* is best planted out as small as possible (under one metre) as larger trees never establish as well as smaller specimens. This species tends to be quite shrubby when young, with many competing leaders, so make sure you prune out unwanted leaders and train up a single leader to form a straight trunk. Once they reach head height they look after themselves. *P. chinensis* and *P. vera* need full sun but *P. lentiscus* will grow in any aspect.

Varieties

P. chinensis (8 × 5 m, taller in the wild), the Chinese pistachio, is a deciduous tree from western and central China. It is an excellent tree for backyards and is commonly planted as a street tree in inland cities like Canberra and Armidale. In summer the tree is generously clothed with glossy, dark green pinnate leaves a bit like those of an ash tree, turning stunning yellows, oranges and reds in autumn. Seedlings can vary in the quality of their autumn colour so it is best to choose a tree in autumn when you can see what you are getting.

P. lentiscus (1–3 × 2–4 m), the mastic tree, is rarely seen in Australia but is widely used as hedging in its native Mediterranean countries. It has glossy, dark, evergreen pinnate leaves which turn bronze during the winter. It is the source of mastic, the dried resin used to scent Middle Eastern desserts and in perfumery. *P. lentiscus* is extremely tough, growing in any soil from pure sand to pure clay to pure limestone, in full sun with driving sea winds or in the shade of evergreen trees. This plant deserves to be more widely grown.

P. terebinthus (8 × 6 m), the turpentine tree, is a deciduous tree from the Canary Islands to Turkey, via Portugal, Morocco and Egypt. Most often seen as a rootstock for grafted edible pistachio nuts in Australia, it is a beautiful tree in its own right, with orange and red autumn colour.

P. vera (3 × 3 m, taller in the wild) is the edible pistachio nut. An attractive small deciduous tree with very large, rounded, apple green leaves native to Greece, Turkey,

Pistacia lentiscus.

Syria, Iran and Afghanistan. To produce nuts both a male and a female tree are needed. Grafted, named varieties give the best results, such as 'Kerman' or the CSIRO selection 'Sirora'. Pistachios need a very long, very hot summer and a cold winter to fruit well so they thrive in inland areas, although fruit has been produced even in southern coastal Victoria. Pistachios are being grown commercially in WA and the Sunraysia region of Victoria and NSW.

Drought rating: very tough to super tough

Plumeria – frangipani
Origin
Frangipanis are a small genus of succulent, evergreen or deciduous trees from winter-dry tropical climates in Central and South America and the West Indies.

Season of interest
Frangipanis are mostly grown for their fragrant summer flowers but they look beautiful all year round. Their foliage is neat and generous and in the dry season their bare form is very architectural – almost their finest incarnation!

Garden uses
Frangipanis are excellent compact trees for small gardens and courtyards and are tough enough to be grown in pots on a balcony or paved areas.

Cultivation
Frangipanis need a frost-free climate, the hotter the better. They require water in summer when they are growing but not during the winter when they are dormant. They grow in any well-drained soil in full sun.

Varieties
P. alba (5 × 5 m) has familiar white, fragrant frangipani flowers but very narrow, lance shaped leaves giving it an almost palm-like appearance.

P. obtusa (5 × 5 m) sometimes called the Singapore frangipani, is evergreen, with dark green, round-tipped leaves and sparkling white, salverform flowers. It is the least cold tolerant frangipani, thriving in Darwin but not doing so well in Sydney.

P. rubra (5 × 5 m) is the common frangipani. The wild form has pink flowers, as the name 'rubra' suggests, but more commonly seen in Australia is the white variety *P. rubra* var. *acutifolia*. It is the most cold tolerant variety.

There are innumerable hybrids becoming available in Australia with flower colours from whites, through yellows, pinks, violet purples, reds to beetroot and much larger flowers than the wild species. These are sure to become very popular for subtropical and tropical gardens in the coming years.

Drought rating: very tough

Prunus – flowering plums
Origin
Prunus are a large genus of shrubs or trees from the northern hemisphere. Stone fruits such as peaches, cherries, apricots and plums are members of this genus (*Prunus* is Latin for plum).

Prunus mume is the first blossom to come into flower in mid-winter.

Flowering peaches come in a variety of colours and degrees of doubleness.

Season of interest

Prunus flower in winter to spring.

Garden uses

Prunus are the well-loved 'blossom' trees which herald the coming of spring in southern Australia. They are useful fast-growing trees, compact enough to fit even into small gardens.

Cultivation

Prunus prefer climates with cool to cold winters such as inland and southern coastal areas. *P. persica* and *P. dulcis* have short dormancy requirements and do well as far north as the NSW central coast. Prunus are not fussy about soils, although they prefer water-retentive clays to sand. They need full sun and plenty of air flow around them. Ornamental prunus don't need pruning except to remove occasional dead or crossing branches. This is best done in the spring as the tree enters active growth in order to minimise the spread of bacterial canker, a debilitating disease which causes gum to ooze from lesions in the bark and can ultimately kill the tree.

Varieties

P. mume (3.5 × 3.5 m) is the Japanese flowering apricot seen in Japanese and Chinese art, often mistakenly called a 'plum'. It is a fast-growing deciduous tree which bears single or double, white or pink flowers on naked twigs in mid-winter, long before any other blossom trees flower. The cheery flowers are strongly almond-scented.

P. × blireana is a hybrid of *P. mume* with burgundy foliage and pale pink, semi-double flowers. It flowers slightly later than its parent.

P. dulcis (4 × 4 m) is the almond, probably originally from the Middle East or central

Almond trees have exquisitely fragrant blossoms.

Asia. Fruiting almonds have sublimely scented, single white flowers. There are a few ornamental cultivars with double pink or purple flowers.

P. persica (4 × 4 m) is the peach, probably originally from China. Like the almond there are several double-flowered ornamental varieties in shades of white, coral red, pink and magenta. 'Versicolor' has white flowers striped and splashed with red. This is one of the few 'blossom' trees which does well in humid coastal climates.

Drought rating: very tough

Pyrus – pears
Origin
Pears are deciduous trees from Europe and Asia. Some of them come from quite dry climates in western Asia and south-eastern Europe.

Season of interest
Ornamental pears are grown for their spring blossom, attractive summer foliage and bright autumn colours.

Pyrus calleryana 'Capital'.

Garden uses
Many of the pears are relatively compact trees very well suited to small gardens.

Cultivation
Pears prefer a well-drained soil in full sun; however, they are quite tolerant of seasonally wet, heavy soils. They are best suited to climates with a distinct cold winter.

Varieties
P. calleryana comes from China. It has given rise to many selections of varying quality, some of them being very brittle, prone to splitting and jettisoning limbs. Others are excellent. Bunches of white flowers appear in

Pyrus salicifolia 'Pendula'.

spring and autumn colour varies from coppery to purple-red. 'Capital' (10 × 3 m) and 'Chanticleer' (10 × 5 m) are both very neat selections of upright, conical form. They are well suited to smaller gardens where height is needed without bulk.

P. nivalis (10 × 6 m) called the snow pear, is a native of central and south-eastern Europe. It has oval-shaped, silver, velvety leaves with yellow autumn colour.

P. salicifolia (8 × 6 m) from Turkey and Iran has willow-like, grey leaves. It is best known in its weeping form *P. salicifolia* 'Pendula' (4 × 4 m).

Drought rating: very tough

Quercus – oaks

Origin

When we think of oaks we tend to think of the huge, deciduous English oak *Quercus robur* (which is, incidentally, quite drought tolerant); however, the genus is very widespread in the northern hemisphere and includes many species from Mediterranean and semi-arid climates. These tend to be

Quercus canariensis.

evergreen, sclerophyllous trees whereas the species from summer-wet climates tend to have very large, soft, deciduous foliage.

Season of interest

Evergreen oaks look unchanging throughout the year. Deciduous oaks look their best in summer and autumn when they may turn colour before shedding their leaves.

Garden uses

Oaks are trees for large gardens only. They can achieve impressive proportions although their growth can be painfully slow. Oaks make beautiful shade trees.

Quercus suber.

Cultivation

Oaks grow in Mediterranean climates and climates with cold winters. They prefer deep soils but are reasonably adaptable. Although oaks are painfully slow growing, always start off with the smallest specimen you can find. Many oaks have substantial tap roots and few fibrous roots so they do not transplant well much over a metre in height. Advanced specimens take many years to establish (during which time a smaller specimen would have caught up) and the success rate of transplanting is far from perfect, which, if you are spending big money on an advanced tree, is disappointing. Planting small oak trees ultimately gives more satisfactory results than planting advanced trees. Oaks hybridise freely so if you want a purebred specimen make sure you obtain your tree from a reliable source, but in many cases the hybrids are just as lovely as the species.

Varieties

Q. canariensis (20 × 20 m) is the Algerian oak from Mediterranean Europe and North Africa. It looks very much like a semi-evergreen, large-leaved version of the English oak. It is much more tolerant of shallow soils than other oak species.

Q. cerris (20 × 20 m), the Turkey oak, is a very tough, deciduous species from central and southern Europe and Turkey. Its leaves are narrow with attractive jagged lobes. They turn yellow and then brown in the autumn, hanging on the tree until the end of winter.

Q. ilex (20 × 20 m) is the evergreen holm oak so characteristic of Mediterranean gardens. It has small, holly-like, sclerophyllous leaves which are dark green on top and grey-green beneath. Holm oak makes a good hedge. It is one of the most important host trees for black Perigord truffles.

Q. suber (20 × 20 m) from the western Mediterranean and North Africa, is *the* cork oak. It looks very similar to the holm oak, but is paler in both leaf and trunk. Its thick, spongy bark is harvested to make cork.

Quercus ilex.

Quercus cerris.

Tabebuia impetiginosa.

Q. wislizeni (20 × 15 m) is the interior live oak of California. It is a sclerophyllous evergreen with small holly-like, mid green leaves. Its leaves are quite sparse but this gives a nice, light effect.

Drought rating: very tough to super tough

Tabebuia

Origin

Tabebuias come from tropical savannah in South America, such as the *cerrado* biome of Brazil, northern Argentina, Bolivia and Paraguay.

Season of interest

Tabebuias flower in the dry winter season.

Garden uses

These are tough, pretty, fast growing trees for larger gardens.

Cultivation

Tabebuias are adapted to hot, wet summers and warm, dry winters. They thrive in frost-free subtropical and tropical climates in Australia in any soil in full sun.

Varieties

T. impetiginosa (30 × 15 m but usually much smaller in gardens), the pink ipe, pink lapacho or pau d'arco tree, comes from winter-dry tropical and subtropical parts of South America. It is related to the jacaranda and like it is adapted to shed its leaves during the dry season and flower on bare branches. It does this in spectacular style, covering itself in bright pink foxglove-like flowers in the middle of winter.

Drought rating: very tough

Ulmus parvifolia – Chinese elm

Origin

Chinese elms are native to northern China, Korea and Japan, which doesn't automatically recommend them as candidates for dry gardens. Yet they are proven reliable, tough trees.

Season of interest

Chinese elms look good throughout the year. In cold inland climates they are fully deciduous, displaying their mottled bark and fine tracery of twigs in winter. In frost-free climates they are semi-evergreen.

Chinese elms display much variation in form. All are lacy and delicate in appearance, but very tough.

Garden uses

These are good small-to-medium trees for backyards. They are ideal for courtyards or around buildings where light shade is needed.

Cultivation

Chinese elms grow happily anywhere in the southern half of the country. They grow in any soil in sun or light shade. It is important to remove any competing leaders for the first few years on young trees as they have a tendency to become multi-trunked.

Varieties

Usually growing to 10 × 10 m, Chinese elms display an enormous variety of forms, from upright to weeping, light and lacy to dense and shady. If you want to know what your tree will look like at maturity it is best to buy a budded tree propagated from a known parent such as 'Burnley Select', which is very symmetrical and upright in form. 'Frosty' is a very elegant, spreading variety which grows to around 5 × 5 m and has green foliage speckled with cream.

Drought rating: very tough

Vitex

Origin

Vitex is a widespread genus, represented in Australia by the rainforest tree *V. lignum-vitae.*

Season of interest

Different *Vitex* species flower in a variety of seasons. The evergreen species look attractive throughout the year, as do the deciduous species with their neat summer foliage and pretty tracery of twigs in winter.

Garden uses

Vitex are excellent small trees, very amenable to being grown in small courtyards and

Vitex agnus-castus.

gardens. *V. agnus-castus* can be pollarded to keep it even more compact if necessary.

Cultivation

V. agnus-castus is a plant for dry summer, Mediterranean-type climates. *V. lucens* is suitable for frost-free climates in southern Australia. Both grow in any well-drained soil in full sun or part shade.

Varieties

V. agnus-castus (4 × 3 m) rejoices in the common names 'chaste tree' and 'monks' pepper' due to its Medieval monastic use of suppressing libido! A handsome small tree from the Mediterranean basin with deciduous, hand-shaped leaves forming a neat, dome-shaped canopy. In summer it bears long spikes of lavender-blue flowers above the foliage. White and pink forms are also available. **Drought rating: very tough to super tough**

V. lucens (15 × 15 m but usually half this in gardens) from the north island of New Zealand, is commonly known by its Maori name, puriri. It has large, evergreen leaves not unlike those of an umbrella plant. In autumn and winter it bears spikes of bright pink flowers. **Drought rating: very tough**

Shrubs and structural plants

Abutilon – Chinese lanterns
Origin
Abutilons are evergreen, shrubby members of the hibiscus family from subtropical and tropical regions.

Abutilon 'Ashford Red'.

Season of interest
Abutilons' main flowering season is from late spring to autumn although they often flower throughout the year in warmer climates.

Garden uses
Abutilons are good fillers in shrub plantings and background shrubs for mixed plantings. They are very useful in shady areas under trees.

Cultivation
Suitable for anywhere in the tropics, subtropics and Mediterranean type climates, abutilons require a well-drained soil in full sun to dappled shade in a sheltered position. They can become leggy over time and benefit from being cut back by half every so often.

Varieties
A. megapotamicum (2 × 2 m), from Brazil, is a straggly shrub grown for its pretty, lantern-shaped flowers. These are made up of an inflated red calyx from which yellow petals emerge, the orange-brown stamens peeping

Abutilon vitifolium.

out of these. A variety with yellow-mottled leaves is also available.

A. vitifolium (4 × 2 m) is a leggy shrub from Chile. It bears flat, lavender-blue flowers in summer.

A. × suntense (3 × 3 m) is a hybrid of *A. vitifolium*, slightly less rangy than its parent. It bears pale violet flowers. Pink, white and purple forms are sometimes available.

There are many beautiful hybrids and selections, mostly derived from *A. pictum*. They feature lantern-shaped flowers in sunset colours or white, some with speckled or variegated foliage. 'Boule de neige' is white, 'Apricot' is apricot, 'Canary Bird' is yellow, 'Ashford Red' is bright red and 'Nabob' is purple red.

Drought rating: very tough

Aeonium

Origin

Aeoniums are succulents native to Morocco, Madeira and especially the Canary Islands. They grow in a range of dry, inhospitable habitats including barren volcanic lava flows.

Season of interest

Aeoniums look good all year round, with spring flowering an extra bonus.

Garden uses

We tend to think of aeoniums as 'succulents' but another way to think of them is as shrubs which happen to have succulent foliage. They can be used as shrubs in mixed plantings where they exert a very muscular presence. They contrast particularly well with grasses, whose lightness is a perfect foil to their chunky

Abutilon × suntense.

Aeonium 'Sunburst'.

Aeonium 'Zwartkop'.

Aeonium haworthii.

solidity. Aeoniums are beautiful in pots and work very well with masonry and man-made structures. They are useful in very hot sites with reflected heat from concrete or paving.

Cultivation

Aeoniums thrive in any climate which is not too wet in summer, though high humidity does not seem to bother them. They are reasonably frost hardy if sited well. They need a position in full or partial sun. Coloured forms like A. 'Zwartkop' colour better when grown in full sun. They need perfectly drained soil but are not fussy as to soil type. Once a rosette has flowered it will not flower again and should be cut off completely. The plant will branch from the cut point. Aeoniums 'stress beautifully' in times of extreme drought by closing up their leaf rosettes like rosebuds. They lose none of their ornamental value for this and soon recover when moisture becomes available.

Varieties

A. arboreum (1 × 1.5 m) is a succulent shrub from the Canary Islands. It has rounded rosettes of apple green leaves at the end of sausage-like branches. In late winter–early spring these give rise to large torches of cadmium-yellow flowers (cut these off if you don't like them). This species is better represented by its black-leaved cultivar 'Zwartkop' in Australia and there is an ethereal pink-and-cream variegated form called 'Sunburst' occasionally available.

A. canariense (50 × 50 cm) is low growing and fairly unbranched but has enormous rosettes of light green leaves, to 50 cm across, and an impressive spire of pale yellow flowers.

A. haworthii (1 × 1 m) forms a rounded shrub with purple-edged, bronze-grey leaves in rosettes. Its flowers are cream, held in drooping heads. A useful filler shrub.

Aeonium arboreum.

A. holochrysum (1.5 × 1.5 m) is an imposing sculptural succulent shrub from the Canary Islands. It has very large, chunky rosettes of apple green leaves, topped with cadmium-yellow flowers atop grey, sausagey stems. This species is sometimes mislabelled *A. canariense* or *A. arboreum* in Australia.

Drought rating: very tough to super tough

Agapanthus – Nile lilies
Origin
Agapanthus are native to South Africa, Swaziland, Lesotho and Mozambique, inhabiting a range of different ecosystems from coastal areas to grassy subalpine meadows. Therefore, not all agapanthus species are drought tolerant.

Season of interest
Evergreen varieties have foliage which looks good year round but deciduous varieties are dormant in winter. Agapanthus are mainly grown for their flowers which appear mostly in late summer.

Garden uses
Agapanthus are great in mixed borders with shrubs and other perennials or in herbaceous borders with perennials and grasses. Evergreen varieties can be used for edging paths and structures.

Agapanthus have a bad reputation in Australia which is not totally deserved. Only one species (*A. praecox* subsp. *orientalis*) is considered a weed and even this species is not particularly widespread or rapacious. It is only liable to be problematic in very localised areas with relatively high summer rainfall or near waterways. It does not cover vast acreages to the exclusion of all other plants

Agapanthus 'Purple Cloud'.

Agapanthus 'Margaret Olley'.

Agapanthus 'Perpetual Peace'.

in the way that, say, Paterson's Curse or Scotch broom do.

The overwhelming majority of *Agapanthus* species, and particularly their many hybrids, are perfectly well behaved. Many of them rarely set viable seed so they are unlikely to make a nuisance of themselves. If you must grow *A. praecox* subsp. *orientalis* simply ensure that you deadhead it as soon as it finishes flowering to stop it from setting seed. This activity might only take half an hour per year.

Cultivation

Cultivation requirements vary by species. The evergreen species are very robust and will put up with almost any soil type so long as they are sited in full sun or part shade. They compete very well with the roots of gum trees. Although the evergreen species are from the summer rainfall parts of South Africa, they are nevertheless extremely tolerant of drought thanks to their dense, fleshy root system which retains water.

The deciduous varieties are more exacting in their requirements than the evergreens. In most parts of Australia they need some supplementary water in summer to look their best – not much, but some. They require a cold winter to thrive so they are not suitable for coastal NSW north of Sydney or Queensland. Although they are slightly more tricky to grow, the deciduous agapanthus have a delicate beauty not shared by their evergreen cousins and they are well worth growing if you live in the right climate. The deciduous agapanthus should be treated like other herbaceous perennials; cut back, mulched and fed in winter.

Varieties

There are dozens of varieties available. Some worth seeking out include:

A. 'Bressingham Blue' (80 × 40 cm) is a deciduous variety derived from *A. campanulatus*. It has heads of hanging flowers of deep cornflower blue on stems which seem very tall for the size of the leaves.

A. 'Margaret Olley' (100 × 80 cm) is an Australian selection. It is very neat and compact, with large heads of the darkest blue flowers over bright, glossy foliage.

Agapanthus 'Pallidus'.

Agapanthus 'Zella Thomas'.

A. 'Pallidus' (90 × 90 cm) is a neat evergreen variety with abundant icy blue flowers.

A. 'Perpetual Peace' (80 × 60 cm) is white with an extended flowering period from late spring until autumn.

A. 'Purple Cloud' (180 × 90 cm) is a very tall variety with intense, violet-blue flowers.

A. 'Snowball' (30 × 40 cm) is a dainty miniature variety with surprisingly large, white flowers.

A. 'White Orb' (100 × 50 cm) has very large heads of white flowers.

A. 'Isis' (50 × 30 cm) is a dainty deciduous variety descended from *A. campanulatus* with light cornflower-blue flowers.

A. 'Zella Thomas' (70 × 30 cm) has cute, 10 cm heads of cornflower-blue flowers across on long, thin stems.

A. 'Guilfoyle' (150 × 80 cm) has intense, dark blue flowers on dark blue flushed stems arising from very neat foliage clumps. One of the best evergreen varieties.

A. 'Inky Tears' (70 x 50 cm) is derived from *A. inapertus* and shares that species' drooping, tubular flowers although they are very dark purple-blue as the name suggests.

Drought rating: very tough (evergreen species); tough (deciduous species)

Agave
Origin
Agaves are a well-known genus of spiky, rosette-forming succulents from the Americas, especially Mexico. Many species are native to arid and semi-arid climates although some are from more humid areas. Agaves are farmed for the production of sisal fibre (from

Agapanthus 'Guilfoyle'.

Agave attenuata.

Agave attenuata 'Variegata'.

Agave geminiflora.

A. *rigida* var. *sisalana*) and tequila (from A. *tequilana*).

Season of interest

Agaves are evergreen and look unchanging throughout the year. In flower they are spectacular, but flowering is by no means an annual event.

Garden uses

Agaves are the ultimate structural plants but they are not to be planted without some forethought as many are very large and

Agave attenuata 'Nova'.

extremely spiky. They are capable of causing painful puncture wounds to people and pets. This is not a reason not to grow them, however. They simply need to be sited well away from paths and thoroughfares, *taking the final size of the plant into account*. It might feel ridiculous to plant a baby agave out of a 15 cm pot three metres back from a pathway but in five or 10 years time you will be glad you did. It is extremely unpleasant work weeding in and around agave rosettes. It is best to remove weeds thoroughly *before* planting a new agave, and lay a deep gravel mulch around the plant to suppress further weed growth.

The larger agaves are robust enough to be used in the grandest-scale plantings with trees, large shrubs and boulders. The smaller ones look good with low-growing sub-shrubs. Agaves are traditionally planted with cacti and other succulents but they look very hostile and foreboding in such a context. Planting them with softer-textured plants lends a bit more movement and 'give' to the effect, and enhances the sculptural nature of the agaves. Bear in mind that in most species

Agave stricta.

Agave americana.

of agave the rosettes are monocarpic, dying after flowering. Most species produce pups around the base of the parent plant, however, which can be used as replacements. Some species are stoloniferous and sucker to form small colonies.

Cultivation

Agaves will grow in any soil type as long as it is well drained. They need an aspect in full sun or light shade. They compete well with gum tree roots. They are fairly frost hardy as long as they are sited in a hot, dry spot. They do not like cold, wet positions.

Varieties

A. attenuata (1.5 × 2 m) is a shrubby, trunk-forming species from central Mexico. It has the softest foliage of all agaves, its leaves being supple and spineless. The broad leaves are frosted green, with blue and variegated varieties available occasionally ('Nova' is a blue form). It flowers fairly regularly for an agave, producing a spectacular 3 m tall inflorescence, drooping at the tip, in summer. *A. attenuata* is a beautiful plant but unfortunately it is not frost tolerant. It grows very well in humid coastal areas.

Agave americana 'Mediopicta alba'.

Agave americana 'Marginata'.

A. filifera (50 cm × 1 m) is a stoloniferous species from Mexico. It forms spherical rosettes of sword-shaped, dark green leaves with a sharp black point at the tip and the margins covered with shaggy, white threads. It bears a thin flower stem 3 m tall.

A. stricta (50 × 50 cm) is a stoloniferous species from Mexico with very narrow, dagger-like leaves with smooth margins and a black spine at the tip. The leaves are arranged in a perfect sphere, giving the plant beautiful geometry. The flower spike is up to 2.5 m tall.

A. americana (2 × 3 m) from Mexico is the best known agave, with awesome rosettes of giant

spiny grey-green leaves. It gets its common name 'century plant' because the rosettes take many years to flower (usually only a decade or so, however) after which they die. There are some beautiful coloured forms – 'Mediopicta alba' grows to half the size of the species and bears a broad, cream band up the centre of each leaf, 'Marginata' has gold-edged green leaves.

A. geminiflora (1 × 1.2 m) also from Mexico has narrow, pale green leaves with white threads curling along the leaf margins. Its flower stem is 3 m tall. The foliage takes on beautiful pale yellows, oranges and reds when

Agave victoriae-reginae.

drought stressed (this does no harm to the plant).

A. parryi (50 cm × 1 m) is a chunky species from the deserts of Arizona, New Mexico and Mexico. It forms a compact rosette of broad, short chalky blue leaves with large chestnut spines and hooks on the margins. A very handsome agave and small enough to fit into most gardens. Its flower stem is up to 4 m tall.

A. victoriae-reginae (50 × 50 cm) from California and Mexico has neat, spherical rosettes of dark green leaves with chalky white, untoothed margins but a vicious, black terminal spine. There is a stunning geometry in the leaves' white-edged 'facets', which show where the leaves were pressed together as they formed. In summer it produces unbelievably tall flower spikes for the size of the rosette – up to 5 m tall.

Drought rating: super tough

Aloe
Origin
Aloe is a genus of 300–400 succulent perennials, shrubs and trees from Africa, including the islands of Madagascar and Cape Verde, and the Arabian Peninsula. They are especially well represented in the South African Cape Province, where they have diversified into many interesting forms, from ground covers to trees, filling a variety of ecological niches. Aloes look superficially similar to agaves but they are in fact unrelated to them. They are closely allied to the red hot pokers (*Kniphofia*) of South Africa. *Aloe vera* is the best known species; its mucilaginous sap is used to treat burns and in cosmetics.

Season of interest
Aloes are evergreen and look good throughout the year. Most species have

Agave parryi.

Aloe polyphylla.

Aloe barberae.

Aloe plicatilis.

colourful flowers which are an added bonus when they appear.

Garden uses

Their use depends very much on the scale of the species chosen. Tree-like aloes have incredibly architectural forms, making them great as specimens or for planting within mixed shrub and perennial borders. The shrubby species make good background shrubs or for filling in difficult spots. They are excellent plants for stabilising erosion on slopes.

Cultivation

Most (but not all) aloes are indestructible. Once established they need no attention whatsoever; however, in very hot climates they look less wizened with an occasional bucket of water thrown over them. Aloes grow happily in the hottest, most exposed positions, or in light shade. They need good drainage and some species are not frost hardy. On the other hand, some come from subalpine areas where they are routinely dusted in snow. The sprawling shrubby aloes can become leggy with time and benefit from being cut back by half occasionally.

Varieties

A. arborescens (2 × 2 m) is a chunky, trunk-forming aloe from South Africa. It has cow

Aloe striatula.

Aloe ferox.

horn-shaped, blue-green leaves. In winter it bears orange-red flowers in long, single heads. It is not especially frost tolerant.

A. barberae (up to 15 m tall in nature but usually a third this height in gardens) is a wonderful, whimsical tree aloe with scimitar-shaped leaves up to one metre in length. It forms a single trunk flaring into a rounded canopy at one end and a swollen buttress at the other. Site it at least 2 m from buildings to leave room for the buttress to grow.

A. excelsa (3 × 1 m) from southern Africa forms a single, unbranched trunk with long, scimitar-shaped leaves on top. In winter it

Aloe excelsa.

produces torch-like flower heads of orange-red. It looks very much like a single-trunked version of *A. barberae* but is more tolerant of cold winters.

A. ferox (2 m × 80 cm) is a single-trunk forming species. It has large, curving leaves covered with soft spines. In winter it bears candelabra-like heads of red-brown flowers borne in long flower heads.

A. plicatilis (1.5 × 1.5 m), the fan aloe, is a slow-growing shrub from the western Cape of South Africa. It forms a chunky framework of branches, each ending in a dozen or so overlapping leaves like succulent paddlepop sticks. The leaf bases are interwoven, forming a beautiful pattern. In winter open heads of orange-red flowers are produced. This species is moderately frost hardy.

Aloes have pretty flowers which combine easily with perennials and grasses.

A. polyphylla (40 × 80 cm) is a species from the mountains of Lesotho which forms a single, huge rosette of leaves spiralling outwards from the centre. This feature is particularly pronounced in older plants. The spiral may run clockwise or anticlockwise. Heads of orange, hanging flowers are produced in spring or summer. This plant is adapted to cool, misty summers and in Australia it is a great drought-tolerant plant for mountain districts but it does not flourish in the hot, dry areas favoured by most of its kind.

A. striatula (1.5 × 3 m) is a rather straggly shrub with narrow, dark green succulent leaves. From late spring to early summer it produces dozens of bright yellow, candle-like flowers. One of the most cold-tolerant aloes.

Drought rating: very tough to super tough

Alyogyne – native hibiscus
Origin
Alyogynes are shrubby wild hibiscus native to south-west WA, around the Great Australian Bight to South Australia, growing in scrub and rocky places.

Season of interest
Alyogynes flower in spring and summer.

Garden uses
Good shrubs for seaside gardens and exposed places. They mix well with other shrubs, succulents and grasses.

Cultivation
Alyogynes come from a dry-summer climate and do not like hot, humid summer conditions. They are best in the southern half of the continent although they do not tolerate heavy frost. They need a soil which drains perfectly, in full sun. They are leggy shrubs and easily split apart in windy conditions. Pruning them back by half after flowering helps to keep them compact.

Varieties
A. huegelii (2 × 2 m) is a straggly evergreen shrub with foliage reminiscent of rose-scented geranium. It bears large, funnel-shaped, lavender blue flowers over a long season. White and pink varieties are available.

Drought rating: very tough to super tough

Arctostaphylos – the manzanitas
Origin
Manzanitas are members of the Ericaceae family, closely related to arbutus. They are a genus of evergreen shrubs and small trees which, like the arbutus, bear white or pink bell-shaped flowers and have interesting, often brightly coloured bark. A few *Arctostaphylos* species come from subarctic

Arctostaphylos pungens (bark).

Arctostaphylos pungens (foliage).

areas and need regular water (*A. uva-ursi* and *A.* 'Emerald Carpet' for example) but the majority are native to the desert states of the USA and Mexico and are extremely tough and drought tolerant.

Season of interest
Year round, with flowers a bonus in late winter.

Garden uses
The manzanitas are all but unknown to Australian gardeners. They are difficult to propagate so the nursery industry has not embraced them. They are well worth seeking out at specialist nurseries, however, as once established, they are extremely tough and beautiful garden plants, particularly for arid and semi-arid regions, and for planting near gum trees and conifers. Do bear in mind that arctostaphylos are reported to be highly flammable.

Cultivation
Manzanitas will grow in very dry, poor soil and in fact *require* dry soil in summer. They do best in full sun or light shade and will grow near gum trees and conifers.

Varieties
A. manzanita 'St Helena' (2 m × 2 m) has satiny red bark on beautifully gnarled branches, dark green foliage and pink, bell-shaped flowers.

A. pungens (1.5 m × 1.5 m) has similarly red, satiny bark but grey, furry foliage.

Drought rating: tough to very tough to super tough

Aristea capitata (syn. *A. major*)
Origin
Aristea is a genus of strap-leaved, clumping perennials from Africa, especially South Africa. Most of them are diminutive collectors' plants but one species, *A. capitata*, is robust enough to earn a place in the garden.

Season of interest
A. capitata flowers in spring and summer. Its bold evergreen foliage clumps look good throughout the year.

Aristea capitata.

Garden uses

A. capitata is a multi-dimensional plant. Its foliage clumps are very structural and its flowers are beautiful, too.

Cultivation

Any well-drained soil in full sun suits *A. capitata*. It is happy in Mediterranean or subtropical climates. It is very slow to establish, taking three or four years before it begins to flower. It is not a plant for the impatient but like all the best things in life it is worth the wait.

Varieties

A. capitata has bright green, strap-like clumps of foliage to 90 cm with electric blue flowers

borne successively on spikes 60 cm above the foliage.

Drought rating: tough to very tough

Artemisia – wormwoods
Origin

Artemisia is a genus of perennials and shrubs from Mediterranean and semi-arid climates around the world, particularly Europe, Africa and Asia. The herb tarragon is an artemisia (*Artemisia dracunculus*) and the spirit absinthe is derived from *A. absinthium*.

Season of interest

Artemisias look good from spring to autumn. While evergreen species retain their foliage in winter, they can look a bit tired.

Garden uses

The larger artemisias are useful filler shrubs. They set off old roses perfectly and work well in mixed borders. The smaller artemisias make good ground covers to hide the bare shanks of roses or lanky perennials and marry well with other low, hummocky perennials like *Anthemis* and *Nepeta*.

Artemisia canescens.

Artemisia 'Powis Castle'.

Artemisia 'Valerie Finnis'.

Cultivation

Artemisias are more or less indestructible. They grow in any well-drained soil in full sun. They benefit from being cut back in winter to keep them tidy. The flowers of many of the smaller species do nothing at all for the plant and are probably better clipped off as they form.

Varieties

A. absinthium 'Lambrook Silver' (40 × 50 cm) is a small shrub with ferny, silver foliage.

A. arborescens (2 × 2 m), the tree wormwood, is a large shrub with strongly scented, silver, feathery foliage. It is very fast growing and useful for filling gaps quickly.

A. canescens (30 × 50 cm) is a neat little bun of very finely cut, almost thread-like, bright silver foliage.

A. pedemontana (20 × 30 cm) looks like a miniature silver coral, with its very finely cut foliage.

A. ludoviciana 'Valerie Finnis' is an herbaceous ground cover to 30 cm high which suckers enthusiastically to form a dense mat of long, silver, ragged-edged leaves. It does very well in clay soils.

A. 'Powis Castle' (1.2 × 1.5 m) looks similar to *A.* 'Lambrook Silver' but is three times the size.

Drought rating: very tough to super tough

Arthropodium cirratum – the rengarenga or New Zealand lily

Origin

New Zealand. Several *Arthropodium* species are also native to Australia but these tend to be tiny, delicate grassland herbs with little garden value.

Season of interest

Rengarenga lily's foliage has year-round interest. Masses of widely spaced, white, star-shaped flowers appear in mid–late spring.

Garden uses

This is just about the ultimate foliage plant for dry shade. It will grow happily in the most thankless areas of the garden – under the

Arthropodium cirratum.

Cultivation

Rengarenga lilies will grow in almost any type of soil from sand to heavy clay. They will grow in full sun in mild, humid climates like coastal NSW but in most places they benefit from a degree of shade and in fact thrive in full shade. Once established, rengarenga lilies are very drought tolerant, thanks to their ability to store water in their fleshy, succulent roots and leaves. Heavy frosts turn their foliage to mush but well-established clumps soon regenerate from the crown. In very cold areas they are best grown in full shade where they will receive some protection from frost. In wet weather snails will do some damage to the foliage though never as much as they do to hostas.

Varieties

A. 'Matapouri Bay' and *A.* 'Parnell' are named selections but they are not *that* much different from the wild species.

Drought rating: very tough

Aspidistra elatior – the cast-iron plant
Origin

Aspidistras are native to the islands of southern Japan, as an understorey plant in dry thickets. Although aspidistras look lush and tropical, they have several adaptations to help them survive very dry conditions. They possess thick, deep-searching, water-storing roots and tough, leathery leaf blades. Aspidistras get their common name from their indestructibility as house plants. They happily tolerate the dry heat and darkness of indoor conditions without so much as turning a leaf blade.

eaves of a house, on the southern side of a building, right up to the trunk of a dense tree – always looking reliably neat, tidy and handsome. The foliage of this plant has a slightly retro-reflective quality so it helps to light up dark areas of the garden (as opposed to clivias, whose black-green foliage is wonderfully light absorbent). The frothy, white flowers rising above the foliage in spring are a bonus. This first-class plant is becoming better known in Australia but has still not achieved its full potential. Rengarenga lilies are a great substitute for hostas which are so beloved of northern hemisphere gardeners but so dependent on cold winters and wet summers for their success (a rare climatic combination in Australia).

Aspidistra elatior.

Aspidistra lurida.

Season of interest

Aspidistras' foliage looks handsome all year round but the flowers could hardly be described as spectacular. They resemble small, beige and puce starfish and they appear at ground level, often below the mulch, as they are pollinated by litter-dwelling springtails.

Garden uses

Aspidistras are one of the very best plants for dry shade. They withstand extremes of temperature and humidity and tolerate root competition from trees. They will grow in very deep shade and in fact look better in such conditions. They are slow to increase but eventually form imposing colonies.

Cultivation

Aspidistras will grow just about anywhere in temperate and subtropical areas. The only requirement they have is leafy (humusy), well-drained soil and shade. Incorporate plenty of compost or leaf mould at planting time. Once established they require little attention but if you can top up their leaf mould or compost from time to time they will repay you in kind. The better conditions you can afford aspidistras, they quicker they will spread and the healthier they will look.

Varieties

Aspidistras have creeping rhizomes which spread indefinitely but very slowly. They send up single, dark green, paddle-shaped leaves 50 cm–1 m high every few centimetres. A variegated variety is commonly available and more rarely the Chinese species *A. lurida*, some varieties of which sport gold-spattered leaves. Variegated and speckled varieties can revert to plain green, so remove any plain green leaves right to the roots if they appear.

Drought rating: tough

Aucuba – Japanese laurel or gold dust plant

Origin

The main species grown in Australian gardens, *Aucuba japonica*, comes from southern Japan, Korea and Taiwan – predominantly wet, summer rainfall climates.

Aucuba 'Rozannie'.

Aucuba 'Variegata'.

Yet surprisingly, this particular region has given gardeners some very tough garden plants. *A. japonica* is one such plant.

Season of interest

Evergreen shrubs, aucubas look excellent throughout the year but really come into their own in winter when other plants are bare. Female forms can bear glossy, red berries but only if they are pollinated by a male form.

Garden uses

Aucubas are one of the best shrubs for dry shade, lending a cool, generous mood to the garden. They are useful for difficult positions like the south side of a house or in the root zone of trees. They are slow growing but worth the wait.

Cultivation

Aucubas are shade plants. They will take sun but their foliage tends to bleach. In shade they grow lush and glossy. Aucubas cope well with competition from tree roots. They are tolerant of any soil type but the more

organic matter you can add to the soil the better they look and the better able to cope with drought they are. This is especially important in hotter inland areas. Aucubas rarely need pruning.

Varieties

A. 'Rozannie' (1.2 × 1.5 m) is a compact, bisexual form with very dark green foliage. It sets large, red fruits without a pollinator.

A. 'Picturata' (2 × 3 m) is a female form with very dark green leaves with a large cream blotch in the middle and the occasional cream fleck elsewhere.

A. 'Variegata' (2 × 3 m) is the best-known female form, its leaves evenly speckled with gold.

Drought rating: tough to very tough

Ballota – False dittany
Origin

Ballotas come from dry, rocky slopes and wasteland in the Mediterranean basin, particularly Greece, Crete and Turkey.

Ballota pseudodictamnus 'Nana'.

Season of interest
Although technically evergreen, ballotas look their best from late winter until late autumn.

Garden uses
Ballotas have the classic hummocky, bun shape of garrigue plants. This form is great in gardens for making undulating ground covers, for planting around the base of bold succulents like agaves or to contrast with more humble ones like *Senecio serpens*; for underplanting roses and other shrubs and for blending with perennials and grasses. Ballota is never a star performer but it makes a versatile support act.

Cultivation
Ballotas grow in any climate which has a dry summer and a reasonably cool winter. They are incredibly tough and grow happily in hot, exposed positions and also in light shade under gum trees or pine trees. They tolerate salty or alkaline soils and salt spray very well and grow well in pure sand or pure clay. The only things they will not tolerate are hot, humid conditions and being engulfed by other plants. They like full access to the sky above them and a good stiff breeze through them at all times. They are naturally very neat plants but they benefit from being cut back by half to three-quarters in late autumn. Soil which is too rich or moist makes them grow floppy so save your toughest spot for this plant.

Varieties
B. pseudodictamnus 'Nana' (50 × 60 cm) is a compact form of the false dittany. It forms a dense bun of furry, sage-green, rounded leaves 1.5 cm across. In spring it bears fairly insignificant flowers which can be clipped off if they annoy you.

Drought rating: very tough to super tough

Beschorneria – Mexican lilies
Origin
Beschornerias are stout succulent perennials from Central America.

Season of interest
Beschornerias are evergreen and look stunning all year round. Their enormous

Beschorneria yuccoides.

BAMBOOS

Bamboos are giant members of the grass family. Their characteristic feature is their long, woody, jointed stems. Each individual joint is called a *culm*.

Bamboos are concentrated in the tropics but there are also some species from more temperate climates. Many bamboos are quite drought tolerant in humid, coastal climates and a few are drought tolerant even in Mediterranean climates.

Many people got burned by bamboos in the 1970s when only running varieties were available in Australia. Today, dozens of clumping varieties are also available. Clumping bamboos do not run at the roots, instead forming tight clumps. Running bamboos are useful in the right situation, but some thought must be given to how far you want them to spread. For more vigorous running varieties, HDPE (high-density polyethylene) root barriers may be installed to restrict their spread or they may be controlled by maintaining a 20 × 20 cm trench around the bamboo. Wandering rhizomes can be removed as they emerge into the trench during late summer and autumn.

Bamboos are expensive to buy because of the difficulty in propagating them. They thrive in any

Bambusa textilis var. *gracilis*.

Bambusa multiplex 'Alphonse Karr'.

soil type so long as they are not standing in water. They appreciate the addition of organic matter to the soil at planting, a good mulch and regular moisture until they are established. It takes two or three years before they begin to make vigorous full-size growth but they are worth the wait as they are among the most atmospheric and elegant of all garden plants.

Different varieties of bamboo can be used for screening, as specimen plants and in mixed borders with other foliage plants.

Otatea acuminata.

Bambusa eutuldoides 'Viridivittata' (6 × 4 m) is a clumping bamboo with bright yellow, green-striped culms. Its foliage grows right to ground level but may be pruned off to expose the ornamental culms.

Bambusa multiplex (4 × 4 m) is a versatile clumping bamboo from China. It is very cold tolerant. The varieties are more commonly seen than the species, including 'Alphonse Karr' which has pink-striped yellow culms and 'Fernleaf' which is smaller growing with dainty, ferny leaves.

Bambusa textilis var. *gracilis* (6 × 4 m) is a clumping bamboo from China. It has upright bright green culms which are bare of foliage to a quarter their height. The tips of the culms arch gracefully outwards to give the clump a tree-like shape.

Otatea acuminata (5 × 5m) from Mexico, is one of the most drought tolerant of all bamboos. It has a clumping habit with very fine, wispy foliage and

Bambusa vulgaris 'Vittata'.

arching, solid stems. A rare, but very atmospheric bamboo for drier climates.

Phyllostachys vivax 'Aureocaulis' (20 m × indefinite spread) is a stunning bamboo with thick, yellow culms striped with apple green. This bamboo needs to be restricted but if you have sufficient space to accommodate it, makes a breathtaking addition to the garden.

Drought rating: tough to very tough

inflorescences appear in spring and summer as an added bonus.

Garden uses

Beschornerias make dramatic punctuation points in mixed plantings with shrubs and perennials. A free-standing clump of beschornerias makes an imposing specimen, or they can be used as size XL bedding around the base of trees or structures. They complement the strong lines of architecture beautifully. Unlike the similar-looking agaves and yuccas, beschornerias have mercifully soft, spike-free foliage and can be planted next to paths without fear of injuring visitors to your garden.

Cultivation

Beschornerias are suited to all of southern Australia, growing equally well in semi-arid, Mediterranean and humid subtropical climates. They grow in any well-drained soil in full sun or part shade (part shade is preferred in very hot, dry areas).
They cope well with root competition from trees but flowering is reduced in overly shady conditions.

Varieties

B. yuccoides (1.2 × 1.2 m) forms clumps of blue-green, upright, sword shaped leaves which curve inwards at their tips. The 2 m flower stem is dusky red bearing many small, green-tipped, bell-shaped flowers. A truly magnificent plant.

B. septentrionalis (1 × 1 m) has apple-green, outward-spreading leaves and a coral-red, branching flower stem bearing green-tipped, bell-shaped flowers. This plant is perhaps not as neat in form as *B. yuccoides*.

Drought rating: very tough to super tough

Buddleja or (*Buddleia*) – butterfly bush
Origin

Buddlejas come from a wide range of habitats in Asia, Africa and the Americas. There are some very drought-tolerant buddlejas from Africa and South America but they are of little garden merit. The best garden varieties come from slightly damper climates but they are nevertheless fairly tough.

Buddleja 'Lochinch'.

Buddleja × weyeriana.

Season of interest
Buddlejas are mostly grown for their profuse, fragrant flowers which appear in mid-summer (spring for *B. alternifolia*).

Garden uses
Buddlejas are beautiful in flower but can look untidy and shabby at other times. Plant them where they will be unobtrusive when not in flower and don't be afraid to prune them ruthlessly – more than once a year if necessary – to keep them neat. Note that in high rainfall mountain areas *Buddleja davidii* and its varieties can self-seed and become weedy. Be circumspect if growing them in these areas. Don't grow them if you live near bushland and always deadhead immediately after flowering.

Cultivation
Buddlejas are very easy to grow. They will grow in any soil type in full sun in any climate which is not too hot and wet in summer. They are very fast growing and excellent for providing quick screens and plugging gaps in the garden. They can also look very ragged

Buddleja 'Black Knight'.

and ropey, however, if not properly cared for. They need to be pruned heavily in winter, by up to three-quarters, back to a framework of branches. They also benefit from being deadheaded after flowering. This is best done with hedge clippers and again, don't be shy! Buddlejas are drought tolerant in climates with a bit of humidity in the air but in very dry climates they can look pretty sad.

Varieties
B. alternifolia (4 × 4 m) is a thin-stemmed, willowy shrub from China. In spring it bears very fragrant, lilac flowers directly on the

Buddleja 'Fascinating'.

stems produced in the last season. Its leaves are also narrow and willowy. Properly pruned this is an extremely elegant shrub. Unlike other buddlejas it must be pruned immediately *after* flowering in early summer by cutting back flowered shoots to their base unless they are needed to build a framework of branches.

B. crispa (3 × 3 m) is grown more for its foliage than its flowers. The woolly, grey leaves are up to 15 cm long and 10 cm wide. The flowers are lilac pink in quite small, loose heads. This buddleja benefits from regular

hard pruning to keep it neat and to induce it to produce the largest possible leaves.

B. davidii (3 × 3 m) is the best known variety. It bears long, conical, lilac-like panicles of fragrant flowers in mid-summer on a bush with felty, green and silver leaves. There are many named varieties. 'Black Knight' bears dark royal purple flowers. 'Fascinating' has huge panicles of pink flowers. 'White Profusion' has white flowers which unfortunately look slightly dirty once past their peak.

B. globosa (5 × 5 m), from Chile and Argentina, bears egg yolk-yellow flowers in small, spherical heads – quite a cute effect.

B. 'Lochinch' is probably a hybrid and certainly one of the most handsome buddlejas. It is a vigorous but neat shrub, well clothed in large, silver leaves on silver stems and large flower heads in a bluer shade of lilac than most of the *B. davidii* varieties.

B. × *weyeriana* (4 × 3 m) is a hybrid of *B. davidii* and *B. globosa*. It bears flowers in the same yellow shade as *B. globosa* but in conical panicles the same shape as *B. davidii*.

Drought rating: tough to very tough

Bupleurum fruticosum – shrubby hare's ear

Origin

The shrubby hare's ear is actually a woody relative of carrots and parsley (family Apiaceae), native to rocky cliffs around the Mediterranean coast.

Bupleurum fruticosum.

Season of interest

All year, with umbels of tiny yellow flowers a bonus in summer.

Garden uses

Shrubby hare's ear is almost unknown in Australia yet it is incredibly tough, beautiful and suited to a wide range of climates and soils. It forms a hummocky shrub which is structural, but not aggressively so, useful in both formal and informal contexts. Its foliage is extremely neat and handsome and blends particularly well with grasses. This plant should be in every garden.

Cultivation

Any well-drained soil in full sun or partial shade suits *Bupleurum fruticosum*. It will grow in a wide range of climates as long as they are not too hot and wet in summer. It does very well in seaside conditions. *Bupleurum fruticosum* benefits from a haircut with hedge clippers in winter and again after flowering to keep its outline smooth and globular, otherwise it can get a bit leggy and sticky.

Drought rating: very tough

Bystropogon – Canary Island smoke bush

Origin

Bystropogons are shrubby members of the mint family (Lamiaceae) from dry places in the Canary Islands.

Season of interest

Bystropogons flower in summer and autumn. Unfortunately there is not much to them when not in flower.

Garden uses

Use in shrub or mixed borders. They are great for softening the hard-edged muscularity of large succulents like agaves and look fantastic among roses.

Cultivation

Bystropogons grow in any well-drained soil, including very sandy soils, in full sun or part shade. They prefer climates with a cool to cold winter and don't enjoy heat and humidity at the same time.

Varieties

B. canariensis (1.5 × 1.5 m) is the Canary Island smoke bush. It forms a rather twiggy

Bystropogon canariensis.

evergreen shrub with slightly mint-scented foliage. In summer and autumn it is completely engulfed in fluffy grey flowers. This sounds rather unprepossessing on paper but this is in fact a very romantic, atmospheric plant and a real survivor.

Drought rating: very tough to super tough

Ceanothus – the California lilacs
Origin
The majority of *Ceanothus* species come from California, hence their common name. They grow in a variety of habitats, most species enjoying very tough conditions on dry, rocky slopes or in sclerophyllous live oak forest.

Season of interest
Although most varieties look very similar to one another, they flower at different times of the year, from late winter through until late autumn so bear this in mind when choosing them. When in flower ceanothus' aniline colours are very impressive. When not in flower they are rather quiet dark green shrubs.

Ceanothus 'Trewithen Blue'.

Garden uses
These are good plants for very dry, tough positions such as westerly aspects which are shaded for most of the day before receiving a blast of afternoon sun. The ground cover varieties are great for covering hot, exposed banks and slopes. The larger species are good for background planting in mixed borders.

Cultivation
Ceanothus like it tough. They thrive in dry Mediterranean and semi-arid climates. They do not like hot, muggy climates although in humid climates they will tolerate perfectly drained, exposed positions such as in seaside gardens. They need full sun or part shade in a well-drained soil and they like a good stiff breeze going through them. They do not appreciate close, still conditions. Many ceanothus grow happily under gum trees and other evergreens which cast light shade. Ceanothus are quite short lived so be prepared to replace them every 5–10 years. They are very fast growing so this is not such a bad thing. The larger varieties are prone to splitting with age.

Varieties
Ceanothus vary considerably in their size. Some are large shrubs of 3 m × 3 m, others are ground covers growing only 60 cm high but several metres in spread. All ceanothus have flowers in shades of blue; some quite pale, others the most lurid shade of ultramarine imaginable. Some white (and rarely pink) varieties are also available. Unless noted otherwise, their foliage is very dark black-green.

Ceanothus 'Yankee Point'.

C. 'Concha' (3 × 3 m) is a large shrub with purple-blue flowers in spring.

C. 'Gloire de Versailles' (2 m × 2 m) has very pale dove-grey flowers over a long season in summer and autumn and glossy apple-green foliage.

C. 'Trewithen Blue' (6 × 8 m) is an umbrella-shaped small tree with cornflower-blue flowers in spring.

C. 'Yankee Point' (1 m × 3 m) is an excellent ground cover variety with bright blue flowers in early summer and glossy dark green foliage when not in flower.

Drought rating: very tough to super tough

Chaenomeles – japonica or Japanese flowering quince

Origin

Chaenomeles is a genus of three suckering shrubs from China, Japan and Korea.

Season of interest

Chaenomeles flower on bare branches over a long season from winter to mid-spring. Their naturally sprawling habit does not have much presence in summer unless clipped into a ball or other geometric shape.

Garden uses

Chaenomeles make good background or foundation shrubs. They are best planted where they are unobtrusive during the summer but can be allowed to shine during their winter bloom period. They make an excellent hedge, able to be clipped reasonably formally. Chaenomeles are related to true quinces and like them bear large, yellow, fragrant fruits which may be stewed or made into jellies.

Cultivation

Despite their East Asian origins, chaenomeles are incredibly tough. They are frequently encountered growing and flowering beautifully around old farm homesteads and in old, neglected gardens. They perform best in climates with a cool to cold winter, in a position in full sun to partial shade (flowering is better in sunny positions). They grow well in any soil type including heavy, wet

Chaenomeles 'Moerloosei'.

A red chaenomeles.

clays. Too much rich fertiliser makes them very leafy at the expense of flowers. They do not require pruning except for the removal of suckers that appear too far from the main shrub, and the removal of dead stems. They take hedging very well.

Varieties

The species *C. speciosa* and *C. japonica* look very similar, each forming a tangled, spiny shrub, 2 × 3 m in size, with bright red flowers. Of the two *C. japonica* has a slightly more dainty look, bearing smaller flowers on finer

Chaenomeles are usually sold by colour, not name, in Australia.

twigs. *C. speciosa* has flowers 3.5 cm across and has several named varieties. 'Moerloosei' (syn. 'Apple Blossom') has flowers which open salmon pink and fade to white. 'Nivalis' is pure white.

More often seen in Australia is *C. × superba*, a hybrid of *C. japonica* and *C. speciosa*. It bears single or double flowers in shades of white, pink, salmon, peach, coral and red. These are rarely sold by name, rather by colour.

C. cathayensis is rarer in cultivation. It is a much larger plant; tree-like in form and up to 4 m tall. It has long, very narrow leaves, pink flowers, long thorns and very large yellow fruits.

Drought rating: tough to very tough

Cistus – rock roses
Origin
Cistus are evergreen shrubs from rocky places and garrigue scrub in the Mediterranean and Canary Islands.

Season of interest
Cistus flower in late spring and early summer. Their flowering season is unfortunately quite short.

Garden uses
Cistus are not star performers but they can put in a solid supporting act. They are useful background shrubs in mixed plantings with other shrubs or large succulents like agaves. Be aware that *C. salviifolius* self-seeds vigorously and is considered a weed in some parts of Australia.

Cultivation

Cistus grow in any well-drained soil in full sun. They prefer dry climates but will tolerate humidity if planted in exposed positions, such as by the sea. Cistus benefit from a trim after flowering to keep them neat. Bear in mind that, like many Mediterranean shrubs, they are quite short lived; however, they are easily replaced and grow quickly to full size.

Varieties

C. creticus (1 × 1 m) has undulating, sage-like leaves and 4 cm pink flowers. Its scented foliage produces a resin once harvested for use in perfumes by combing it out of goats' beards!

C. 'Bennett's White' (2 × 2 m) has glossy, sticky yellow-green foliage and large white flowers with ruffled petals to 10 cm across

C. ladanifer (1.5 × 1.5 m) has sticky, aromatic foliage. It bears white flowers with a maroon blotch at the base of each petal, 7.5 cm across.

C. 'Peggy Sammons' (1 × 1 m) has pretty, rounded leaves and clear pink flowers 6 cm across.

C. × *skanbergii* (1 × 1 m) has dense, sage-green foliage. It bears masses of 2.5 cm-wide, pale pink flowers. It is one of the more attractive species when not in flower.

Drought rating: very tough to super tough

Clivia

Origin

Clivias are native to forests and ravines in the eastern part of South Africa, which has a very similar climate to Brisbane (a wet, humid summer and a drier winter).

Season of interest

Clivias are evergreen and look handsome year round. Their flowers appear mostly in winter–spring, and sporadically thereafter.

Garden uses

Clivias are superb plants for dry shade. They have very thick, succulent roots which compete well with root competition from trees, so they are great for mass planting around tree trunks. They are very useful

Cistus creticus.

Red clivia.

Cream clivia.

Clivia × cyrtanthiflora.

plants for planting along the shady side of a house or other structure.

Cultivation

Clivias do best in frost-free coastal areas. Although they can *exist* in frosty areas they grow very slowly and rarely flower. Clivias need a position in dappled to full shade. They prefer a humusy soil but are amazingly adaptable.

Varieties

C. miniata (60 × 90 cm) is the best-known variety with pale orange flowers nestled

Clivias are an excellent ground cover for dry shade.

among the broad, strap-like leaves. *C. miniata* has given rise to numerous selections which are in many ways superior to the wild form. Their larger, heavier-textured flowers are held well above the foliage in dense heads. They come in a much larger range of colours from cream through yellows to dark oranges and scarlet red. They are more expensive than the wild form (because they are slow to propagate) but are much more telling in the garden so are worth the extra outlay.

C. gardenii and *G. nobilis* (60 × 90 cm) are similar to *C. miniata* but bear hanging, tubular flowers. They are orange-red, tipped with green.

C. × cyrtanthiflora (60 × 90 cm) has hanging, tubular flowers of bright orange-red.

Drought rating: very tough

Convolvulus – morning glories
Origin

The morning glories are a genus of around 250 plants from around the world, including Australian native species. Most of them are creeping annual or perennial vines but

Convolvulus cantabricus.

Convolvulus cneorum.

others are woody sub-shrubs or ground covers. The much-feared, weedy morning glories which take over vast areas of suburbia and bushland are *not*, in fact, convolvulus. They are members of the related genus *Ipomoea* (notably *I. indica* and *I. cairica*) which also includes the important food crops kumara (*I. batatas*) and kang kong or water spinach (*I. aquatica*). Lesser bindweed (*Convolvulus arvensis*) is an agricultural weed in some parts of Australia, similar in appearance to the pretty native species *C. erubescens*.

Season of interest

Flowers appear in flushes from spring to autumn. *C. cneorum* is ornamental year round thanks to its dense, metallic foliage.

Garden uses

These are great plants for hot, exposed positions such as by the sea, adjacent to hot concrete or brick work or near roads. *C. sabatius* is one of the most useful drought-tolerant ground covers and *C. floridus* is a good foundation shrub. They are quick to fill

their allotted space and do their job with a minimum of maintenance.

Cultivation

The species mentioned below are extremely tough. Their only requirements are full, belting sun and a good stiff breeze through them. They do not like humid, close conditions. They are not fussy as to soil so long as it is well drained. They grow well even in pure sand and they love alkaline soils. The addition of some lime or dolomite helps them along in acid soils. *C. sabatius* and *C. floridus* benefit from an annual hard cut back in winter but be judicious with *C. cneorum* as, like echiums and lavender, it does not respond well to being cut back into dry, brown wood. In any case it is relatively short lived and is best replaced every five years or so.

Varieties

C. cantabricus (40 cm × 1 m) is often encountered growing out of limestone cliffs around the Mediterranean coast where it usually looks quite straggly. In gardens it is

Convolvulus sabatius.

much neater, forming a mound of thin stems with very few leaves and pretty, mallow-pink round flowers.

C. cneorum (1 m × 1 m) is a shrub from coastal Italy, Croatia and Spain with dense, metallic silver foliage and round, white flowers 3 cm across. This is a very attractive small shrub for introducing an ethereal silver colour into the garden. Unfortunately like many Mediterranean shrubs it can be short lived.

C. floridus (3 m × 3 m) is a shrub from the Canary Islands. It has long dark green leaves and in summer it bears large conical heads billowing with small white flowers 1.5 cm across on thin silvery stems. *C. floridus* has a tendency to get leggy but it responds very well to hard pruning to keep it compact. It is inexplicably difficult to obtain in Australia, though if you can get one it is a very rewarding garden shrub indeed.

C. sabatius (20 cm × 1.2 m) commonly known as the Moroccan glory vine, is a ground cover from North Africa. It has small, green, hairy foliage and masses of round, mauve-blue flowers 2.5 cm across over a long season from spring to autumn. This is an excellent plant for growing over retaining walls, between pavers or to soften hot concrete paths and driveways.

Drought rating: very tough

Cordyline – the cabbage trees
Origin
Cordylines are widespread in the Pacific region including Australia. The most useful garden varieties come from New Zealand.

Season of interest
Cordylines are evergreen and look good throughout the year. Frothy, white flowers in spring are a bonus but not the main object of growing them by any means.

Cordyline 'Red Star'.

Cordyline australis.

Garden uses

The New Zealand cabbage tree has wonderful structural presence. In both youth and old age it is one of the most useful plants for making a visual exclamation mark in the garden. A small grove of cabbage trees lends an impressive primeval effect. Cabbage trees branch and become broad headed in old age, but they are easily pruned to keep them looking youthful if this is what you prefer. They resprout easily from around pruning wounds; keep as many of the new shoots as you need and pull off the rest.

Cultivation

Cultivation varies by species. The rainforest species like *C. fruticosa* require sheltered, humid, frost-free conditions. By contrast the New Zealand cabbage tree and its varieties will grow just about anywhere, even in very poor soils and under gum trees, though some sunlight and soil improvement are appreciated. Bear in mind that cabbage trees have very tough root systems and the soil around their trunks is often very dry so they can be difficult to underplant.

Varieties

C. australis (5 × 4 m with time, but easily maintained at a smaller size), the New Zealand cabbage tree, is the best-known and most versatile garden species. Several cultivars are available, including a full-sized purple-leaved variety ('Purpurea') and several smaller-growing cultivars with red-purple foliage (e.g. 'Red Star') or variegated foliage (e.g. 'Albertii') and a miniature green form ('Karo Kiri') which grows just one metre high.

C. fruticosa (4 × 2 m) is the ti plant, probably originally from the western Pacific but spread further afield by Polynesian travellers. The wild form is shrubby with 10 cm wide, glossy dark green leaves but there are innumerable forms with brightly coloured leaves, often striped with cream, bright rosy pink, maroon and purple, some with narrower leaves, others with very wide paddle-shaped leaves. These are foliage plants for humid subtropical and tropical gardens *par excellence*, lending both structure and colour.

C. 'Red Fountain' is a red-leafed selection of the hybrid between the NZ species *C. pumilio* and *C. banksii*. It is not as tough as *C. australis*,

Cordyline australis 'Albertii'.

requiring some shade, soil moisture and humidity to look its best.

C. stricta (3 × 2 m) is native to coastal eastern Australia. It has long, narrow leaves on multiple, rather floppy, canes. A good textural plant for shade.

Incidentally, the spectacular mountain cabbage tree, *C. indivisa*, is sometimes encountered in Australian nurseries labelled as 'drought tolerant'. Nothing could be further from the truth. This plant is endemic to *very* high rainfall (2000 mm+), high altitude regions of New Zealand. It is anything *but* drought tolerant and it is notoriously difficult to cultivate outside its home range, even within New Zealand itself.

Drought rating: tough to very tough

Correa – native fuchsia
Origin
A genus of evergreen Australian shrubs mostly from scrubby or wooded habitats.

Season of interest
Different correas flower in flushes at different times but there are often a few sporadic flowers outside their main flowering season. Some species are very leggy and ungainly but a few are more densely foliaged and regular in form, making them more useful garden shrubs.

Garden uses
Although they bear small, colourful, tubular flowers, they are hardly spectacular and correas are best thought of as filler shrubs for sheltered areas near gum trees. *C. alba* is a

Correa pulchella.

seaside plant in the wild and is very useful in coastal situations.

Cultivation
Correas do well away from very hot, humid areas. They are good plants for southern

Correa lawrenciana.

Correa alba.

Australian and inland gardens. They need a well-drained soil in part sun to shade. They respond well to clipping, which keeps them neat and dense. Like many native shrubs, correas are short lived so be prepared to replace them every five to 10 years.

Varieties

C. alba (1.5 × 1.5 m) comes from coastal southern Australia and Tasmania. It forms a dense shrub with round leaves which are dark green on top and grey underneath. Its flowers are white and nestle among the foliage in late summer to autumn.

Correa baeuerlenii.

C. baeuerlenii (1 × 2 m) has shiny, dark green leaves and a fine, twiggy habit. Its autumn–winter flowers are pale green tubes emerging from flattened calyces. They look for all the world like little chefs' hats, hence its common name, the chef's hat correa.

C. lawrenciana comes from cooler, damper mountain areas of eastern Australia where it can grow up to 6 m high, but is usually half this height in gardens. It is a very light, airy shrub with handsome dark green leaves and tubular, pale green flowers in autumn and winter.

C. pulchella (50 cm × 1 m) is a variable, sprawling shrub from SA. It bears bright coral, bell-shaped flowers in winter.

Drought rating: very tough

Cotinus – smoke bush
Origin

There are two species of *Cotinus*. *C. coggygria*, the most widely grown species, is native to a large area ranging from Southern Europe to central Asia where it grows on dry, poor soils. The other, *C. obovatus*, is native to the southern-central states of the USA from Tennessee to eastern Texas.

Season of interest

Spring to autumn. In summer smoke bushes bear fluffy flower heads which look like smoke billowing around the plant. They are best thought of, however, as foliage plants with their handsome, oval, matte-textured foliage in shades of blue-green, purple or gold, giving way to brilliant autumn colours before losing their foliage in winter.

Cotinus 'Flame'.

Cotinus 'Grace' grown as a coppice.

Garden uses

Smoke bushes have autumn colour to rival the best Japanese maples but they are a whole lot tougher, growing happily in poor, dry soils in very exposed sites. They make a perfectly sized tree for small garden spaces such as courtyards although one of the best ways to grow them is as a *coppice*. Essentially this means that the plant is prevented from forming a trunk and is grown as a kind of shrub. When grown as a coppice, smoke bushes can be used as you would any herbaceous perennial in mixed border plantings. They look particularly good planted with ornamental grasses.

Cultivation

Smoke bushes are extremely tough, growing just about anywhere as long as they have at least half sun and well-drained soil. They are initially a little slow to establish (with the exception of *C.* 'Grace') but they are worth the extra patience involved. When training a smoke bush as a tree you will need to encourage a single trunk to form by pruning out competing leaders for the first few years.

You will find it difficult to form a straight trunk but the sinuous, winding trunks of smoke bushes are part of their appeal. To grow a smoke bush as a coppice, cut all growth back to within 10 cm of the ground each winter. The shrub will respond by sending up many straight, unbranched rods to around 1.5 m tall, almost like an herbaceous perennial. This pruning technique has the effect of enlarging the foliage and preventing the plant from producing its smoky flower heads, which some people find unattractive.

Varieties

The wild form of *C. coggygria* (4 × 4 m if left to its own devices but easily maintained as a medium-sized shrub by pruning) has blue-green foliage, pinkish flower heads and variable autumn colour. Better to track down one of the named varieties:

C. 'Flame' looks like the wild species but reliably develops bright orange autumn colour.

C. 'Golden Spirit' has beautiful acid-yellow foliage but is weaker growing than other varieties and tends to burn out in hot, dry weather. It should only be grown where regular water and protection from heat can be given.

C. 'Grace' is a hybrid of *C. coggygria* and *C. obovatus* and displays amazing hybrid vigour. It has very large leaves which emerge purple, fade to matte blue-green over summer before changing to stoplight red in autumn. This variety is the most suitable for coppicing

C. 'Royal Purple' has foliage which emerges purple and darkens to almost black over summer.

Drought rating: very tough

Cotyledon

Origin

Cotyledons are shrubby succulents native to dry karoo and fynbos regions of South Africa, where they are rather unflatteringly known as pig's ears in both English and Afrikaans.

Cotyledon orbiculata 'Silver Waves' combines easily with architecture.

Cotyledon orbiculata 'Tall Form'.

Season of interest

Cotyledons look good throughout the year but are at their best in summer when they flower and their foliage is at its whitest.

Garden uses

These are great plants for bedding and mixed borders with shrubs, perennials and grasses. Cotyledons look great in planter boxes and pots. They are useful for growing under gum trees.

Cultivation

Any well-drained soil in full sun or part shade suits cotyledons. They are not fussy as to climate although they look more impressive in summer-dry climates where they grow very tight and white.

Varieties

C. orbiculata (40 × 40 cm) has oval, blue-grey, succulent leaves covered with a white waxy bloom which gives the plant a brilliant silver colour. It bears apricot, bell-shaped flowers in summer and autumn. 'Silver Waves' is a form with larger, whiter, ruffled foliage. 'Tall flowered form' has flower stems to 1.2 m high.

Drought rating: very tough to super tough

Cussonia

Origin

Cussonias are slow-growing small trees from South Africa. In many ways they look like dry-climate versions of their rainforest cousins the umbrella trees. Instead of the umbrella trees' dark green, glossy, rounded leaflets, cussonias have blue-green or blue-grey, jagged-edged leaflets. Instead of the umbrella trees' slender branches, cussonias are gnarled and corky. They form a swollen caudex as an adaptation to drought.

Season of interest

Cussonias are evergreen and look good throughout the year.

Garden uses

Use in the back of a mixed border or as a free-standing tree. Cussonias are very tolerant of life in a pot.

Cultivation

Cussonias are very tolerant of climate although they take longer to establish in very frosty areas. They thrive in any well-drained soil and appreciate the addition of some organic matter at planting. They need a position in full sun to part shade.

Varieties

C. paniculata (5 × 5 m) has blue-grey, jagged-edged leaves.

C. spicata is similar but with greener foliage. It does not tolerate frost and prefers moister conditions than *C. paniculata*. It is better suited to warmer, humid coastal climates.

Drought rating: very tough to super tough

Dierama – fairies' fishing rods

Origin

Dieramas come mostly from South Africa with some species further north in east Africa. They generally grow in damp grasslands in summer rainfall areas but display considerable drought tolerance in a garden context.

Cussonia paniculata.

Dierama pulcherrimum 'Blackbird'.

Dierama pulcherrimum.

Dierama igneum.

Season of interest

Dieramas flower in summer but their evergreen foliage is attractive throughout the year.

Garden uses

Dieramas are grown for their masses of hanging, bell-shaped flowers produced on tall, wiry stems in summer but their narrow, grass-like foliage is beautiful in itself. Dieramas are very useful in mixed perennial and shrub plantings (e.g. with roses), in gravel gardens, or they can be used as freestanding specimens.

Cultivation

Dieramas will grow in full sun anywhere with a reasonably cool winter. Although they are native to summer rainfall areas they are amazingly tough and resilient in drier parts of Australia, especially when grown in clay soils. They appreciate the occasional handout of water in summer. Dieramas are slow to establish and usually take around three years to flower after transplanting.

Varieties

Dierama dracomontanum (1 m × 1 m) has mallow-pink flowers.

D. igneum (60 cm × 60 cm) is a rarer species with tiny coral-pink, star-shaped flowers.

D. pulcherrimum (1.5 × 2 m) is the most commonly available species. It is available in several colours from white, through pinks to very dark purple.

Drought rating: tough to very tough

Dietes – wild iris
Origin

There are five species of *Dietes* native to South Africa with a sixth endemic to subtropical Lord Howe Island.

Season of interest

Dietes are grown for their long succession of delicate, iris-like flowers which appear in flushes throughout the summer. Each individual flower only lasts a day or two, but they are borne successively over a very long period. Dietes' evergreen foliage is attractive year round.

Dietes bicolor.

Garden uses

Dietes are among the toughest of the tough garden plants. They are extremely useful in dry, exposed positions which is no doubt why they are commonly planted in shopping-centre carparks and median strips. They can quickly fill bare patches in very heavy or degraded soils, in the root zones of trees (as long as it is not too shady) and in south-westerly situations which are shaded for most of the day but receive a few hours of brutal afternoon sun. On larger properties dietes can be used to line driveways or to demarcate borders and fence lines, but a warning: using more than two or three dietes in smaller gardens is guaranteed to make them look like a carpark!

Cultivation

The South African dietes must be the unfussiest plants on earth. Any position which receives at least a few hours of sun, in any climate and any soil type suits them fine.
D. robinsoniana comes from subtropical Lord Howe Island and while it grows well in humid coastal areas of mainland Australia it does not

Dietes robinsoniana.

perform well in dry, frosty inland areas. Having said this, there are some fine specimens at the Australian National Botanic Gardens in Canberra, so it is worth a try if a suitable microclimate can be found.
D. robinsoniana prefers more shade and shelter than its South African relatives.

Varieties

Dietes bicolor (1 × 1 m) has pale yellow flowers.

D. grandiflora (1 × 1 m) has two-tone white and mauve flowers.

D. robinsoniana (1.5 × 1.5 m) has white flowers but is grown primarily for its impressive clump of broad, sword-shaped foliage.

Drought rating: very tough to super tough

Echium – the Pride of Madeira

Origin

The genus *Echium* contains around 60 species from Europe, North Africa, and especially Madeira and the Canary Islands. One of Australia's most serious agricultural weeds, Paterson's Curse, is actually an echium (*E. plantagineum*).

Season of interest

Echiums are grown mostly for their brilliant flowers which appear in late winter and spring. When not in flower the herbaceous varieties form very sculptural foliage rosettes and the shrubby varieties can form attractive mounds if well maintained.

Garden uses

There are two kinds of echium. The woody varieties form mounding shrubs to 2 m tall and 3 m wide and are permanent garden fixtures. The monocarpic ('once-fruiting') varieties are herbaceous. They do not form shrubs but grow in a manner similar to foxgloves; that is, they form a rosette of foliage in their first year before flowering and dying their second. The two varieties are used differently in the garden because of their different stature and lifespan. The shrubby varieties are very useful as foundation shrubs in seaside gardens as they will happily grow in thin, sandy, soils and are impervious to salty sea winds. They will also grow in difficult spots under pine trees and gum trees. They grow very quickly so are useful for plugging gaps in the garden. The monocarpic echiums are best used in mixed plantings between shrubs and structural plants where they will not cause too much disturbance to the design of the garden when they die after flowering.

Cultivation

Echiums like open, airy conditions. They do not like close, humid sites or very frosty

Echium candicans.

Echium candicans 'Heronswood Blue'.

Echium wildpretii.

conditions. They prefer full sun but the shrubby varieties also grow well in half shade. They will grow in any soil so long as it is well drained, but they perform best on poor soils where their growth tends to be more compact and less prone to snapping. Like many Mediterranean plants, echiums are quite short lived. The shrubby echiums live for 10 years or so before becoming woody and rank. When this happens they are easily replaced and will soon fill up the gap. Sadly the monocarpic echiums flower once only before dying. They live for two or three years at best; however, they are unbelievably spectacular when in flower so their short lifespan cannot be considered sufficient reason not to grow them. All echiums self-seed readily (though not as readily as Paterson's Curse) and the seedlings can be transplanted to where they are needed. Transplanting is best done when the seedlings are smaller rather than larger. Shrubby echiums need to be pruned judiciously after flowering to stop them becoming leggy. The best way to do this is to cut back spent flower heads as far as possible into wood which is still green and fleshy. If cut back too hard, into brown, dry wood, the whole branch will die back.

Varieties

E. candicans, the Pride of Madeira, is the best known garden echium. It forms a shrub with silvery, sage-green foliage to 2 m × 3 m. It has heart-stopping, electric-blue flower heads to 30 cm long in late winter. There are several selections and hybrids of this species available, such as 'Heronswood Blue' and 'Heronswood Candles'. All have flowers in various shades of blue, some with glowing purple stamens.

E. pininana is a monocarpic species which forms an imposing rosette of large, hairy leaves in its first year followed by a single, spectacular conical inflorescence up to 3 m tall, covered with hundreds of tiny lilac-blue flowers. *E.* 'Cobalt Tower' is a hybrid of *E. pininana* with the shrubby *E. candicans*. It looks very similar to *E. pininana* but forms several flower spikes on a candelabra shaped plant.

E. simplex is a monocarpic species which forms a rosette of highly decorative broad, silvery dark green leaves. It forms a single, conical spire of white flowers up to 2.5 m tall. This is a very classy echium.

E. virescens is a shrubby species (2 × 3 m) with narrow silver foliage and pale, silvery-pink flowers. It is the most cold tolerant of the shrubby echiums.

E. wildpretii, Tower of Jewels, is a monocarpic species from the Canary Islands. It has a rosette of narrow, hairy, silvery leaves followed by a single, conical spire of flowers up to 2 m tall. It is unusual in the genus in that its flowers are a lurid shade of coral pink. Plant this echium if you want visitors to your garden to rub their eyes in disbelief!

Drought rating: very tough to super tough

Elaeagnus

Origin
Elaeagnus mostly come from dry thickets in Japan, Korea and China but some come from Europe and central Asia.

Season of interest
Evergreen elaeagnus look good throughout the year. Their insignificant but strongly scented flowers are borne in autumn. Deciduous elaeagnus look good when in leaf during the summer. Their flowers are borne in late spring.

Garden uses
The evergreen species make handsome background shrubs and take hedging very well. They are good amongst deciduous plants in a mixed border, coming into their own during winter. The oleaster is a useful fast-growing small tree for areas which need height and cover quickly. Bear in mind that oleasters sucker, have thuggish root systems

Elaeagnus angustifolia.

and are prone to shedding branches. If you are prepared to deal with these eventualities they are very useful trees in the right position.

Cultivation
Elaeagnus grow in any soil in climates which are not too hot and humid in the summer. They grow in full sun and the evergreen species tolerate quite a bit of shade.

Varieties
E. angustifolia (6 × 6 m) is the oleaster tree from southern Europe to central Asia. It resembles the willow-leafed pear (*Pyrus*

Elaeagnus macrophylla.

salicifolia). It is a fast-growing, suckering, deciduous tree with blackish, fissured bark and silvery elongated leaves which shine in the sun. In spring it bears tiny yellow flowers with a sweet perfume. 'Quicksilver' is a smaller, neater selection with shorter, more silver leaves.

E. × *ebbingei* (3 × 3 m) is an evergreen shrub with leathery leaves, matte dark-green on the upper surface, paler and scaly beneath, to 10 cm long. It bears tiny beige flowers in autumn which are very strongly perfumed. Several variegated selections are available including 'Gilt Edge' and 'Limelight'.

E. macrophylla (3 × 5 m) is a sprawling evergreen shrub with wide leaves to 10 cm long which are silvery when they emerge, becoming glossy dark green with age.

E. pungens (4 × 4 m) is a spiny shrub similar to *E.* × *ebbingei* but with glossier foliage. Again, several variegated selections are available including 'Variegata', 'Maculata' and 'Goldrim'.

Drought rating: very tough

Eriogonum – wild buckwheat
Origin

Eriogonum is a large genus of perennials and shrubs related to rhubarb from North America. Many grow in very dry places such as the Californian chaparral and deserts. They are almost unknown in Australia but

Elaeagnus × *ebbingei.*

Eriogonum arborescens.

Eriogonum giganteum.

ought to be more popular as they are super-tough but very pretty plants.

Season of interest

Wild buckwheats flower in spring and summer. Their individual flowers are tiny but they are borne in clustered heads which completely hide the foliage in some species. They look decorative into autumn, turning a rusty colour as they fade.

Garden uses

These are great plants for mixed borders and are useful for softening the strong lines of large succulents like agaves. They are incredibly tough and will grow in quite thankless positions including under gum trees and pine trees.

Cultivation

Eriogonums do well in any summer-dry climate. They do not like muggy conditions during summer. They need a well-drained soil in full sun or part shade but apart from that will grow pretty much anywhere. Remove spent flower heads and cut back the branches by half in autumn to winter.

Varieties

E. arborescens (1 × 1 m) is commonly called Santa Cruz wild buckwheat. It is a small shrub with leaves like short, furry pine needles. It bears small heads of cream flowers which fade to pink and then rusty brown.

E. giganteum (1.2 × 1.2 m) is commonly called St Catherine's lace. It is a shrubby plant not unlike sage with rounded, furry grey leaves. It bears large heads of cream-pink flowers which age to rusty brown.

Drought rating: very tough to super tough

Erysimum – wallflowers
Origin

Wallflowers are annuals and shrubs of the cabbage family native to Europe and North America. The old-fashioned bedding annual wallflowers are derived from *E. cheiri*, sometimes placed in its own genus *Cheiranthus*. Shrubby *Erysimum* species from the Mediterranean are very tough and drought tolerant being native to rocky, limestone soils.

Erysimum 'Bowles' Mauve'.

Season of interest
Wallflowers seem to flower forever but their main season is from late winter to spring.

Garden uses
These are wonderful plants for mixed borders and for underplanting flowering shrubs like roses.

Cultivation
Wallflowers grow in any climate that is not too humid in summer. They like full sun, perfect drainage and plenty of airflow. Seaside positions are ideal. They need to be cut back by half to two-thirds after flowering (it can be difficult to decide exactly when this is). Bear in mind that they are short lived so be prepared to replace them every five years or so. They are very fast growing so this is not such a problem.

Varieties
The shrubby garden wallflowers grow to around 60 × 80 cm. They bear huge numbers of 1.5 cm flowers in succession on flower stems which continue to elongate over many months.

E. 'Chelsea Jacket' has flowers which open yellow and age to dark pink and then purple, creating a pretty multi-coloured effect.

E. 'Terracotta' has terracotta orange flowers.

E. 'Bowles' Mauve' has mauve flowers.

Drought rating: very tough

Escallonia
Origin
Escallonias are evergreen shrubs from scrub and woodland in South America, especially Chile.

Season of interest
Escallonias' summer flowers are a bonus but they are mainly grown for their glossy evergreen foliage.

Garden uses
Escallonias make excellent fast-growing hedges. They take straight lines quite well, so can be used for quite formal hedges. Escallonias can be used in background

Escallonia bifida.

Escallonia 'Iveyi'.

plantings and as fast growing windbreaks for establishing new gardens. They thrive in seaside conditions.

Cultivation

Escallonias grow in any climate with a reasonably cool to cold winter. They need a well-drained soil in full sun to part shade. When not grown as hedges they can become

Escallonia 'Langleyensis'.

quite leggy quickly and benefit from being hard pruned from time to time.

Varieties

E. bifida (6 × 5 m) is more tree-like, with long, oval, dark green leaves and masses of white blossom.

E. 'Apple Blossom' (2 × 2 m) has pink flowers.

E. 'Donard Seedling' (2 × 2 m) has shell-pink flowers.

E. 'Iveyi' (3 × 3 m) has elegant, glossy, very dark green leaves and large panicles of icy white flowers in late summer. A first-class plant.

E. 'Langleyensis' (3 × 3 m) has hot-pink flowers.

Drought rating: very tough

Euphorbia – spurges
Origin

Euphorbia is an enormously diverse genus of over 2000 species of annuals, perennials, succulents, woody shrubs and trees found throughout the world. The ubiquitous red

Euphorbia amygdaloides 'Purpurea'.

Euphorbia characias 'Ascot Gnome'.

poinsettia of subtropical gardens is in fact a member of this genus (*E. pulcherrima*) as is the old-fashioned snow-on-the-mountain (*E. marginata*). Many euphorbias come from semi-arid and arid climates which makes them of particular interest to Australian gardeners.

Season of interest

Most euphorbias look good year round, peaking at flowering time which, for Mediterranean climate euphorbias, is late winter and spring.

Garden uses

Euphorbias come in every conceivable shape from classic herbaceous perennials to neat,

Euphorbia 'Tasmanian Tiger'.

Euphorbia lambii.

lush shrubs to leafless, sea-urchin-like blobs to giant cactus-like trees. Most euphorbias have flowers in shades of brilliant lime green or acid yellow in late winter or spring, which doesn't sound terribly exciting but is in fact a wonderfully refreshing colour at that time of year, blending beautifully with daffodils and emerging spring foliage on deciduous trees. There is a euphorbia to suit just about any situation in the dry garden.

Cultivation

The species mentioned below are Mediterranean climate euphorbias which thrive in places with dry, hot summers or in exposed places by the sea. They prefer full sun and plenty of air movement in humid coastal areas but will take half shade in drier,

Euphorbia × *martinii* 'Slow Life'.

Euphorbia × *martinii* 'Ascot Rainbow'.

inland climates and in fact are useful for difficult spots in the root zone of trees in such climates. Euphorbias need a well-drained, moderately fertile soil. Too much nitrogen makes them floppy and prone to blowing apart in winds but they appreciate the addition of a modest amount of well-rotted organic matter to the soil before planting. Stems which have borne flowers will not do so again and should be cut back as low as possible when flowering has finished, taking care not to get the caustic sap in your eyes or on sensitive skin. In certain climates euphorbias self-seed vigorously so it is best to deadhead them before the seed is released, especially if they are grown near bush areas. This is not an onerous task and in any case unwanted seedlings are shallow rooted and easily removed.

Varieties

E. amygdaloides, known as wood spurge, grows to 50 × 50 cm. It has thinner leaves than the other species and needs shade from the hottest part of the day. It is useful for tucking in around shrubs and large grasses.
E. amygdaloides 'Purpurea' is the most commonly grown form, featuring dark purple foliage and bright yellow-green flowers in late winter. *E. amygdaloides* 'Robbiae', sometimes called 'Mrs Robb's bonnet' is a running form with black-green glossy foliage. It can be extremely invasive so plant it with care.

E. characias (1.2 × 1.2 m) is a blue-grey-foliaged shrub from Mediterranean Europe. It bears large heads of acid-green flowers with a red eye in late winter. More frequently seen in Australia is *E. characias* subsp. *wulfenii* which bears tighter heads of flowers of a clear yellow-green. 'Ascot Gnome' is a very neat, compact selection from Lambley Nursery in Victoria. 'Tasmanian Tiger' is an excellent cream variegated selection by Tasmanian plantswoman Sally Johannsohn. It is extremely elegant and ethereal, but requires some protection from the hottest summer sun.

Euphorbia mellifera.

Euphorbia rigida.

E. lambii (3 × 3 m) is a small tree from the Canary Islands. It has a very neat, umbrella-like canopy over a single or divided trunk. Its foliage is extremely neat, blue green, with acid-green flower heads in spring. Sadly it does not survive in frosty areas.

E. × martinii is a hybrid of *E. characias* and *E. amygdaloides*. There are several selections of this hybrid, some of the best made by Australian plantsman David Glenn. 'Ascot Rainbow' is a larger form at 90 × 90 cm. Its leaves emerge plum purple before becoming gold variegated. Its spring flowers are similarly variegated and have a red eye. 'Michael McCoy's form' and 'Slow Life' (90 × 90 cm) look much like larger versions of *E. amygdaloides* 'Purpurea', with dark claret foliage and yellow flowers.

E. mellifera comes from Madeira and the Canary Islands where it grows into a 15 m tree. Oddly, in gardens it never exceeds a 2 × 2 m shrub. English gardeners are mad about this plant, with good reason. It forms an extremely handsome, round shrub clothed in 20 cm long, velvety, apple-green leaves with a paler midrib. In spring it bears caramel-brown, honey-scented flowers. Although drought tolerant, this plant looks happier if given an occasional drink in summer.

E. myrsinites is similar to *E. rigida* but more creeping and smaller in all its parts. You could almost call it 'cute'. A great plant for tumbling over retaining walls or edging raised beds.

E. rigida (40 × 80 cm) comes from the Mediterranean basin from Portugal to Greece and Turkey and Morocco in north Africa. It forms a neat tuft of stems, each with short blue-grey leaves spiralling around its length. In late winter these are topped with flat heads of bright, acid-green flowers.

E. stygiana (1.5 × 1.5 m) is a close relative of *E. mellifera* from the Azores. Sadly there are only 15 specimens left in the wild. *E. stygiana* looks like a smaller version of *E. mellifera* but with typical yellow-green flowers rather than brown. One nice bonus is that the old leaves turn bright pink and red in autumn before falling, forming a crimson carpet around the bush.

Drought rating: very tough

Fatsia japonica – Japanese aralia
Origin
Coastal woodland and scrub in Japan and Korea.

Season of interest
Fatsias are evergreen and look good throughout the year.

Garden uses
Most of us think of fatsias as indoor plants and this is how they are usually sold to us. The thing which makes them such outstanding indoor plants, just as with aspidistras, is their incredible resilience in the face of the most adverse growing conditions imaginable. They have to put up with very low light levels, very low atmospheric humidity, wildly fluctuating temperature and a high degree of neglect. For a fatsia, being given a place in the garden, even a pretty horrible place, must seem like a holiday in paradise by comparison. With their huge, glossy, palm-shaped leaves they exert quite a presence and are well worth finding a spot for. They are an excellent choice for planting under evergreen

Fatsia japonica 'Variegata'.

trees (including gum trees in not-too-dry areas) and they work very well with architecture so they are very effective up the shady side of the house.

Cultivation
Fatsias prefer half to full shade. They will grow in sun but their foliage will be permanently yellow instead of dark, glossy green. Incorporate plenty of organic matter at planting time and mulch them deeply. They are not especially fast growing but get better year by year. They can be cut back hard if they become spindly. The occasional watering in summer will keep them looking their best, but so long as the soil contains plenty of organic matter and they are sheltered from hot winds fatsias are amazingly tough.

Varieties
Fatsias grow to 3 × 3 m but are easily kept smaller with pruning. The variety 'Moseri' is more compact. There is also a very rare variegated variety.

Drought rating: tough to very tough

Fatsia japonica.

Garrya elliptica – silk tassel bush
Origin
Dry chaparral scrub in California and southern Oregon, USA.

Season of interest
Garryas are evergreen so they look good throughout the year. They come into their own in winter when they are dripping with the long, soft catkins which give them their common name.

Garden uses
Garryas are not glamorous enough to use as feature plants but they shine in their own quiet way, deserving a place in any garden. Their even, dark green foliage can be used as a background for flowers, autumn foliage, or silver-foliaged plants, or it can be used as an informal screen or hedge for privacy. Garryas can be planted in just about any position and relied on to do their job without screaming for attention.

Cultivation
Garryas grow in any climate which is not too humid and wet in summer. They are not fussy about soil, growing equally well in pure sand or pure clay. They are likewise not fussy about position so long as they get at least some sun.

Varieties
Named varieties are not commonly available in Australia. Garryas grow to 4 × 4 m but are easily kept smaller with pruning.

Drought rating: very tough to super tough

Genista – the brooms
Origin
The common name 'broom' is applied to at least four genera (*Genista, Cytisus, Spartium, Retama*). Some of the environmental and agricultural weeds commonly referred to as 'brooms' are the Scotch broom (*Cytisus scoparius*), Spanish broom (*Spartium junceum*), Cape broom (*Genista monspessulana*) and Dyers' broom (*Genista tinctoria*). Not all brooms can be tarred with the same brush as these nightmare weeds, however. The brooms described below have so far been unproblematic in Australian gardens. The responsible gardener will keep an eye on them and remove them if they look like they might be weedy in your local climate.

Season of interest
Late spring to summer is the main flowering period for brooms. They make good background shrubs the rest of the time.

Garden uses
Good plants for mixed borders with shrubs, perennials, grasses and succulents. *G. lydia* has such a strong character that it can be used as a focal point in low ground cover plantings.

Garrya elliptica.

Cultivation

Any well-drained soil in full sun suits brooms. They prefer dry climates, languishing in summer-humid areas.

Varieties

G. frivaldszlcyana (1.5 × 1 m) has soft, green foliage and masses of pale yellow flowers in late spring to summer.

G. lydia (1 × 1 m) is very unusual in form. It is leafless, forming a thatched dome of arching, dark green twigs. In late spring to summer it is completely hidden by hundreds of cadmium yellow flowers.

Drought rating: very tough to super tough

Hedera – ivies

Origin

Ivies are a genus of evergreen woody creepers native to Europe, North Africa and Asia. They suffer from the same affliction as agapanthus and brooms; unjustly maligned as 'noxious weeds'. In actual fact, the ACT is the only jurisdiction which recognises just one of the 11 *Hedera* species as such (*H. helix*).

Hedera canariensis.

Season of interest

Ivies look great all year round.

Garden uses

Ivies make wonderful ground covers for dry shade. English ivy (*H. helix*) only flowers and sets seed when its creeping runners find something vertical to climb up, like a fence or a tree, which enables it to form its shrub-like adult growth when it reaches the top. This can take many years. As long as you prevent your ivy from running up trees, walls or fences it will not flower and set seed. If you are still concerned about weed potential, grow one of the other species of ivy.

Cultivation

Ivies grow in all but tropical climates. They tolerate any soil type in part sun to full shade. They will grow in full sun as long as there is sufficient moisture available. Be on the lookout for runners heading up trees, fences and buildings and remove the offending runners. This should only take a few minutes per year. Once ivies form their woody adult growth, it takes an enormous amount of work to remove them.

Varieties

All species spread several metres, rooting as they go.

H. canariensis from North Africa has large, triangular, floppy leaves, 12 cm long. It has a gold-variegated selection 'Gloire de Marengo'.

H. colchica from Iran and the Caucasus has large, oval-shaped leathery leaves.

H. helix from Europe is the common or English ivy, with strong three to five-lobed leaves. It has given rise to an amazing array of selections with different leaf shapes, sizes and colours, most of them much less vigorous than the parent.

Drought rating: very tough

Hedychium – ornamental gingers
Origin
Ornamental gingers come from tropical and subtropical Asia at a range of altitudes and therefore from a range of different climates. Many of them are suitable for cooler, drier climates than their tropical distribution would suggest.

Season of interest
Hedychiums have beautiful foliage from spring to autumn, being deciduous in cooler climates. In warmer climates they tend to be evergreen, looking good year round. Their beauty is enhanced when they flower in summer and early autumn.

Garden uses
These are wonderful plants for shade. They can be massed around the base of trees or used as feature plants, almost like a shrub.

Cultivation
Hedychiums are best for humid coastal climates with a minimum of frost, although they can be surprisingly cold tolerant in inland areas if sited correctly. They look their best in sheltered positions in light shade with cool, humid air, and out of hot, drying winds.

Hedychium gardnerianum.

They will tolerate more sun as long as there is sufficient soil moisture. They can also tolerate more shade although their flowering will be reduced. Hedychiums grow in any soil type but appreciate the addition of plenty of organic matter. This improves their ability to withstand dry periods considerably. Flowered stems need to be cut back to the ground to keep the plant tidy.

Varieties
H. coccineum (1.8 m × 3 m) has bright orange-red flowers in large heads over narrow mid-green foliage in summer.

H. coronarium (1.5 m × 3 m) bears beautifully fragrant white, butterfly-like flowers in summer.

Hedychium coccineum.

H. greenei (1.2 m × 3 m) has very decorative dark green leaves, bronze underneath, held on bronzy stems. The autumn flowers are pale orange.

Alpinia zerumbet 'Variegata'.

Elettaria cardamomum.

H. gardnerianum (1.8 m × 3 m) bears big heads of sweetly fragrant yellow flowers with orange anthers.

Other tough gingers worth growing include:

Alpinia zerumbet (2.5 m × 3 m), shell ginger, forms upright clumps of bright green paddle-shaped leaves. In summer and autumn it produces long, pendant inflorescences of orchid-like flowers which are white with a yellow and red-striped lip. The flowers are exquisitely scented. There is also a gold-variegated form.

Elettaria cardamomum (60 cm × 1 m) is the cardamom plant. It has cardamom-scented foliage but its flowers are fairly insignificant. It makes a nice ground cover for full sun to part shade.

Drought rating: very tough in humid climates, tough in drier climates

Helichrysum – everlasting daisies
Origin
The everlasting daisies comprise around 500 species from Europe, Asia and especially South

Curry bush (*H. italicum* subsp. *serotinum*) makes an excellent low silver hedge.

Helichrysum petiolare looks much neater when clipped. Here with *Anthemis* 'Susanna Mitchell'.

Africa and Australia. They usually grow in dry, hot habitats. Some are short-lived shrubs, some are perennials and others, like our familiar native ornamental species, are annuals.

Season of interest
The shrubby helichrysums are evergreen and look good all year round.

Garden uses
Helichrysums make useful filler shrubs in mixed borders or for underplanting flowering shrubs or large succulents like agaves.

Cultivation
Helichrysums are plants for dry summer climates or in exposed positions such as by the seaside in more humid places like Sydney and Brisbane. Any well-drained soil in full sun suits them. *H. petiolare* will grow happily in part shade or dappled shade as long as it is not too moist. The shrubby helichrysums respond well to being clipped and *H. petiolare* is a good short-lived topiary specimen. The flowers of the shrubby species are not very interesting and tend to make the bush flop under their weight. They can be clipped off before they open if this irritates you. All species are short lived and need to be replaced every five years or so.

Varieties
H. argyrophyllum (20 × 40 cm) from rocky places in South Africa forms a mat of silver foliage with pretty yellow paper daisies in summer and autumn.

H. italicum subsp. *serotinum* (60 cm × 1 m) is the curry bush of Mediterranean Europe. It forms a dense bun of strongly aromatic, silver, thread-like foliage. Its summer flowers are yellow, fading to brown.

H. petiolare (1.5 × 2 m) is a dense, sprawling shrub from South Africa. It has neat, small round leaves which are grey covered with white velvet, and heads of straw-coloured flowers in summer. The selection 'Limelight' has pale yellow-green leaves. It is rather sickly and performs better in shade.

H. thianschanicum 'Icicles' (40 × 40 cm) forms a tiny mini-shrub with silver, needle-like foliage. It bears yellow flower heads in summer.

Drought rating: very tough to super tough

Helleborus – the hellebores

Origin

A genus of around 20 perennials from Europe, especially the Balkans, and one species from China. Best known are the colourful 'winter rose' type hellebores which are hybrids between *H. orientalis* and other Balkan species. These varieties, while somewhat *tolerant* of a certain amount of summer dry, do not thrive in such conditions and should not be thought of as plants for dry gardens unless you live in high rainfall mountain climates. The species from Mediterranean Europe do thrive in dry climates, however, and while their flowers are

Helleborus foetidus 'Wester Flisk'.

not as showy, they are nevertheless very attractive garden plants.

Season of interest

Hellebores are evergreen and look good throughout the year but their greatest value is during the wintertime when they are in flower.

Garden uses

The Mediterranean hellebores fade into the background during summer but step into the limelight in the winter garden when their handsome foliage and modest flowers can be appreciated. These species work very well planted around the perimeter of deciduous shrubs with coloured stems, like *Rosa glauca* and *R. moyesii* 'Geranium' where they benefit from some shade in the summer and contrast beautifully with the coloured stems in winter. They look fantastic interplanted with spring bulbs and work well with winter-flowering euphorbias, which have quite a similar colour scheme.

Cultivation

The Mediterranean hellebores prefer more sun than the 'winter rose' types although some protection from the hottest part of the day is preferred. Having said that, *H. argutifolius* loves full sun and *H. foetidus* is happy even in very difficult dark shade. Well drained soil is essential and the addition of well-rotted organic matter and a thick mulch helps them along. Hellebores love lime or dolomite added to the soil. The only maintenance necessary is to cut back in late spring any stem which flowered earlier in the year.

Helleborus argutifolius.

Helleborus × sternii.

Varieties

H. argutifolius (syn. *H. corsicus*) comes from the Mediterranean islands of Corsica and Sardinia where it often grows in fairly exposed situations by the sea or in low scrub. It is the largest of the hellebores growing to an impressive 1.2 m × 1.2 m. It has leathery, three-lobed leaves of verdigris-green, overtopped with 5 cm wide, jade-green flowers in winter.

H. foetidus is known, rather unfairly, as the 'stinking hellebore'. It has an extensive natural distribution, occurring in many parts of Europe from the British Isles to Hungary. *H. foetidus* has finely cut, finger-like leaflets of dark, matte green, growing on a stout trunk to 50 cm tall. In winter it doubles this height when masses of small, bell-shaped flowers are borne on tall, branching flower spikes. Both the flowers and flower stems are of a fresh, pale green which contrasts beautifully with the foliage. There are several named varieties of *H. foetidus* each with its own subtle beauty. 'Wester Flisk' has distinctly pewter-green foliage and dark red markings on the stems and flowers. 'Sienna' has particularly finely

cut, black-green foliage. 'Sopron' has dark green foliage overlaid with silver while 'Gold Bullion' has bright acid-green foliage.

H. lividus is an exquisite diminutive species from the Mediterranean island of Majorca, growing just 40 cm tall and wide. Like its close relative *H. argutifolius*, *H. lividus* has leathery, three-lobed leaves, dark green marbled with silver above and dusty pink below. The stems and 4 cm flowers are also dusty pink. This species is difficult to obtain in Australia, and reasonably slow growing but well worth the effort. It prefers slightly more sheltered conditions than *H. argutifolius*, and can be tucked under a deciduous shrub for protection from the midday summer sun.

H. × sternii (60 cm × 60 cm) is an easy-to-grow garden hybrid of *H. argutifolius* and *H. lividus*. It has inherited its beautiful dusty-pink stems from *H. lividus* and its robustness and ease of culture from *H. argutifolius*. Seedlings display a lot of variation from one another, some having heavily veined leaves, or more pink flush than others. Named strains are sometimes available, including the 'Blackthorn Strain' with reliably pink flowers and heavily veined foliage and the rare 'Ashwood Strain' with its deeply serrated, silver foliage and dusty pink flowers.

Drought rating: very tough

Hesperaloe parviflora
Origin
Hesperaloe are a small genus of rosette-forming succulent perennials from deserts in Texas and Northern Mexico.

Season of interest
A beautiful plant throughout the year but stunning when in flower during the summer months.

Hesperaloe parviflora. It is hard to do this stunning plant justice in photographs.

Garden uses
Hesperaloe parviflora is wonderful in mixed plantings with shrubs, perennials, succulents and grasses because it contributes both handsome foliage and beautiful flowers. It makes a great feature or specimen plant, surrounded by gravel, or in a very large pot. It has even been used mass-planted in streetscapes to great effect. This plant should be in every inland garden.

Cultivation
Hesperaloes like full sun and well-drained soil, preferably not too heavy in texture. They are quite happy in the hottest, driest spot in the garden and are a great plant for arid climates.

Varieties
H. parviflora is a clump-forming plant to 60 cm × 1.2 m. Its leaves are long and thin, and almost tubular in cross-section, to funnel rain and dew into the centre of the plant. They are dark green with white threads along their edge and although they look sharp they are actually quite soft. The yellow-tipped coral, bell-shaped flowers open successively on tall (1.2 m), elegant stems throughout the summer, quite indifferent to heat. There is a yellow variety of hesperaloe but this does not seem to be available in Australia at present.

Drought rating: super tough

Iris
Origin
Iris is a genus of around 300 species of bulbs and perennials widespread in the northern

Iris confusa.

hemisphere. They inhabit a range of habitats from standing water to semi-arid climates.

Season of interest

Different species of iris flower from mid-winter until mid-summer. Some varieties have handsome evergreen foliage which looks good throughout the year. In fact, some iris have leaves that are more interesting than their flowers. Such species are best thought of as foliage plants.

Garden uses

I. foetidissima, *I. japonica*, *I. confusa* are excellent ground cover plants for dry shade. The bearded iris are good plants for hot, dry, exposed sites in full sun.

Cultivation

I. foetidissima, *I. japonica*, *I. confusa* will grow in any climate south of the tropics. They prefer a leafy, moisture-retentive soil in part shade to full shade. Bearded iris only succeed in areas with cold, frosty winters. They need a well-drained, poor soil in full sun. They especially like well-drained clay soils. Bearded iris need

to be lifted and replanted every few years to keep them fresh. They do not appreciate having mulch over their rhizomes.

Varieties

I. foetidissima (60 × 60 cm), from southern Europe and the Azores, has the rather unfortunate common name of 'stinking gladwyn'. Its leaves smell like vitamin B tablets when actively crushed – not really that offensive. It is a wonderful plant for dry shade, forming dense, evergreen clumps of narrow, very dark green leaves. Its flowers are small, beige and nestle among the foliage but the seed pods are large and split open in late autumn to reveal large, orange seeds which are very ornamental. There is a silver-variegated form, 'Variegata', which does not set seed.

I. japonica (40 cm, spread indefinite) forms little fans of evergreen, glossy foliage. Its flowers are small and very pale mauve.

I. confusa (one metre, spread indefinite) is the big brother of *I. japonica*. It forms fans of bright green leaves atop short, bamboo-like rhizomes. Its flowers are flat and very pale mauve-blue.

Iris foetidissima 'Variegata'.

Iris unguicularis.

I. unguicularis (50 × 90 cm), the Algerian iris, is native to the Mediterranean basin. It forms a clump of long, narrow, evergreen leaves. In winter it bears beautiful, lavender blue, apricot-scented flowers nestled in the foliage. A very tough plant, it benefits from being cut back to 15 cm in late autumn before the flowers emerge so that they can be appreciated easily.

Bearded irises are complex hybrids of several southern European species, grown for their highly coloured flowers (in ancient mythology Iris was the goddess of the rainbow). They come in three sizes; large, median and dwarf. There are hundreds of varieties in every conceivable colour combination – too many to discuss here!

The Pacific Coast Iris are just beginning to gain popularity in Australia. These are hybrids derived from *I. douglasii* and other iris species native to the dry sclerophyll live oak forests of California. They form clumps of narrow, evergreen (summer deciduous in very dry seasons) foliage to 50 cm with 8 cm-wide flowers in spring, in shades of purples, maroons, pinks, creams and peachy sunset shades. They are a little bit tricky to establish but once established they are very tough.

Drought rating: tough to very tough

Jasminum – the jasmines
Origin
Many of us think of jasmines as delicate and exotic. They don't spring to mind when we think of drought tolerant plants. Yet jasmines are members of the same family as the olive (the Oleaceae) and like the olive most of them are incredibly tough. Jasmines are a genus of deciduous and evergreen creepers and shrubs from scrubby, rocky places in Europe, Africa and Asia.

Season of interest
Different species of jasmine flower in winter, spring and summer, some in flushes, others in one massive display.

Garden uses
The climbing jasmines are very dense and vigorous. They don't mix well with other plants (as they tend to engulf them) but they do work very nicely with buildings. They need a very sturdy structure to support their considerable bulk. Paling fences will *not* do the job, as many Australian gardeners have discovered over the years. Brick walls are ideal, with a framework of heavy wires attached to them for guidance.

Cultivation
Jasmines are very adaptable, growing in a variety of climates in full sun in any soil type. In cooler climates the evergreen species

benefit from reflected heat from brick walls or other structures. The shrubby species benefit from being cut back if they become rangy. The climbing species can be clipped with hedging shears at any time to keep them neat.

Varieties

J. nudiflorum (3 × 3 m) is a deciduous shrub from western China. It bears bright yellow flowers in winter. Sadly, it is not fragrant. This species grows best in areas with a cooler winter.

J. polyanthum (4 × 3 m) is an evergreen climber with dark green, glossy leaves. The vines are completely engulfed in white, star-shaped flowers opening from pink buds with the first warm days of spring. Their heady fragrance is a sign that the cold weather is over in southern Australia.

J. sambac (3 × 3 m) is a scrambling shrub probably from south Asia though it has been cultivated and traded for so long that its origins are unclear. This is the jasmine used to scent jasmine tea and sold in garlands at temples throughout South East Asia. It bears exquisitely scented, white, star-shaped flowers in flushes throughout the warmer months. In Australia it is more commonly encountered in its double form, 'Grand Duke of Tuscany'. Although hardy in cooler inland areas this plant looks much better when grown in frost-free coastal areas in a sheltered position. It does tend to become a bit sticky at times and benefits from being cut back to 10 cm above the ground now and then.

Drought rating: very tough

Kalanchoe

Origin

A genus of succulent perennials, shrubs and trees from semi-arid climates of the Middle East, Africa, Asia, tropical America and especially Madagascar.

Season of interest

Kalanchoes' foliage looks good throughout the year. The flowers are a seasonal bonus.

Garden uses

The tree-like species make imposing structural plants in mixed borders or in pots. The smaller varieties make good filler plants in mixed borders with shrubs, grasses, perennials and other succulents.

Cultivation

Kalanchoes do best in frost-free climates in areas including humid summer areas and

Kalanchoe beharensis.

Kalanchoe fedtschenkoi 'Variegata'.

Kalanchoe luciae.

inland areas. They thrive in any well-drained, preferably sandy soil in full sun or part shade.

Varieties

K. beharensis (3 × 3 m), sometimes called the velvet plant, is a small succulent tree from Madagascar. It has large, arrowhead-shaped leaves with wavy margins up to 40 cm long. The leaves are velvety in texture, bronze above and sage-grey below.

K. fedtschenkoi 'Variegata' (50 × 60 cm) is a pretty succulent perennial with scalloped, blue-green leaves covered with a waxy bloom.

The edges of the leaves are variegated with cream and pink.

K. pumila (20 × 50 cm) is a very dainty miniature succulent with blue-green leaves covered with a waxy bloom, making them appear steel grey. It bears pink, bell-shaped flowers in spring. This must surely be the prettiest of all succulent plants.

K. luciae (30 × 30 cm – one metre tall in flower) comes from rocky hillsides in South Africa. It has large, round, saucer-like leaves growing in a flattened basal rosette. The leaves are green with a paler bloom, turning dark reds and pinks during cold weather. Tall flower spikes of small, cream flowers appear in spring.

Drought rating: very tough to super tough

Kniphofia – the red hot pokers
Origin
A genus of perennials mostly from South Africa, where they grow by stream sides and in wet meadows.

Kalanchoe pumila.

Season of interest

There is a kniphofia to flower in every month of the year but the majority of species flower in either early spring or late summer.

Garden uses

These are great plants for giving vertical emphasis to flower borders along with more nebulous perennials and grasses.

Cultivation

Kniphofias are often sold as super drought tolerant. Their various habitats in nature suggest otherwise. Almost all kniphofia species are found with their feet standing

Kniphofia 'Blaze'.

either permanently, or seasonally, in water. However, their thick, succulent roots and succulent foliage give them a high degree of drought *tolerance* and so long as they can recharge their water reserves for at least part of the year most species seem perfectly happy to accept periods of drought. They do not thrive in climates with permanently low rainfall, however.

Kniphofias need a position in full sun in subtropical- or Mediterranean-type climates. They grow in any soil type including heavy clays, in which they prove especially tolerant of drought. In sandy soils they benefit from the addition of plenty of organic matter to aid water retention. Kniphofias are mostly evergreen (a few are deciduous) but they benefit from having their foliage cut back to 15 cm in winter to keep them neat.

Varieties

Dozens of varieties are available. Some of the best are:

K. 'Blaze' (1 m × 80 cm) has coral-orange flowers in mid-summer.

Kniphofia 'Lime Glow'.

Kniphofia sarmentosa.

Kniphofia 'Little Maid'.

K. 'Jack de Marco' (60 × 40 cm) is an Australian selection with apricot buds opening to rich yellow flowers in summer.

K. 'Little Maid' (60 × 40 cm) has pale yellow buds opening to ivory flowers. A reliable, floriferous, winter-deciduous variety.

K. 'Lime Glow' (1.2 m × 80 cm) has lime-green buds opening to lime-yellow flowers.

K. 'Percy's Pride'(1 m × 60 cm) has lime-green buds opening to cream flowers over a very long season in summer and autumn. A very neat Kniphofia.

K. 'Prince Igor' (2 m × 1 m) has huge heads of orange buds opening to yellow flowers in summer.

K. sarmentosa (1 m × 80 cm) flowers during winter with dusky apricot flowers over grey foliage.

K. caulescens (1.2 m × 80 cm) is a statuesque plant with neat, blue-grey foliage (most of the

Kniphofia caulescens.

genus has rather messy, green foliage). It bears thick flower heads of cream flowers opening from dusky coral buds in late summer.

Drought rating: tough to very tough

Lavandula – lavenders

Origin

Lavenders are a genus of around 40 species centred around the Mediterranean basin where they grow in dry, rocky, exposed places. They are classic plants of the garrigue scrub characteristic of southern Europe. Lavender is strongly associated with the south of France where one species is extensively grown for the perfume industry.

Season of interest

Lavenders flower from spring to autumn.

Lavandula stoechas is a declared noxious weed in Victoria.

Garden uses

Lavenders are good plants for seaside gardens and exposed, rocky positions. They are traditional plants for underplanting roses, especially old shrub roses. They work well in combination with perennials and large-scale succulents like aloes. If you want to grow lavender for the classic lavender fragrance then only one species will do the job: *Lavandula angustifolia*, the English lavender. Despite its common name English lavender is native to southern Europe, not England. The drawback of English lavender is that it has one spectacular flowering in mid-summer and then the show is over. Other species of lavender flower over a *much* longer season – three months or more – but they don't have the classic lavender perfume, instead smelling rather camphory.

Cultivation

Lavenders need an exposed position in poor, well-drained soil. They detest muggy, still air so are no good for very humid coastal areas, with the exception of the

These lavenders have been clipped back after flowering to keep them neat. Even with no flowers they can add structure to the garden.

Lavandula pinnata is one of the few lavenders which thrives in humid subtropical climates.

ferny-leaved lavenders such as *L. canariensis* and *L. multifida* from the Canary Islands, which seem impervious to it. In southern Australia lavenders thrive in seaside gardens and other open, airy positions. Lavenders can get quite leggy and split in the centre of the bush. Clip them back after flowering as hard as you can *without* going into dry, brown, leafless wood, which will not reshoot. Like many Mediterranean shrubs lavenders are short lived and should be replaced every few years.

Varieties

L. angustifolia (1 × 1 m) is the so-called English lavender, but native to France and Spain. It has, unsurprisingly, lavender-purple flowers on long, thin stems held well above a bun of silver, needle-like leaves. Several varieties are available including the compact, bluer 'Munstead' (60 × 60 cm) and the dwarf, dark purple 'Hidcote' (40 × 40 cm).

L. stoechas (80 × 80 cm) is variously called French, Spanish or Italian lavender. Along with its relative *L. stoechas* subsp. *pedunculata* it forms a variable complex of plants. Its tiny purple flowers are borne in relatively large, furry bracts topped with several long, petal-like appendages, or 'flags'. The flowers are held just above the foliage. Many named varieties are available, including a great many selections in the 'Bee' and 'Bella' series made by Australian plantsman Robert Cherry (e.g. 'Bee Pretty'and 'Bee Happy'). All are lovely variations on a theme, featuring different permutations of colour based on pale pink to dark reddish purple flowers and 'flags' on neat, compact and floriferous plants. *L. stoechas* is possibly the best of all lavenders from an ornamental point of view.

Note that *L. stoechas* is a declared noxious weed in Victoria (only) and may not be traded or grown in that state.

L. pinnata (1 × 1 m) has large, silver, ferny leaves and tight flower heads with relatively large purple flowers. It comes from the Canary Islands and grows in warm, humid conditions better than other varieties, as does its relative *L. canariensis*. *L. pinnata* is possibly the parent of the Australian selection 'Sidonie' which looks almost exactly the same.

Drought rating: very tough to super tough

Lavatera

Origin

A genus of perennials and shrubs in the hibiscus family, native mostly to the Mediterranean region and central Asia.

Season of interest

Lavateras flower spectacularly in flushes through summer and autumn.

Garden uses

Lavateras are good shrubs for exposed sites, especially in seaside gardens. They are good background or filler shrubs for mixed plantings with other shrubs and perennials.

Cultivation

Lavateras hate humid, muggy conditions and are best suited to the southern half of the country, both coastal and inland. They are plants which thrive on exposure, enjoying plenty of sun and air movement. They do not like being hemmed in by other plants. Any soil suits them as long as it drains perfectly. Lavateras are prone to debilitating fungal diseases and are in any case fairly short lived. Be prepared to replace them every five to six years. They quickly grow to full size. In very frosty areas lavateras should be planted out as soon as your frosts are finished in spring, giving them a full growing season to establish before the onset of winter.

Varieties

L. 'Barnsley' (2 × 1.5 m) has white, hibiscus-like flowers with a reddish eye, which fade to shell pink.

Lavatera 'Kew Rose'.

L. 'Blushing Bride' (2 × 1.5 m) has a succession of white flowers with a pink eye.

L. 'Kew Rose' (2.5 × 2 m) bears masses of mid-pink flowers like small hibiscuses over a very long season from summer to autumn. This is by far the best variety of lavatera. It is the most robust and telling variety.

Drought rating: very tough

Lupinus – lupins

Origin

Lupins are a large genus of annuals, perennials and shrubs in the pea family, widespread in the Americas, Europe and Africa. They grow in a variety of habitats including some very dry ones. Best known are the magnificent Russell lupins, hybrids derived from *L. polyphyllus* which is native to Alaska and British Columbia. Russell lupins require lots of water and a cold climate to do well. There are extensive naturalised populations in the New Zealand alps and Scotland where such conditions prevail.

Season of interest

Dry-climate lupins flower in winter and spring.

Lupinus variicolor.

Garden uses

Lupins are excellent, very fast-growing filler shrubs. They are not long lived but they are so useful that this can be forgiven. They can be used as a quick, low windbreak around vegetable beds, or to nurture slower growing woody shrubs or trees. They can achieve their full size in a single season from a cutting or seedling.

Cultivation

Dry climate lupins grow in any well-drained soil in full sun. They are best suited to dry-summer climates and prefer cold winters. They can be cut back severely if they become leggy.

Varieties

L. arboreus (1.5 × 2 m) comes from California. It has pale yellow or cream flowers in heads 15 cm long, scented like sweet peas. It has a propensity to self-seed in certain climates so be vigilant for weediness.

L. variicolor (1.2 × 1.2 m) is also a Californian native. It looks almost identical to *L. arboreus* but with blue and white flowers instead of yellow.

Drought rating: very tough to super tough

Mahonia

Origin

A genus of around 70 evergreen shrubs from wooded, rocky parts of North America and Asia. They are grown for their dark, glossy green, pinnate, holly-like foliage and their golden yellow, often fragrant flowers which appear from autumn to spring.

Season of interest

Mahonias are handsome throughout the year. They are at their best in winter when their architectural form can be appreciated.

Mahonia bealei.

Mahonia aquifolium.

Garden uses

These are great shrubs for difficult dry-shade areas. Mahonias have a quiet beauty which, like all the best things in life, is an acquired taste.

Cultivation

Mahonias can grow in sun but they are happier in half to full shade. They are unfussy as to soil but grow faster and look healthier if they are given some well-rotted organic matter at planting time and a deep annual mulch. No pruning is required except to remove dead branches occasionally.

Mahonia lomariifolia.

Varieties

M. aquifolium, the Oregon grape, is a suckering species which forms a dense ground cover one metre tall. Its golden yellow flowers are followed by blue berries, which, like all Mahonias, are edible but not very nice.

M. bealei is a neat shrub to 2 × 3 m. It has very long leaves with very broad leaflets and lily of the valley-scented flowers.

M. japonica is very similar to *M. bealei* but has narrower leaflets.

M. lomariifolia has a very erect habit to 3 × 2 m. Its leaves have up to 40 very narrow leaflets, giving the effect of a fish skeleton – quite a unique effect.

M. nervosa is a rarely available suckering ground cover just 50 cm high, with surprisingly large, fern-like leaves.

Drought rating: tough to very tough

Melianthus – honey bush
Origin

Melianthus are evergreen sub-shrubs native to South Africa.

Season of interest

Melianthus are grown primarily for their bold, evergreen foliage. Their winter–spring flowers are a nice bonus.

Garden uses

Melianthus are excellent feature plants, working very well with architecture. They make good background shrubs in large-scale mixed plantings, lending a lush, tropical feeling to dry gardens.

Melianthus major.

Cultivation

Melianthus are plants for Mediterranean and subtropical climates. They prefer positions in full sun to part shade. They do sucker but the suckers are easy to remove by hand. The plants can get leggy by the end of the season and benefit from being cut back to near ground level occasionally. If cut back every year they are prevented from flowering, which, as they can self-seed in high rainfall areas, isn't such a bad thing.

Varieties

M. major (2 × 3 m) is a suckering sub-shrub with large, pewter-coloured pinnate leaves which look like they have been cut out with pinking shears. In winter–spring it bears 60 cm dark red inflorescences.

Note that *M. comosus* is a declared noxious weed; regionally controlled in Victoria, prohibited in WA.

Drought rating: tough to very tough

Metrosideros
Origin
Metrosideros are evergreen trees and shrubs from Polynesia and especially New Zealand, related to our gum trees.

Season of interest
Metrosideros are evergreen and look good throughout the year. Their brilliant flowers make them a seasonal highlight.

Garden uses
The larger metrosideros make good screening trees while the smaller ones make good background shrubs, hedges and screens. The dwarf varieties can be used in mixed borders for seaside conditions.

Cultivation
Metrosideros are plants for humid coastal climates and the subtropics. They like positions in full sun in any well-drained soil. They love seaside conditions. They don't need any routine pruning but can be cut back hard if they get out of hand, and they respond well to hedging.

Varieties
M. excelsa (15 × 10 m but usually half this height in gardens) is the well-known New

Zealand Christmas tree or pohutukawa. It forms a dense tree with dull grey-green leaves and striking red, eucalyptus-like flowers in summer. Several selections are available including 'Pink Lady' with dusty pink flowers, 'Lighthouse' with pillar-box red flowers, 'Moon Maiden' with creamy yellow flowers and 'Fire Mountain' with orange-red flowers.

M. kermadecensis (15 × 10 m but usually half this size in gardens) is similar to *M. excelsa* but finer textured in foliage and flower.

Drought rating: very tough

Miscanthus

Origin
Miscanthus are semi-evergreen or deciduous perennial grasses mostly from Africa and Asia.

Season of interest
Miscanthus look beautiful for much of the year thanks to their bright green foliage in spring and summer, fluffy flower heads in late summer and autumn, autumn-coloured foliage in cooler areas, and dying off to a beautiful straw colour in winter, while retaining their upright form. The only time they don't look beautiful is in the short time between cutting them back in late winter and re-sprouting in the spring.

Garden uses
Miscanthus are incredibly useful garden plants. They are at the same time inconsequential and imposing, forming dense visual masses but made of the airiest, lightest stuff, moving and rustling in the slightest

Miscanthus transmorrisonensis has a solid presence and fluffy lightness at the same time.

breeze. They marry perfectly with perennials, shrubs and small trees or they can be used on their own in massed plantings. Miscanthus self-seed negligibly if at all in most climates (although it might be worth keeping an eye out in very wet parts of Australia). Miscanthus can do no wrong: they are ornamental grasses *par excellence*.

Cultivation
Miscanthus are suitable for Mediterranean and subtropical climates. They prefer a cool to cold winter to look their best. They grow in any water-retentive soil in full sun or part shade (but no more). In dry, shallow soils they need to have plenty of organic matter added at planting and a good, deep mulch. They are definitely not xeriphytes but once established they display a fair degree of drought *tolerance*, surviving happily on the occasional handout of greywater.

Varieties
M. sinensis comes from China, Korea and Japan where it displays much variation in

Miscanthus 'Sarabande' displays beautiful autumn colour in cold climates.

Miscanthus flower heads are airy and light.

nature. This has allowed many interesting selections to be made, some more drought tolerant than others. All cultivars have narrow, green leaves with a white midrib. Flowers are borne in large, spidery heads which vary in colour from burgundy through pinks to silver. Among the best are 'Yakushima' (1 × 1 m) a dwarf selection from the Japanese island of Yakushima, 'Gracillimus' (1.8 × 1.5 m) a formal, upright, fine-leaved form which does not flower in cooler climates, 'Sarabande' looks similar but is more relaxed in outline, 'Variegatus' (1.5 × 1.5 m) has wider, cream-variegated foliage edged in pink (more tasteful than it sounds). This variety prefers some shelter from the hottest part of the day.

M. transmorrisonensis (2 × 2 m) comes from Yushan (formerly known as Mt Morrison) in Taiwan. This species has wide, emerald green, arching foliage and very large heads of fluffy, pink flowers which quickly age to silver. It is officially evergreen, but it does benefit from being cut back in late winter to clean it up. A surprisingly drought-tolerant grass given its natural distribution in wet Taiwan.

M. × giganteus (3 × 1.2 m) is a sterile hybrid. It looks quite a lot like miniature sugar cane. It forms tight, very upright clumps which rarely flower in cool climates. This is probably the least drought-tolerant miscanthus in inland areas, but very happy in coastal climates where, because it is sterile, it cannot set seed.

Drought rating: tough

Myrtus communis – myrtle
Origin

Myrtus communis comes from the Mediterranean basin – southern Europe and north Africa. It is the sole member of its genus but gives its name to the huge Myrtaceae family which includes such

Myrtus communis.

Myrtus communis subsp. *tarentina.*

familiar plants as eucalypts, bottlebrush, lillypillies, New Zealand Christmas tree, cloves, guavas and feijoas. In Roman times myrtle was sacred to the goddess Venus. Today it is widely used in Mediterranean gardens.

Season of interest

Myrtle is evergreen. It looks glossy and beautiful throughout the year. Its fluffy white flowers are a summer bonus. Myrtle's foliage has a beautiful, fruity fragrance and can be used in the kitchen to flavour meats and desserts.

Garden uses

Myrtle is an excellent foundation hedge in mixed plantings and takes clipping well in formal gardens. Dwarf myrtle makes an excellent hedge, similar in appearance to box but faster growing.

Cultivation

Myrtles grow in any soil as long as it is well drained. They like full sun or partial shade.

They take clipping well but do not require any special pruning.

Varieties

M. communis grows to 4 × 4 m in nature but is usually seen at half this size.

M. communis subsp. *tarentina* (1 × 1 m) is a dwarf form of myrtle with smaller, narrower leaves. It is more cold hardy than the type and is in many ways a better plant.

M. communis 'Variegata' is full size with cream variegated foliage.

Drought rating: very tough

Nerium oleander – oleander
Origin

There are two subspecies of oleander, one from the eastern Mediterranean (*N. oleander* subsp. *oleander*) and the other (*N. oleander* subsp. *indicum*) from Iran to western China. Oleanders are evergreen shrubs which grow wild in dry, rocky river beds. They are members of the same family as

Nerium 'Docteur Golfin'.

Nerium oleander.

frangipani, star jasmine and periwinkle (the Apocynaceae family).

Season of interest

Oleanders flower over a long season from spring to early autumn and often sporadically thereafter.

Garden uses

Mention at a dinner party that you are going to plant oleander in your garden and watch your fellow diners recoil in horror. Every Australian knows that oleanders are

Nerium 'Petite Salmon'.

poisonous and a good many people claim to know of a friend-of-a-friend's second cousin who died of it. What they may not know is that many of the English dainties in their own gardens are also poisonous – daffodils, daphnes, delphiniums, hellebores, foxgloves and lily of the valley, to name but a few. The Australian native white cedar tree (*Melia azedarach*), so widely planted in shopping-centre carparks, and the castor oil plant (*Ricinus communis*), found along train lines in many coastal cities, are *much* more poisonous than oleander; fatally so, in fact. Putting urban myth and hysteria to one side, oleander poisoning is actually quite rare as the sap tastes horribly bitter.

Oleanders are first-class garden plants for dry climates. They always look neat, generous and handsome in the face of total neglect and they seem to be constantly in flower. They can be used as foundation shrubs, informal hedges or specimen shrubs. Many of their relatives are succulent plants, such as the *Adenium* species, and like these, oleanders are slightly succulent in nature, storing water in their thick, fleshy leaves which have specialised stomata (pores) which limit water

Nerium *'Splendens Variegatum'*: variegated foliage *and* lurid pink, double flowers. Is it possible to have too much of a good thing?

Nerium oleander 'Album'.

loss. They have extremely deep, searching roots which can find water where shallower-rooted shrubs cannot.

Cultivation

Oleanders are tolerant of any soil type, including salty soils, as long as they are in full sun. They can be pruned back hard, to within 10 cm of the ground, to rejuvenate them if they become leggy. During times of extreme hardship they tend to drop many of their leaves as a survival mechanism, but they will recover with the next rain, or if you slosh a bucket of greywater on them now and then.

Varieties

All varieties grow to 3 × 3 m unless otherwise noted.

'Album' has white, single flowers.

'Docteur Golfin' (syn. 'Italia') has hot cherry-red flowers and is said to be one of the most cold-tolerant cultivars.

'Petite Salmon' and 'Petite Pink' (1 × 1 m) are dwarf varieties with salmon and pale pink coloured flowers, respectively.

'Splendens' has dark pink, double flowers.

Drought rating: very tough

Phlomis
Origin

Phlomis is a genus of shrubs and herbaceous perennials in the mint family. They come from the Mediterranean basin through to central Asia and China, where they grow in rocky places, dry grasslands and dry woodlands, often under pine trees.
Most of them are exceptionally tough plants, which are sadly underrated in Australia. Perhaps this is because, like euphorbias, they are not star performers and are easily taken for granted.

Phlomis samia.

Season of interest

Different *Phlomis* species flower from spring through to autumn. Their seed heads are just as beautiful as their flowers and last into winter.

Garden uses

The herbaceous perennial species are useful in mixed plantings with other perennials and grasses. Their flowers could not really be described as showy, but coupled with their strong upright form phlomis nevertheless make quite a strong statement in a perennial border. The shrubby species work well as foundation shrubs in mixed plantings.

Cultivation

Phlomis need a position in full sun or half shade. The herbaceous perennial species prefer deeper soils than the shrubby species, which thrive even on very thin rocky soil.

Varieties

P. fruticosa (1 × 1.5 m) is commonly called Jerusalem sage but it is neither a sage nor is it from Jerusalem, coming instead from the Balkans through to Greece, Turkey and Cyprus. It forms a mounding shrub with sage green foliage and whorls of yellow flowers.

P. russeliana (100 × 80 cm) is commonly called Syrian rue. Happily it *does* come from Syria (as well as Turkey) but it is not remotely related to rue! *P. russeliana* is an herbaceous perennial species from dry woodland with large arrow-shaped leaves and yellow flowers. It flowers over a relatively short season but even when the flowers themselves have finished the whorls of bracts stay upright on their stems right into winter, looking particularly beautiful when covered with frost.

P. purpurea (1 × 1 m) is a shrubby species from Spain and Portugal with grey foliage and mauve-pink flowers. In very dry seasons this species is liable to shed its foliage and become a bit sticky. It pays to deadhead the spent flower heads and clip it into a ball shape after

Phlomis fruticosa.

PALMS

The palm family (Arecaceae) contains 2600 species from around the world. Palm species are mostly concentrated in the tropics but they are also found in cooler climates. Palms are adapted to an amazing variety of habitats from rainforests to mangroves and deserts. Two of the best-known palm species are the date palm (*Phoenix dactylifera*), native to the desert sands of north Africa and the coconut palm (*Cocos nucifera*), native to beach sands of the western Pacific.

Many palms are extremely ornamental and make excellent garden subjects. Palms have such strong architectural form that they can only really be used as feature plants. When grown in the right climate they need no extra water and tolerate long periods of drought. Palms ask only a well-drained soil and a bit of extra water and attention in their first few years. Forest palms like the bangalow palm and the lady palm prefer some shelter and shade when young whereas those from more open habitats, like *Chamaerops humilis,* revel in exposed positions.

Archontophoenix cunninghamiana (up to 12 m, but usually half that height in gardens), the Australian native bangalow palm, is surely one of the most beautiful of all cultivated palms. It forms a head of graceful, bright-green, frond-shaped leaves atop a smooth, grey, ringed trunk. It is a very tidy palm, shedding its entire leaf very neatly from the trunk leaving no unsightly leaf base as many palms do. It bears very attractive violet flowers followed by bunches of red fruits. It is suitable for any frost-free climate but prefers some humidity in the air to look its best.

Bismarckia nobilis (10 m) is a stunningly beautiful palm from Madagascar. It forms a single trunk topped with massive, fan-shaped foliage of

Archontophoenix cunninghamiana.

Bismarckia nobilis.

Butia capitata.

Chamaerops humilis var. *cerifera.*

Chamaerops humilis (4 × 5 m with time) is a clumping palm native to southern Europe and north Africa. It bears stiff, neat, dull green, fan-shaped leaves in dense clusters around the apex of its trunks. There is a beautiful blue form occasionally available (*C. humilis* var. *cerifera*). This palm prefers areas with cooler winters – southern coastal regions and inland climates. It languishes in subtropical and tropical areas.

Livistona australis (20 m but usually half that size in cultivation), the Australian cabbage tree palm, is a single-trunked palm from the east coast of Australia as far south as the Victorian border. It

metallic silver-blue. It is suitable for frost-free climates only. It needs a hot microclimate in southern parts of Australia. There are some magnificent specimens growing in inner Sydney city where they seem to benefit from the heat reflected by roads and paving.

Butia capitata (5 m), the jelly palm, is a single-trunked palm from Brazil and Paraguay. It has long, palm-shaped leaves of a silvery blue-green. If pollinated by a nearby male tree, female jelly palms bear delicious, bright red fruits the size of a 10 cent piece, tasting very much like a tart nectarine. The jelly palm is very tough and will grow in a range of climates including frosty inland areas.

Chamaerops humilis.

Rhapis excelsa.

has bright green, fan-shaped leaves on thorny leaf stems and a shaggy brown trunk.

Rhapis excelsa (4 × 4 m eventually, though easily kept smaller), the lady palm, is a suckering, thicket forming palm from southern China. Usually grown as a houseplant, it makes a beautiful, bamboo-like screening plant for shady areas in humid, frost-free climates.

Trachycarpus fortunei (10 m), the windmill palm, is one of the most cold-tolerant of palms, native to the foothills of the Himalayas. It was very popular in Victorian times and is commonly seen in Melbourne gardens. It has bright green, fan shaped leaves atop a brown, shaggy trunk. A good palm for mild mountain climates, it does not like heat and humidity at the same time. Its rare relative *T. latisectus* is sometimes available. It looks similar but sheds its leaf bases and so has a bare trunk.

Palms for Mediterranean gardening zone

Butia capitata

Chamaerops humilis

Phoenix canariensis (also grows in humid regions but is quite weedy in these)

Trachycarpus fortunei.

Rhapis excelsa (with shelter)

Trachycarpus fortunei

Washingtonia filifera

Palms for humid subtropical and tropical climates

Archontophoenix cunninghamiana

Bismarckia nobilis

Livistona australis

Phoenix roebelenii

Rhapis excelsa

Washingtonia filifera

Phlomis' beautiful seed heads give interest to the garden long after their flowers have finished.

flowering to keep it neat. *P. italica* is a similar, but smaller, species from the Balearic Islands.

P. samia (120 × 80 cm) is an herbaceous species from pine forests in the Balkans and Turkey with woolly, oval leaves and unusual, smoky pink flowers with a darker pink lip.

Phlomis tuberosa.

P. tuberosa is an herbaceous species from the Balkans, Greece, Turkey, Iran and central Asia. It has large, dark green, nettle-like leaves and whorls of mallow pink flowers on purple stems.

Drought rating: very tough to super tough (shrubby species); very tough (herbaceous species)

Pittosporum

Origin

A genus of shrubs and trees from Asia, Africa, Australia and the Pacific region, especially New Zealand.

Season of interest

Pittosporums flower mostly in spring and summer but they are primarily grown for their evergreen foliage.

Garden uses

Pittosporums are good screening plants, responding well to clipping. *P. tenuifolium* has become inordinately popular in recent years but there are many other beautiful

Pittosporum tobira.

varieties. Some species can be trained as small trees. They are very adaptable plants, particularly good for seaside gardens. The Australian native *P. undulatum* is considered a weed in some parts of Australia as human activity has allowed it to expand its range unchallenged into urban bushland fringes.

Cultivation

Pittosporums are not fussy as to climate, doing well anywhere south of the tropics. They are not fussy about soil, either, performing well on both sand and clay. They don't need regular pruning but respond well to both hedging and hard pruning if they become leggy.

Varieties

P. tobira (6 × 6 m but slow growing and easily contained), the Japanese mock orange, is a native of Japan but is widely planted in Mediterranean countries as a street tree, such as on Madrid's broad avenues. It has glossy, dark green leaves 10 cm long and white, beautifully perfumed flowers borne in clusters in summer. 'Wheeler's Dwarf', sold as 'Miss Muffett' in Australia (1 m × 1 m) is a dwarf, bun-shaped cultivar. 'Variegata' is full-size but with cream-variegated foliage.

Drought rating: tough to very tough

Pseudopanax – lancewoods
Origin

Pseudopanax is a genus of evergreen shrubs and small trees related to ivy and umbrella trees, endemic to New Zealand.

Pseudopanax lessonii 'Gold Splash'.

Season of interest

Pseudopanax are evergreen and look good throughout the year.

Garden uses

The shrubby *Pseudopanax* species are good foundation shrubs. The tree-like species are usually planted for their unique juvenile growth which makes a stunning punctuation mark in mixed borders. The juvenile tree-like species look especially good emerging from a sea of grasses. All are good plants for dry shade, including under gum trees, in areas with a modicum of air humidity.

Pseudopanax 'Cyril Watson'.

Pseudopanax crassifolius juvenile form.

Pseudopanax crassifolius mature form.

Cultivation

Pseudopanax do well in subtropical and Mediterranean-type climates. They grow in full sun in mild, humid climates but prefer shade in hotter, drier climates. They are excellent in seaside gardens. Pseudopanax need a very well-drained soil and appreciate the addition of organic matter. They are painfully slow growing but quality is worth waiting for.

Varieties

P. ferox (5 × 3 m), the toothed lancewood, has two phases of growth. In its juvenile phase it has a single, spindly trunk with 40 cm long leaves which look like nothing so much as a collection of brown hacksaw blades hanging from a piece of dowel. When it reaches 4 m or so the tree branches out and gets its adult foliage which is softer, shorter and greener, resulting in a tree that looks like it was drawn by a kindergarten student. The related *P. crassifolius* is very similar but its juvenile foliage is very narrow and smooth-edged and its adult foliage is oval and bright green. *P. crassifolius* is not quite as drought tolerant as *P. ferox*. It is thought that the bizarre form of these trees is an adaptation to avoid being

Pseudopanax lessonii 'Purpurea'.

browsed by moa; the extinct, giant flightless birds of New Zealand.

P. lessonii (6 × 6 m but usually half that size in gardens) is commonly called by its Maori name, houpara. It is a shrub with leathery, bright green leaves composed of three to five leaflets from coastal scrub and forest. It has given rise to many selections, including 'Gold Splash' with gold splashed leaves and 'Purpurea' with bronze-purple leaves.

P. 'Cyril Watson', has bright apple green, three to five shallowly lobed leaves.

Drought rating: tough to very tough

Punica granatum – pomegranate
Origin
The pomegranate is probably native to Iran but it is difficult to tell since it has been cultivated in many countries since time immemorial.

Season of interest
Pomegranates look beautiful in all seasons. Their summer foliage is glossy and cool, their flame-orange flowers are borne over a long season from summer to autumn, they have pale yellow autumn colour and their fine twigs look attractive dripping with winter raindrops.

Garden uses
Pomegranates can be used as foundation plants in mixed plantings, as small specimen trees (bear in mind they are very slow growing) or in pots. They take clipping well and can be used as topiary shrubs.

Cultivation
Pomegranates are Mediterranean climate plants but also grow well in subtropical

Pseudopanax ferox.

Pomegranates have ornamental flowers, fruit and foliage.

climates. They need nothing more than a position in full sun and a well-drained soil. Adding plenty of well-rotted organic matter to the planting hole and giving a deep annual mulch will help get them off to a good start. Pomegranates are slow growing but they respond well to any extra attention you can give them.

Varieties

Pomegranates can become small trees of 6 × 5 m eventually, but are usually seen as shrubs half this size in gardens.

There are several ornamental varieties grown for their large, double orange, apricot, cream or cream and orange flowers. These ornamental varieties do not produce useful fruit. For fruit, grow 'Kazake', 'Elcite', 'Wonderful' or 'Galusha Rosavaya', all of which produce large, juicy, commercial-quality fruit and single orange flowers. 'Nana' is a dwarf variety growing to 1 × 1 m.

Drought rating: very tough to super tough

Puya

Origin

Puya is a genus of ground-dwelling bromeliads from high altitude deserts and Mediterranean climates of the Andes.

Season of interest

Puyas are evergreen and look impressive all year. They do not flower often but when they do it is in spring. A flowering puya is a very impressive phenomenon. Be sure to invite everyone you know to see it. To witness this spectacle for yourself, try visiting the Mt Tomah Botanic Gardens in the Blue Mountains of NSW in November when their massive clump of *Puya berteroniana* is in jaw-dropping full bloom.

Garden uses

Puyas are viciously armed with backward pointing spines along the leaf margins. They are definitely not plants for the faint-hearted. They should be planted no closer than 1.5 m from paths, with plenty of clear access around the clump. They are a nightmare to weed around so make sure they have a deep gravel mulch to make the task as easy as possible. Having said all that, puyas are also among the most magnificent plants you can grow in your garden. If you can find the right spot for them they are very rewarding.

Cultivation

Puyas are best suited to dry-summer regions although there are some excellent specimens at the Royal Botanic Gardens in Sydney. They need a well-drained soil in full sun.

Puya berteroniana.

Varieties
P. alpestris (1.5 × 1 m) has long shaggy leaves. It bears a large spike of metallic turquoise flowers.

Puya coerulea.

P. berteroniana (3 × 2 m) has long silver-green leaves. Its inflorescence is huge and club-shaped, with hundreds of metallic green flowers with bright orange stamens. This puya is for large gardens only.

P. coerulea (1.5 × 2 m) has blue-purple flowers which emerge from pink-red flower stems and bracts over silver foliage.

P. venusta (1.5 × 1 m) has bright silver leaves. Its flowers are dark blue, borne in a red torch-like inflorescence.

Drought rating: very tough to super tough

Rhaphiolepis – Indian hawthorn
Origin
Indian hawthorns are evergreen shrubs of the rose family from East Asia. Despite their natural distribution in rather rainy countries, Rhaphiolepis are incredibly drought tolerant.

Season of interest
Rhaphiolepis are evergreen so they look interesting all year round. They flower from autumn to spring and bear attractive blue berries in autumn.

Garden uses
These are excellent, reliable plants for dry shade. They make good low hedges and background shrubs.

Cultivation
Rhaphiolepis grow in subtropical or Mediterranean climates. They are just about indestructible, growing in any soil type in full sun or shade. They grow happily in difficult

Rhaphiolepis indica.

south-westerly aspects which experience gloomy shade for most of the day with a blast of westerly sun in the afternoon. Rhaphiolepis also compete very well with tree roots. They do not need any pruning or attention yet always look neat.

Varieties

R. indica (2 × 2 m) from China has very dark green, rounded, leathery leaves. It bears bunches of white flowers in spring and sporadically at other times.

R. umbellata (1.5 × 1.5 m) from Japan has dark green, toothed leaves and bunches of pinkish white flowers in spring, and then sporadically at other times.

R. × delacourii is a hybrid of *R. indica* and *R. umbellata*. Several selections have been made in different sizes and colours. 'Oriental Pearl' (1 × 1 m) has white flowers from autumn to spring. 'Rajah' (1 × 1 m) has masses of dark pink flowers from autumn to spring. 'Springtime' (1 × 1 m) has shell-pink flowers in spring and summer.

Drought rating: very tough

Romneya coulteri – Californian tree poppy or Matilija poppy

Origin

Romneya coulteri is a shrubby relative of the poppies from the deserts of California and Baja California in northern Mexico, where it grows in chapparal scrub.

Season of interest

Romneya is grown for its exquisite flowers which look like enormous poppies with petals made from the most delicate, icy white crepe paper and a fluffy boss of golden stamens in the centre. The blue, ragged-edged foliage is very attractive, too. This is a plant that British gardeners adore but struggle to grow due to a lack of summer heat and dry. This plant is a cinch to grow in much of Australia so be sure to send your British friends photos of your plant! The main flowering period is early-mid summer, with a few sporadic flowers through late summer and autumn.

Garden uses

Romneya works well in mixed borders with other flowering shrubs and perennials or in tough, inhospitable positions.

Cultivation

Romneya is a plant for Mediterranean or summer-dry climates. It does not like the combination of heat and humidity at the same time. It grows in any well-drained soil in full sun or light shade but performs best in positions which are very dry and exposed. It is just about indestructible once established but establishing a new plant can be tricky. Like all members of the poppy family romneya has a

Romneya coulteri is one of the most ethereally beautiful of all desert plants.

Rosa glauca.

fragile root system and resents disturbance. When transplanting them be very careful not to tease out or otherwise disturb the roots. Where possible select smaller seedlings as these transplant more successfully than larger plants. Romneyas are officially evergreen but in very dry summers they can shed their leaves and become dormant immediately after flowering. This is perfectly natural but if it bothers you, cut them back by half and give them a bucket or two of recycled water from the washing up and they will generally push out a new flush of foliage. Romneyas benefit from being cut back to 10 cm above the ground in winter to keep them fresh and neat. Romneya is a suckering shrub. It grows to 2 × 3 m but is easily kept to a smaller width by removing suckers. In high-rainfall areas it can spread quite enthusiastically. Luckily this plant has an insubstantial root system and the suckers are easily removed.

Drought rating: very tough to super tough

Rosa – roses

Origin

Roses are a large genus of plants widespread in the northern hemisphere. They give their name to an enormously diverse plant family, the Rosaceae, which includes stone and pome fruits, cane fruits, strawberries and perennials such as burnets, potentillas and geums.

Season of interest

Roses flower from spring until autumn. But many varieties have a beauty which extends far beyond the flowering season in the form of hips, foliage and even beautifully coloured stems and thorns. The best roses are indeed plants for four seasons.

Garden uses

Roses are great plants for mixed borders with other shrubs, perennials and grasses. They are traditionally underplanted with spring bulbs; an excellent formula in a dry-climate garden. Roses look deeply unconvincing in pure stands (i.e. 'rose gardens') – do not be tempted to plant them in such a way under any circumstances! There are *so* many

Rosa 'Geranium'.

Rosa rugosa 'Scabrosa'.

excellent varieties of rose available that there is simply no excuse for choosing inferior ones; for example sickly, sticky roses or those with huge, ludicrously coloured flowers unable to blend with anything else in the garden.

Cultivation

Roses are suited to southern Australia only. They do not like hot, humid summers but revel in Mediterranean-type climates. They prefer cold winters. Roses grow in any well-drained soil in full sun. In sandy soils add plenty of organic matter at planting time. Some roses have rather particular pruning needs but those listed below can be treated like any other summer flowering shrub; that is clipped with hedge shears after flowering. Species roses can be left to their own devices, simply remove dead or old canes in winter from time to time.

Varieties

R. glauca (syn. *R. rubrifolia*) (2 × 2 m) is a twiggy shrub grown for its leaves and stems which are purple with a bluish bloom like a plum. The flowers are small, single, pale pink and fleeting.

R. 'Geranium' (3 × 2 m) is a hybrid of *R. moyesii* with bright green, dainty foliage on thick, acid green stems. The bare stems are very decorative during the winter. The single, scarlet flowers don't last long in early summer, but give way to extremely ornamental, orange-red, flask-shaped hips which hang on the plant over winter if the birds let them.

R. rugosa (1.5 × 1.5 m) is native to sand dunes in coastal parts of Siberia, Northern Japan, Korea and China. Despite its northerly provenance this is an extremely dependable rose in Australian conditions. The very thorny stems are well clothed in thick, deeply ribbed, dark green foliage which is always healthy and

Rosa rugosa 'Belle Poitevine'.

Some old roses like the Alba 'Königin von Dänemark' are very tough and blend well with other garden plants.

Ruscus × microglossus.

glossy. It turns yellow in autumn before falling. The flowers are large, single or semi-double and beautifully perfumed. They give way to large, orange-red hips which hang on the bush throughout winter (subject to the birds). 'Fru Dagmar Hartopp' has silvery pink flowers and slightly grey foliage. 'Roseraie de l'Haÿ' is double, magenta pink but unfortunately does not form hips; 'Alba' is a single white, 'Scabrosa' has very large, single, magenta pink flowers. 'Belle Poitevine' is double, mauve pink.

Of the old roses some (but not all) Albas, Gallicas and Damasks make good garden shrubs and some of the Noisettes like 'Lamarque' are excellent garden plants if you can support their long, trailing stems.

Drought rating: tough to very tough

Ruscus – butcher's broom
Origin
Ruscus come from dry woodland in Europe, the Caucasus, north Africa, Madeira and the Azores. They used to be included in the lily family (Liliaceae) but are currently placed in their own family (the Ruscaceae) along with aspidistras, lily of the valley, mondo grass and mother-in-law's tongue. Interestingly, most of these genera thrive in dry shade. Ruscus are well adapted to dry conditions thanks to their robust, succulent root system and absence of leaves. Instead of leaves they have stem tissue modified into leaf-like structures called cladodes.

Season of interest
Ruscus look unchanging throughout the seasons (in fact they almost look artificial). Female plants bear red berries in summer and autumn.

Garden uses
Butcher's brooms are excellent plants for tough positions in dry shade. They can be mass planted to form a tall, spiky ground cover.

Cultivation
Ruscus are suitable for a wide range of climates. They grow happily in the most

thankless positions imaginable such as under pine trees or under overhanging house eaves. They are excellent for tough, shady positions in seaside gardens. They grow in any soil type from pure sand to pure clay. The only maintenance needed is to remove dead stems occasionally.

Varieties

R. aculeatus (1 × 1 m) forms a thicket of erect, cylindrical stems covered on their top halves with spiky, dark green cladodes 1.5 cm in length. Female plants bear red berries if pollinated by a male plant nearby. There is a rare hermaphrodite form available which is self-pollinating.

R. × microglossus (60 × 60 cm) has larger, thinner, apple green cladodes and more pliant, arching stems. It is an altogether softer looking plant.

Drought rating: very tough to super tough

Ruta graveolens – rue

Origin

Rue is a small sub-shrub with unique, bluish, lacy foliage from rocky places in Mediterranean Europe.

Season of interest

Rue looks good from spring until late autumn. It has yellow flowers in summer but some gardeners consider these an irritation and clip them off before they open.

Garden uses

Rue can be used in mixed borders with shrubs and perennials or as a low edging plant.

Ruta 'Jackman's Blue'.

Cultivation

Rue grows anywhere as long as it is not too hot and humid in summer. It needs full sun but will tolerate very poor soil. Although technically evergreen, rue usually looks pretty tired and shabby in winter, when it benefits from being cut back by two-thirds. Be careful when cutting rue back as its sap can cause severe skin reactions in some people.

Varieties

Rue grows to around 80 × 80 cm. 'Jackman's Blue' has larger, bluer foliage than the wild species.

Drought rating: very tough

Senecio

Origin

Senecio is one of the largest genera of all plants, with around 1000 species in its broadest sense, although many are now placed in different genera. Senecios take many forms from roadside weeds to climbers and trees. Many of them are succulent plants or adapted to dry climates in some other way.

Senecio cineraria 'Cirrus'.

Senecio serpens.

Season of interest
The succulent and shrubby senecios look good all year around.

Garden uses
The shrubby and succulent senecios are excellent for mixed plantings with shrubs, succulents and perennials. Some make very good ground covers.

Cultivation
Senecios are very adaptable to climate although those with grey-hairy foliage like

Senecio vira-vira.

S. *cineraria* resent high summer humidity. They prefer dry-summer climates. Any position in full sun or half shade in well-drained soil suits them. The shrubby species benefit from being cut back by half to two-thirds after flowering.

Varieties
S. *cineraria* 'Cirrus' (75 cm × 1 m), commonly called dusty miller, is a mounding shrub with scalloped, felty leaves of the brightest white. It contrasts brilliantly with dark, evergreen foliage and sets off dark-coloured perennials perfectly. Its yellow daisy flowers are slightly annoying and are better clipped off.

S. *vira-vira* (80 cm × 1 m) is a neat shrub with ferny silver foliage. It has buttery yellow flowers.

S. *serpens* (syn. *Kleinia repens*) (30 cm × 90 cm) is a succulent species, one of several referred to as 'blue chalk sticks'. It looks like a chalky blue pigface. It makes a striking, neat ground cover, thriving even under gum trees. Unfortunately it is not very cold tolerant.

Drought rating: very tough to super tough

Solanum – nightshades

Origin

Solanum is a huge, widespread genus of plants which includes potatoes, chillies and eggplants as well as numerous garden shrubs and climbers.

Season of interest

Solanums have an extended flowering season with the main flush in summer and autumn.

Garden uses

The shrubby species are useful background plants or for planting in the shade of trees. The creepers are very vigorous and need to be sited carefully, and only on well-built, hefty structures. You may *want* a creeper to neatly cover a fence, but it will want to grow up and up towards the light, perhaps engulfing your neighbour's house in the process!

Cultivation

Any well-drained soil in full sun or partial shade suits most solanums. They resent having wet feet.

Solanum rantonnetii.

Solanum jasminoides 'Alba'.

Varieties

S. jasminoides (6 m) is the well-known potato creeper from Brazil. Usually seen in its white form, 'Alba', the wild form is in fact lilac purple. A very vigorous twining plant, it must be sited with caution. It is not suitable for small gardens.

S. rantonnetii (syn. *Lycianthes rantonnetii*) (2 × 3 m) is a scrambling shrub from Paraguay and Argentina. It bears masses of blue-purple flowers 3 cm across over a long period in summer and autumn. 'Royal Robe' is a particularly dark purple form. It is marginally cold tolerant but much happier in frost-free climates.

S. wendlandii (12 m) is the giant potato creeper from Costa Rica. It is a magnificent large creeper for subtropical and tropical climates, it produces 4 cm, lilac coloured flowers in large trusses over a long season from summer to autumn. Its stems are thick, grey and sausage-like. They do not climb by themselves but are covered with tiny, Velcro-like hooks which help them to straggle their way up through tree branches in nature. In gardens they need to be tied in place firmly.

Drought rating: very tough

Tamarix – tamarisk trees

Origin
Dry, exposed places in Europe, the Mediterranean and central Asia, often in salty soils.

Season of interest
Tamarisks are at their best in spring and summer.

Garden uses
Tamarisks are useful as small trees in mixed plantings, as screens or windbreaks, or they can be coppiced and treated as perennials. Be aware that the athel tree (*T. aphylla*) is a declared noxious weed in all states and *T. parviflora* is also considered a weed in some areas.

Cultivation
Tamarisks will grow in any soil in full sun or part shade. They are extremely tough and will grow just about anywhere *including salty soils*. They are easily pollarded or coppiced to keep them neat. *T. ramosissima* flowers on new wood so this does not affect its flowering.

Tamarix ramosissima growing as a coppice.

Varieties
T. ramosissima (5 × 5 m but easily kept smaller with pruning) has tiny, scale-like leaves, giving a casuarina-like effect. It has clouds of tiny, pink flowers in late summer and autumn.

Drought rating: very tough to super tough

Teucrium – germanders

Origin
Teucriums are evergreen perennials and shrubs of the mint family from the Mediterranean basin, growing in exposed, dry, rocky places.

Season of interest
Teucriums flower during spring and summer.

Garden uses
The lower growing species make excellent ground covers for exposed, dry situations. The larger species are good plants for mixed borders with large shrubs, grasses and succulents.

Cultivation
These are plants for dry Mediterranean climates. They do not cope with humid subtropical and tropical conditions. Teucriums prefer a well-drained, poor soil in full sun in conditions similar to their relatives the lavenders.

Varieties
T. chamaedrys (10 cm × indefinite spread) enjoys the cute common name of 'wall germander'. It is a creeping perennial, forming a mat of small, glossy green leaves

Teucrium chamaedrys.

with pink, lipped flowers in spring. An excellent ground cover for exposed, poor soils and harsh reflected heat from hard surfaces.

T. fruticans (2 × 2 m) is an open, twiggy shrub with silver stems and leaves. Its flowers are pale silvery blue and lipped but they barely show up against the similarly pale foliage. This plant looks much better when clipped neatly.

T. marum (50 × 50 cm) is a small shrubby perennial from the Mediterranean islands commonly known as cat thyme. It forms a bun of silver, petrochemical-scented foliage topped with masses of lolly-pink flowers. A great plant despite its weird smell.

Teucrium betonicum.

T. betonicum (1.2 × 1.2 m) has exceptionally large, light green leaves for the genus and large heads of purple-pink flowers. This plant will withstand quite a lot of shade.

Drought rating: very tough to super tough

Trachelospermum – star jasmine
Origin
A genus of woody, evergreen creepers from the same family as oleander and frangipani, native mostly to Asia.

Season of interest
Star jasmines flower in summer.

Garden uses
Star jasmines' best use is as evergreen ground covers. They happily form a green carpet

Teucrium marum.

Trachelospermum jasminoides.

under evergreen trees. If grown as creepers they need a *very* strong supporting structure (paling fences will not do) and need to be clipped regularly to keep them in check. Of course the main reason they are grown is to bring their sublime fragrance into the garden.

Cultivation

Perfect for any climate that is not too cold and frosty, star jasmines are happy in any well-drained soil. They like a sheltered position in sun or dappled shade. They take hedging well.

Varieties

T. asiaticum (6 m) is less vigorous than its better-known cousin. It has dark green leaves mottled with reddish brown in spring and flowers of a slightly more yellow shade, also beautifully fragrant. It is more cold tolerant than *T. jasminoides* but slower growing.

T. jasminoides (9 m) is the best-known star jasmine with glossy, apple-green leaves and white, highly fragrant flowers.

Drought rating: very tough

Westringia – native rosemary
Origin
Westringias are evergreen, shrubby members of the mint family from Australia.

Season of interest

Westringias look good throughout the year.

Garden uses

Westringias make excellent subjects for hedging or topiary.

Cultivation

Westringias need a well-drained, poor soil in full sun or part shade. They are fully drought tolerant on the coast but may occasionally need some water in very dry inland areas.

Varieties

W. fruticosa (2 × 4 m) is the coastal rosemary of NSW. Specimens growing on windy headlands grow low and dense but plants in sheltered back dunes grow rank and twiggy. In gardens, coastal rosemary forms a neat shrub 2 × 2 m and looks even better when it is regularly hedged. Its foliage does indeed resemble the distantly related rosemary though its whitish-purple flowers are larger. Several varieties are available including 'Morning Light' with variegated foliage, 'Smokey' with silver foliage and 'Jervis Gem' with darker purple flowers.

Drought rating: very tough

Xanthoceras sorbifolium – yellow horn

Origin

Xanthoceras is a genus of just one species, a deciduous large shrub from northern China.

Season of interest

Xanothoceras flowers in spring and has pale yellow autumn colour.

Garden uses

Good in mixed plantings with perennials and grasses or for planting in small copses to make a mini dry-climate woodland.

Cultivation

Xanthoceras grows in any soil in full sun or light shade in the southern half of the country.

Varieties

Xanthoceras sorbifolium (4 × 4 m but easily kept smaller) has divided, light green ash-like leaves. In spring it bears candle-like spikes of white, star-shaped flowers with red-striped centres as the fresh new leaves emerge. From a distance the overall effect is very much like a horse chestnut. This plant looks very temperate and soft, but is incredibly tough. It is rare in Australia at the moment but should become popular once gardeners realise that its beauty is matched by its toughness.

Drought rating: very tough to super tough

Yucca

Origin

Yuccas are rosette-forming plants with sword-shaped leaves from arid parts of the

Yucca rostrata.

Americas, including high deserts which get very cold in winter and low deserts which get exceedingly hot in summer. Many of them form one or more trunks with age and grow into shrubs or small trees. Others remain as single, ground-hugging rosettes. All yuccas bear tall spires of cream, bell-shaped flowers, sometimes utterly spectacular due to their sheer numbers.

Season of interest

Yuccas are evergreen and look good throughout the year. Their spectacular flowers are a bonus, borne in spring, summer or autumn depending on the species.

Yucca aloifolia.

Yucca filamentosa 'Bright Edge'.

Garden uses

Many Australian gardeners take one look at yuccas and think 'yuck'. They don't fit our preconception of a 'proper', English garden plant so most Australian gardeners reject them out of hand. In fact, English gardeners have had a long love affair with yuccas, beginning with the illustrious Gertrude Jekyll, mother of the English herbaceous border, who planted dozens of them in her schemes.

Yuccas are wonderful architectural plants, but it is *how* you use them that can make or break them. When planted exclusively with other sword-leaved succulents like agaves and furcraeas, or with other spiky plants like cacti, yuccas look hostile and lose much of their effect in the company of similarly themed plants. By contrast, when they are used in the company of perennials, grasses, shrubs and soft-leaved succulents, yuccas have real presence. Many yuccas are not viciously spiky compared with some of their ilk. Some of them are actually quite soft and therefore much better suited to smaller gardens where they are more likely to come into contact with humans or pets.

Yucca whipplei.

Yucca recurvifolia.

Yuccas do very well in large pots, which can be moved around as garden features. They marry extremely well with architecture so they are very useful planted close to buildings or structures such as decks. Although yuccas are softer than many agaves and furcraeas, the spines on the ends of their leaves can still cause painful puncture wounds so be very careful not to plant the spiky species closer than 1.5 m to paths. On a more positive note, many people do not realise that yuccas' flowers are edible; not merely edible but delicious! They give a fragrant, beansprout-like crunch to salads.

Cultivation

Yuccas are easy to grow in any well-drained soil in full sun or, for the shrubby species, light shade. They prefer sandy, alkaline soils but are very adaptable. Some are native to climates which receive little or no rain in summer, others are native to the wet east coast of the USA and Mexico but all species are very adaptable to less-than-ideal climates. They are amenable to watering in summer and bulk up much more quickly with some extra irrigation. This is a bonus as they are otherwise very slow-growing plants.

Varieties

Y. rigida (4 × 2 m) is a compact, branching yucca with short, rigid, chalky blue leaves from northern Mexico. Its cream flowers often nestle among the foliage.

Y. rostrata (4 × 1 m) is a very elegant species from Texas, New Mexico and northern Mexico. It has very narrow, pale blue, fairly soft foliage and usually forms a single-trunked shrub. 'Sapphire Skies' is a selection from Mexico with powder blue, even softer foliage.

Yucca elephantipes.

Y. rostrata is one of the faster growing yuccas and very cold tolerant.

Y. whipplei (1 × 1 m) from California is commonly called 'Our Lord's candle'. It is a non-trunk-forming species with narrow, rigid, blue-green foliage. After a few years the rosette sends up a spectacular flower spike to 4 m tall covered with hundreds of cream flowers. The rosette usually dies after flowering although some forms send up pups first. If you want this plant permanently in your garden it is worth planting one or two seedlings every year or two.

Y. filamentosa (1 × 2 m), Adam's needle, is a mounding shrub from the eastern USA. It has dark green, relatively soft leaves with curly white threads along the margins of the leaves and a 2 m tall flower stem covered with cream bell-shaped flowers. 'Bright Edge' is a smaller-growing form with gold-variegated foliage.

Y. aloifolia (8 × 5 m), called Spanish dagger or bayonet, is a tree-like yucca from south-eastern USA, eastern Mexico and the West Indies. Its name alludes to the stiff, toothed, dark green leaves with a sharp spine at the end. Pretty cream flowers appear in late summer to autumn. Although forming a tree in nature, it is very slow growing and can be pollarded to any size.

Y. recurvifolia (2 × 2 m) is a shrubby species with floppy, innocuous dark green-grey leaves and a 2 m high flower spike covered with cream bells. This was the yucca Miss Jekyll planted extensively at Hestercombe – from the wet summer climate of the eastern USA. 'Variegata' has softly variegated foliage.

Y. elephantipes (10 × 4 m) from Mexico is usually encountered as a potted specimen but in the garden can eventually form a small, multi-trunked tree with wide, rich green leaves and a buttressed base. It is not as cold hardy as other species and succeeds better in areas which do not experience frost.

Drought rating: very tough to super tough

Ephemerals: perennials, bulbs and annuals

Achillea – ornamental yarrow
Origin

Achilleas are a genus of herbaceous perennials from Europe and Asia, many of them from

Achillea clypeolata with *Ixia polystachya* and *Teucrium fruticans.*

Achillea 'Credo'.

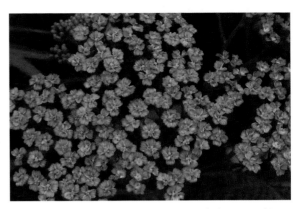

Achillea 'Terracotta'.

dry, rocky places. The best known achillea is the herb (or pasture weed, depending on how you look at it) yarrow (*A. millefolium*).

Season of interest

Achilleas flower from late spring until early autumn.

Garden uses

Achilleas are prime candidates for inclusion in perennial borders or mixed borders with shrubs and perennials. They are good for creating solid blocks of colour.

Cultivation

Many of the old garden cultivars derived from *Achillea millefolium* are rather rapacious, running all over the garden if left unchecked. Most of the other species and newer hybrids are very well behaved, remaining in a single compact clump. Achilleas prefer climates without too much summer humidity and a good, cold winter. They grow in just about any soil as long as it is well drained. The addition of organic matter is a great help to their ability to cope with drought, but giving them

too much nitrogen will cause them to flop and look unsightly. Achilleas benefit from being lifted and divided every few years to keep them fresh. They are very fast growing.

Varieties

A. clypeolata (60 × 60 cm) has a clump of ferny silver basal leaves, above which rise flat heads of golden flowers 7.5 cm across. This plant is very floriferous but it quickly becomes tired and woody so it benefits from being divided and replanted at least every other year. **Drought rating: very tough**

A. 'Coronation Gold' (120 × 70 cm) is similar to *A. clypeolata* and may be a hybrid of it. It is bigger in all its parts with silver foliage and yellow flower heads 10 cm across. **Drought rating: very tough**

A. filipendulina 'Gold Plate' (120 × 100 cm) is a very stately achillea with green, ferny leaves which clothe tall stems topped by flat heads of golden yellow flowers 12 cm across. **Drought rating: very tough**

The hybrids of *A. millefolium* are less drought tolerant but still pretty tough. They come in a much wider range of colours and grow to around 80 × 60 cm. 'Cherry Ripe' has maroon flowers fading to dusty pink. 'Terracotta' has (unsurprisingly) terracotta-orange flowers fading to a straw colour. 'Walter Funcke' has brick-red flowers fading to terracotta. 'Credo' and 'Hella Glashoff' both have lemon-yellow flowers fading to cream and 'The Beacon' has cherry-red flowers fading to lemon. **Drought rating: tough**

Achnatherum calamagrostis
Origin
Achnatherum calamagrostis is native to rocky hillsides in central and southern Europe.

Season of interest
This grass looks its best from spring to mid-winter. Flowers appear from late spring and

Achnatherum calamagrostis is a perfect foil to more solid plants like Sedum 'Matrona'.

remain upright and beautiful even after the foliage has died back.

Garden uses
This grass is beautiful in perennial and mixed borders. This grass is very effective in large swathes.

Cultivation
Achnatherum calamagrostis (1 m × 1 m) prefers climates where winters are cold and humidity is not too high in summer so it is not a plant for coastal northern NSW and Queensland. In the right climate it is very undemanding in its needs. It is best cut back to the ground in winter to keep it tidy. A handful of blood and bone and an annual mulch are enough to keep it looking its best. Seedlings do occasionally appear around the parent plant in moister parts of southern Australia. This plant has not been widely tested in higher rainfall areas, so be on the lookout for any tendency to self-seed more vigorously in your area.

Drought rating: very tough

Agastache – the hummingbird mints
Origin
Agastache is a genus of perennials and sub-shrubs from North America with one species from east Asia. The species from the eastern states of the USA and the Asian species, *Agastache rugosa*, require constant summer moisture to look their best. However, the species from the desert states of the central and western USA and Mexico are extremely tough. In the wild

Agastache 'Sweet Lili' is one of the best new plants for dry gardens.

they grow in rocky, dry scrub in full sun or very light shade.

Season of interest

Hummingbird mints flower profusely over the entire summer and autumn.

Garden uses

As the name suggests, hummingbird mints are an important food source for desert hummingbirds in the Americas. Australian honeyeaters love the long, tubular flowers of agastaches, too. They are great plants for attracting birds into your garden. The foliage is deliciously fragrant so plant them next to paths where you can brush against them as you pass. The flowers are edible, with a sweet aniseed flavour. Best used in dry perennial borders or mixed borders. Useful as an underplanting for roses.

Cultivation

Hummingbird mints are only beginning to be grown in Australia but are sure to become favourites with Australian gardeners. They are incredibly good performers in the garden, flowering lavishly for months on end with absolutely no attention whatsoever. They are extremely easy to grow in any area which experiences a reasonably cool winter and not too much summer humidity. They ask nothing more than a well-drained soil in full

Agastache aurantiaca.

Agastache mexicana.

sun or very light shade. The only maintenance required is to cut them back to 5 cm in winter to keep them tidy.

Varieties

A. aurantiaca (80 × 80 cm) has masses of apricot-orange flowers emerging from mauve-pink buds and fine, grey, liquorice-scented foliage.

A. mexicana (120 × 40 cm) bears hot-pink flowers on a tall but somewhat floppy plant. It is best planted with grasses and other perennials around it for support and it does benefit from the occasional handout of water in summer. Its foliage is citronella scented.

A. 'Sweet Lili' (120 × 60 cm) is a superlative new selection by Victorian plantsman David Glenn. It bears masses of bubblegum-pink flowers on perfectly upright stems from mid-summer until early winter. It has anise-scented foliage.

Drought rating: very tough

Allium – ornamental onions
Origin

Allium is a very large genus with around 850 members, mostly from the northern hemisphere, particularly the Mediterranean basin and Middle East, as well as the western USA.

Season of interest

Alliums are mostly early-summer flowering bulbs. After flowering, many species' seed heads remain upright and interesting into autumn.

Garden uses

Alliums have one of the most unique forms of any garden plant. The majority have flower

Allium carinatum subsp. *pulchellum.*

Allium 'Globemaster'.

Allium sphaerocephalon.

heads which are absolutely spherical in shape, sometimes surprisingly large, on straight, leafless stems. Even a few alliums make a very strong effect in a garden. *En masse* they are quite breathtaking. They look great in perennial and mixed plantings and marry beautifully with grasses. The flower heads remain attractive long after the tiny flowers have finished so don't be in a hurry to cut them back.

Cultivation

Alliums need an aspect in full sun in a well-drained soil, moist in winter and dry in summer. The large-flowered alliums are slightly more exacting in their needs, preferring well-structured loamy soil and a cold winter to do well. The smaller species are more forgiving of climate and soil type. Alliums flower as their foliage is dying back so it is a good idea to plant low-growing perennials over them to hide the unsightly dying foliage. *Stachys byzantina*, *Anthemis* 'Susanna Mitchell', *Salvia* x *sylvestris* varieties and the smaller *Artemisias* are ideal for this purpose.

Bear in mind that in the correct conditions some of the smaller species of allium self-seed enthusiastically. Three-cornered garlic (*Allium triquetrum*) is extremely weedy in damp conditions and should not be grown. The much-cursed onion weed (*Nothoscordum gracile*) is from a related genus.

Varieties

A. carinatum subsp. *pulchellum* (40 cm) comes from southern Europe to Turkey. It has rosy purple flowers which do not have the alliums' usual spherical form, but are like miniature starbursts, with each tiny flower hanging at the end of a pink, fine stalk. This species increases quickly.

A. cristophii (60 cm) comes from rocky slopes in Iran and central Asia. It has flower heads 20 cm across with large, star-shaped flowers of a metallic, silvery rose colour. After flowering the flower heads break off and blow away like tumble weeds to distribute the seeds.

A. 'Gladiator' (1.2 m) has heads of purple flowers 10 cm across.

A. 'Globemaster' (60 cm) is a hybrid of *A. cristophii* with an enormous head of lavender blue flowers, up to 30 cm across.

A. sphaerocephalon (60 cm) is commonly called 'drumsticks' because of its 3 cm, spherical flower heads on the ends of long, thin stems. The wine-purple flowers bob around in the breeze on their wiry stems: very cute. This species increases well.

Drought rating: very tough

Amaryllis belladonna – naked ladies or belladonna lilies

Origin
Naked ladies are large bulbs from South Africa. They get their charming common name from their pink flowers which arise from the bulbs on flesh-coloured stems, unclad by leaves, in late summer.

Season of interest
Naked ladies flower in late summer–early autumn.

Garden uses
Naked ladies are great planted at the base of structures such as decks or retaining walls, or as a seasonal feature bordering driveways and paths. They can be tucked into any tough spot that has space for their grapefruit-sized bulbs. Naked ladies are dormant for most of the year. It is easy to forget they are there until they surprise you in late summer by sending up their sweetly perfumed flowers almost overnight, and you get to congratulate yourself on your gardening genius.

Amaryllis are available in a range of colours.

Cultivation

Naked ladies are the sort of plant you see growing around old, deserted farmhouses, flowering beautifully despite years of neglect. They are easy to grow anywhere that has a cold, moist winter and a summer that is not too hot and wet (i.e. inland and southern coastal districts). They need plenty of sun in winter when they are in active growth but they don't care one way or the other in summer so they are ideal for planting under deciduous trees. Naked ladies like to be planted with the neck of the bulb above the soil but don't worry too much as they will find their own level eventually. Like many South African bulbs they take a couple of years to establish after they have been transplanted so patience is needed. Once established they get better year on year without making any demands on the gardener except to remove the dead leaves in early summer and the flower stems after flowering.

Varieties

There are several varieties available, most of them actually hybrids with the closely related genus *Brunsvigia*. In Australia naked ladies tend to be sold by colour: white, pale pink and dark pink. Occasionally the creamy white 'Hathor' is offered. In all varieties foliage clumps are 30 × 80 cm, flowers are up to 80 cm high.

Drought rating: very tough

Anemanthele lessoniana – gossamer grass or pheasant tail grass
Origin

This plant is endemic to the drier, eastern side of New Zealand.

Anemanthele lessoniana turns rusty orange in autumn.

Season of interest

Gossamer grass is evergreen and looks good throughout the year but it is particularly good from late summer to winter when it flowers and takes on coppery hues.

Garden uses

This is a great plant for mass planting around the bases of trees, especially in difficult south-westerly aspects which are in shade all day before receiving a blast of brutal afternoon sun. It can be used in flower borders with perennials like *Eryngium* and *Echinops*, which it sets off beautifully.

Cultivation

An amazingly tough plant for part sun to almost full shade. It will also grow in full sun in good, well-composted soil and in cooler areas but does better in part shade in hotter areas. *Anemanthele lessoniana* grows to 80 × 80 cm in size. It grows equally well in pure sand and heavy, wet clay. It shows some propensity to self-seed in wetter climates and irrigated gardens, but usually only within a stone's throw of the parent plant. This plant has not been widely tested in many parts of Australia so be on the lookout for any tendency to seed further afield than your own garden.

Varieties

There is one variety listed as 'Autumn Cascade' but it is not really that different from the wild species.

Drought rating: very tough

Anthemis

Origin

Anthemis are native to rocky places in the Mediterranean and the Middle East.

Season of interest

Anthemis flower from spring to autumn. Some forms flower much longer than others.

Garden uses

Anthemis are wonderful in mixed borders, for underplanting roses or other shrubs. They are great in dry perennial borders combined with other herbaceous perennials and grasses. Anthemis are fast growing and are therefore very useful for plugging up gaps in the garden quickly. Their bright, happy, but not overly strong yellow hues are perfect for brightening up colour schemes which contain a lot of purple, blue or white; these colours can be too sombre when used exclusively on their own.

Cultivation

Anthemis are easy to grow in any well-drained soil in full sun. They benefit from the addition of some well-rotted organic matter but too much nitrogen (or, indeed, water) will make them floppy. In other words, they thrive on neglect! Trim them back to 20 cm after flowering to keep them tidy and cut them back to 5 cm in winter.

Varieties

A. 'Susanna Mitchell' (50 cm × 1 m) has masses of creamy yellow daisies over grey foliage from mid spring until late autumn. A very giving plant.

A. 'E. C. Buxton' (50 × 80 cm) bears butter-yellow flowers over green foliage for just a few weeks in early summer.

A. 'Tetworth' (50 cm × 1 m) is similar to 'Susanna Mitchell' but with milky white petals and more silver foliage.

Drought rating: very tough

Calamagrostis × acutiflora

Origin

A sterile garden hybrid of *C. epigejos* and *C. arundinacea*, widespread in Europe and Asia.

Season of interest

Calamagrostis look good in every season except for the short time between cutting back and reshooting from late winter to early spring.

Anthemis 'Susanna Mitchell'.

Calamagrostis 'Karl Foerster' makes a vertical contrast to the cauliflower-like form of *Sedum* 'Autumn Joy'.

Garden uses

A wonderful grass to plant *en masse* as an herbaceous hedge or large-scale bedding. Its strict upright form is a perfect foil for floppier shrubs and perennials and it mixes extremely well with architecture. A top-class grass.

Cultivation

Calamagrostis is a plant for climates with a cool to cold winter. It grows in any soil type, including seasonally inundated and mildly salty soils, and it particularly loves clay soil. It grows best in full sun but tolerates some shade. Although evergreen it benefits from being cut back to the ground in winter to tidy it up.

Varieties

'Karl Foerster' (1.8 m × 60 cm) has bright green foliage to 75 cm tall. In early summer it bears airy green-purple flower heads which contract into thin, golden, reed-like spikes when the flowers finish.

'Overdam' (1.5 m × 50 cm) is similar to 'Karl Foerster' but with white- and pink-variegated foliage. It is very ethereal and pretty.

Drought rating: tough to very tough

Centranthus ruber – red valerian
Origin

Centranthus ruber is a woody-based perennial from the Mediterranean, related to true valerian.

Season of interest

Red valerian's main flowering is in spring with sporadic flowering through until autumn.

Garden uses

Red valerian is a useful plant for mixed borders with flowering shrubs and other perennials.

Centranthus ruber.

Cultivation

Red valerian is suitable for climates which are not too humid in summer. Any well-drained soil in full sun suits it. It has fluffy, thistle-like seeds which self-seed around the garden so be prepared to pull a few out and make sure it is not going further than your garden fence.

Varieties

Red-pink, red and white varieties are available.

Drought rating: very tough

Colchicum – meadow saffron
Origin

Colchicums are a genus of 60 or so bulbs from the eastern Mediterranean basin to central Asia. They are grown for their goblet-shaped, pink, mauve or white flowers which appear in autumn before the glossy, strapped-shaped foliage emerges during winter. The flowers are often quite profuse, with each bulb bearing up to 20 flowers in succession. Colchicums are quite poisonous; however, a drug used to treat gout is derived from them.

Colchicum agrippinum.

Colchicum byzantinum.

Season of interest

Most colchicums flower in early autumn. They appear at a very useful time when the summer-flowering plants have finished but those with autumn interest haven't properly begun.

Garden uses

Colchicums are excellent bulbs (or more properly, corms) for naturalising under trees, grass or gravel. They can be used to underplant deciduous shrubs such as roses and they are perfect for tucking into nooks and crannies in forgotten areas of the garden. They grow happily with no attention whatsoever and give the gardener a nice surprise by popping up masses of flowers when the rest of the garden is looking tired after the heat of summer.

Cultivation

Colchicums grow in any climate which has a cold winter and dry summer (i.e. southern and inland Australia). They do not like areas which are wet and humid in summer.

Colchicum speciosum.

Colchicums have the same needs as daffodils; that is, they need full sun and some available moisture when they are in growth during the winter months and need to be reasonably dry in summer. The corms are planted in summer, 10–20 cm deep, where they eventually form large colonies which can be left undisturbed for many years.

Varieties

C. agrippinum (8 cm) is probably a natural hybrid of two other, unknown, species. It has small, star-shaped, mauve-pink flowers with a fine tessellated, or chequered, pattern on the petals.

C. bornmuelleri (12 cm) has medium-sized, pink, goblet-shaped flowers with creamy white throats.

C. byzantinum (12 cm) is also probably a hybrid which has been grown since the 16th century. It displays a lot of variation but generally has small, mauve pink flowers with rounded petal tips and a white vein up the middle of each petal. This species is often confused with *C. speciosum* in Australia.

C. speciosum (20 cm) has large, floppy, mauve-pink or rarely white, goblet-shaped flowers with a white throat.

Drought rating: very tough

Cyclamen

Origin

Cyclamen are native to the Mediterranean basin – southern Europe, north Africa and the Middle East. They grow in woodland, grassy meadows and rocky hillsides. They are often encountered growing under pine trees and indeed they are one of the few garden plants which actually relish this position. They are adapted to drought by becoming dormant in summer, surviving underground as a large, woody tuber.

Season of interest

Cyclamen are at their best from autumn to spring. Like many Mediterranean bulbs (daffodils, etc.) they are dormant in summer.

Garden uses

Most of us think of cyclamen as rather temperamental indoor plants but in fact the

Cyclamen hederifolium is tough but dainty.

Cyclamen have beautiful foliage.

Cyclamen coum.

wild cyclamen are tough garden bulbs. They are extremely useful in dry shade, even in thankless spots such as in the root zone of large trees.

Cultivation

Coming from a Mediterranean climate cyclamen prefer distinct seasons – a cool to cold, moist winter and a dry summer. They do very well in inland areas and the southern coastal areas of Australia. All that they ask is a leafy soil (plenty of deciduous leafmould or rotted pine litter added). If happy they self-seed gently to form impressive colonies.

Varieties

Cylcamen grow to 10 × 15 cm (*C. hederifolium* is wider at 30 cm).

Cyclamen coum flowers in mid-winter as the rounded, dark green leaves emerge. Flowers may be white, pale pink or hot pink. This species requires a more sheltered position than the following species.

C. hederifolium is very tough and reliable. Pink or white flowers emerge from the leaf litter in late summer to early autumn like so many dancing fairies. These are followed by decorative, dark green, ivy-shaped leaves marbled with pewter. An excellent plant for dry shade.

Wild cyclamen look delicate but they are tough enough to grow under pine trees, self-seeding gently to form good-sized colonies.

C. persicum, from which the florist's cyclamen is descended, is occasionally available. It has pink flowers with purple centres and pewter-veined dark green leaves. It prefers milder, damper conditions than the previous species and is more suited to coastal conditions.

Drought rating: very tough

Echinops – the globe thistles
Origin
Echinops are herbaceous perennials from the dry, rocky grasslands and steppes of Europe east to central Asia.

Season of interest
Echinops flower from late spring to early autumn.

Garden uses
Echinops are traditional herbaceous border plants. They look fantastic with other herbaceous perennials and especially with ornamental grasses. When in full flower the effect is of hundreds of little coloured blobs floating in mid air – totally unique from a

Echinops bannaticus 'The Giant'.

design point of view and absolutely perfect for combining with some of the more ethereal grasses like *Achnatherum calamagrostis*.

Cultivation
Plants of open grasslands and steppes, globe thistles need full sun. They do not like hot, humid summers. They have deep tap roots and need well-structured, deep soil to give of their best. Digging the soil deeply and adding plenty of well-rotted organic matter will get them off to a good start. A deep mulch is beneficial. In very hot weather echinops' flowering may be attenuated and they may have a summer dormancy before re-emerging in autumn. An occasional handout of water prior to flowering will usually prevent this or you can let nature take its course by cutting the entire plant back to the ground after the summer flowering and waiting for the autumn flush of growth to emerge later on.

Varieties
All species are variations on a similar theme. They have upright, branching silver stems, finely cut, slightly spiky leaves which are green

Echinops ritro 'Veitch's Blue'.

Echinops give a unique texture to perennial plantings, combining beautifully with other perennials and grasses.

above and silver below, overtopped with ping pong ball-sized spherical flower heads on stiff stems.

E. bannaticus (150 × 75 cm); most commonly seen is the form 'Taplow Blue' which is steel blue in bud, opening to dove grey flowers. 'The Giant' is silvery white.

E. ritro (90 × 60 cm) has blue flowers and darker green leaves. Its form 'Veitch's Blue' is superb, with inky blue flowers on bright silver stems.

E. ruthenicus (60 × 40 cm) has pale blue flowers.

E. sphaerocephalus (2 × 1 m) has green-silver buds opening to white flowers

Drought rating: tough

Epimedium – bishop's mitre or barrenwort
Origin
Epimediums are perennial members of the Berberidaceae family which also includes *Berberis* and *Mahonia*. Some epimedium species are used in traditional Chinese medicine as an aphrodisiac; they are now marketed in the west under the moniker 'horny goatweed'! Most epimediums are native to summer-rainfall climates in China however there are a few from drier climates. The toughest species are *E. perralderianum* from the mountains of Algeria and *E. pinnatum* from Turkey, the Caucasus and northern Iran.

Season of interest
Epimediums are evergreen and look good all year. Their flowers in late winter–early spring are a seasonal bonus.

Epimedium 'Fröhnleiten' flowers and new spring foliage.

Garden uses

Epimediums are handsome ground covers for dry shade. They are excellent for edging paths and they are very fashionable in English 'woodland' gardens so if that is the look you long for, these are great plants to grow.

Cultivation

Epimediums prefer half to full shade in climates with a cool to cold winter. They don't like areas which are hot and humid at the same time. The European/North African species are the best varieties to grow as the Chinese species need some summer water to thrive in most Australian climates (although these species are worth a try in mountain districts). Epimediums love leafy, well-prepared soil with an annual topdressing of autumn-leaf litter. Under such conditions they are amazingly drought tolerant once they are established. Epimediums love the conditions under deciduous trees and tolerate root competition well. Although evergreen they benefit from having their foliage cut back to the ground in late winter as the flower buds appear. The flowers are much more effective when not obscured by old foliage.

Varieties

E. × perralchicum (40 × 80 cm) is a hybrid of *E. perralderianum* and *E. pinnatum* subsp. *colchicum*. It has bright, apple green foliage on wiry stems. In late winter it bears racemes of bright yellow, star-shaped flowers. Its new foliage is very attractive, veined with burgundy. *E. × perralchicum* is usually seen in the form of the vigorous, large-flowered selection 'Fröhnleiten'.

Drought rating: tough

Eryngium – sea hollies
Origin

Eryngiums are a widespread genus of perennials which superficially resemble thistles but are in fact members of the carrot family (Apiaceae). There are eryngiums native to many regions of the world including Australia. The best garden varieties come from dry, rocky places from Europe east to central Asia, and from semi-arid parts of South America.

Season of interest

Eryngiums are mainly summer and autumn flowering but their bold foliage is attractive from spring to autumn and the dry seed heads can be beautiful into winter.

Garden uses

Classic herbaceous border plants, eryngiums combine beautifully with other perennials

Eryngium × zabelii 'Blue Hills'.

Eryngium ovinum.

Eryngium amethystinum.

and ornamental grasses, lending a totally unique texture with their spiky, metallic blue and silver flower heads. The strap-leafed species such as *E. eburneum* form a useful bridging element between succulents and herbaceous plants in a flower garden.

Cultivation

Some eryngiums are quite drought tolerant but many others, although spiky and xerophytic-looking, actually have fairly high water needs. For example, *E. agavifolium* from Argentina looks like a succulent plant, with its spiky leaves, but in fact it requires very moist, fertile soil to thrive. Of the drought-tolerant eryngiums, the Eurasian species perform best in well-structured soils which have plenty of organic matter and lime added, and are deeply dug to accommodate their long tap roots. The drought-tolerant species from South America perform well in sandy soils.

Varieties

E. amethystinum (80 × 70 cm) from Italy, Sicily and the Balkans has lobed leaves overtopped with masses of pale silver-blue flowers. Each thimble-shaped flower head is surrounded by decorative, needle-like spines.

E. bourgatii (60 × 50 cm) is native to the Pyrenees. It bears sturdy stems of medium-sized flowers of a good strong blue. Each flower head is surrounded by a spiky collar.

E. eburneum (1 m × 60 cm), from South America, has spiky, strap-shaped leaves. The globular flower heads are silvery-white and lack the decorative ruff seen in European species. They are elegantly presented like silver candles on a candelabra-like flower stem.

Eryngium bourgatii.

E. ovinum (50 × 50 cm) is the Australian native 'blue devil' which grows wild in our increasingly threatened native grasslands. It forms masses of metallic blue, thimble-shaped flowers on metallic blue stems in summer. The flowers are so abundant that they completely engulf the foliage.

E. × *tripartitum* (50 × 50 cm), a garden hybrid, bears small silver-blue flowers in abundant heads.

E. × *zabelii* (60 × 60 cm) is a garden hybrid of *E. alpinum* and *E. bourgatii*. Above a celery-green foliage rosette rise umbels of metallic-blue flowers on stiff blue stems. The cones of tiny flowers are surrounded by large lacy ruffs. 'Blue Hills' is a fine Australian selection.

Drought rating: tough

Francoa ramosa – bridal wreath
Origin
Francoa ramosa (syn. *F. sonchifolia*) is an evergreen perennial from Chile, growing in rocky places and shady forest.

Season of interest
Bridal wreath has attractive foliage which looks good for most of the year. Its main attraction is its flowers which appear in late summer and autumn.

Garden uses
Bridal wreath is a great ground cover for under trees. Although it is quite tough it has a soft, woodlandy feel about it. This is a cheery, giving plant which is inexplicably rare in Australian gardens.

Francoa ramosa.

Cultivation
Francoa is good in all but very hot and humid climates. It prefers a leafy soil in part to full shade, so it is perfect under deciduous or evergreen trees. In good, leafy soil it is quite tough once established. Francoa copes well with root competition from trees. Its foliage can look a bit tired by late winter, when it benefits from being cut back to 5 cm above the ground.

Varieties
F. ramosa (70 × 70 cm) bears dozens of small white flowers on long, wand-like stems, opening successively over an extended season. There is also a rarer, pink-flowered variety.

Drought rating: tough

Gaillardia – the blanket flowers

Origin
Gaillardias are native to North America, where they grow in a wide variety of habitats including dry, rocky places.

Season of interest
Gaillardias look good when they are in flower from late spring to late autumn, sometimes even into early winter.

Garden uses
These are wonderful plants for introducing bold, bright colours into the summer flower garden. Many drought-tolerant, summer-flowering perennials have very small flowers so the gaillardias' big, daisy-like flowers are a welcome contrast. Although not yet well known in Australia, these are plants which deserve to be in every garden.

Cultivation
Gaillardias like full sun or very light shade in a well-drained soil. They will grow on any soil type but they do appreciate the addition of some well-rotted organic matter. Too much water and nitrogen in the summer makes gaillardias floppy so don't be too generous with them. Removing deadheads during the summer will prolong the flowering season and cutting them back to 10 cm tall in winter will freshen them up for the following year. Occasionally a plant will flower itself to death and disappear completely but there will usually be one or two new volunteers either from seeds or roots which remain behind.

Varieties
There are several named varieties, all of them fairly similar at 50 × 60 cm in size with 7.5 cm wide daisy-like flowers in egg yolk-yellow, dark blood-red, or a combination of the two. Varieties derived from *G. aristata* such as 'Burgunder' (red) and 'Heronswood Select' (yellow with a red central band) are perennial while those derived from *G. pulchella* such as 'Lorenziana' are annual. *G.* 'Burgunder' is often incorrectly sold as 'Burgundy' in Australia.

Drought rating: very tough

Gaura

Origin
Gaura grows wild in Texas and Mexico.

Season of interest
Gaura flowers from late spring to late autumn.

Garden uses
A good plant for dry banks or mixing with grasses, shrubs and perennials.

Gaillardia 'Burgunder'.

Gaura 'White form'.

Gaura 'Siskiyou Pink'.

Cultivation

Gauras grow in any climate south of the tropics. They need a well-drained, preferably poor soil in full sun or part shade. In very rich soils they tend to flop. *Gaura lindheimeri* is included in the noxious weed list and is prohibited in Western Australia. Its smaller relation *G. parviflora* is restricted in NSW and prohibited in WA. Be vigilant for it self-seeding too vigorously in your area.

Varieties

G. lindheimeri 'Whirling Butterflies' (1 m × 60 cm) and 'Summer Breeze' (1.2 m × 60 cm) have white flowers opening from pink buds.

G. 'Pearly Pink' (60 cm × 40 cm) is a smaller form with pale pink flowers and red-tinged stems and leaves.

G. 'Siskiyou Pink' (80 × 60 cm) has dark pink flowers and red-tinged stems.

There is also an icy white form of gaura with no pink pigment whatsoever.

Drought rating: very tough to super tough

Geranium – cranesbills

Origin

These are the true geraniums, not the plants Australians call 'geraniums', which are actually pelargoniums. Geraniums are widespread in temperate climates around the world, including Australia. They are found in many different environments, including some quite dry ones.

Season of interest

Geraniums flower in spring and summer. Some species have decorative foliage which extends the season of interest.

Garden uses

Most geraniums are good plants for using as ground covers around shrubs such as roses.

Geranium maderense produces huge heads of pink, or rarely white, flowers.

G. maderense is the exception which, because of its imposing scale, makes a stunning feature plant for shady gardens.

Cultivation

Geraniums like well-drained, well-composted soils. They flourish in full sun or light shade in most climates except humid tropical areas. They benefit from being cut back by half in winter. *G. maderense* is the exception to these rules. It is a forest plant and prefers shade. It is particularly good in coastal gardens where it enjoys the extra humidity and frost-free conditions. It must not be cut back as it is a monocarpic plant – it flowers once then dies.

Varieties

G. incanum (30 × 60 cm) is a ground cover from South Africa. It forms a dense mat of ferny, mid-green leaves with a long succession of magenta-purple flowers 2.5 cm across. A beautiful, soft plant not well enough known in Australia.

G. traversii (10 × 60 cm) is a ground cover from New Zealand's Chatham Islands. It has pale pink flowers 1.5 cm wide over leaves shaped a bit like vine leaves. A beautiful bronze-leaved form called 'Seaspray' is more commonly available.

G. maderense (1.2 × 1.2 m) is a spectacular monocarpic plant from the island of Madeira. In its first year it forms a sculptural dome of large, dissected, glossy green leaves on brown stalks which buttress the plant (its root system is pretty feeble). In this state the plant is quite beautiful enough but in its second or third year the foliage is overtopped with an enormous, fuzzy brown inflorescence which looks like a wig sitting on top of the plant. From the wig emerges a succession of mallow pink, round flowers 3 cm across over many weeks – a magnificent sight. After flowering the plant dies but a few seedlings usually appear here and there and can be transplanted when 5–10 cm high. There is a beautiful but very rare white form of *G. maderense* occasionally available.

Drought rating: very tough

Gladiolus
Origin
Gladiolus are deciduous bulbs mostly from South Africa, with a few from elsewhere in Africa and the Mediterranean basin.

Gladiolus tristis.

Gladiolus × colvillei.

Season of interest

Gladiolus are spring or summer flowering.

Garden uses

The highly bred Dame Edna Everage-type gladiolus are difficult to mix with other plants as they scream for attention and refuse to be team players. On the other hand the delicate wild gladiolus are wonderful garden plants. They can be planted under perennials to pop up and flower from among the clumps.

Cultivation

Gladiolus grow in any soil type in full sun. Heavy, wet soils don't bother them and neither do free-draining sands. They are suited to Mediterranean and subtropical climates.

Varieties

G. communis subsp. *byzantinus* (80 cm) is a species from the Mediterranean basin. It has bright magenta flowers.

G. × colvillei (50 cm) is a hybrid of *G. tristis* and *G. cardinalis*. It shows some variability with flowers in shades of white, salmon pink and red with distinctive markings on the petals. 'The Bride' is pure white.

G. tristis (one metre) is commonly called the marsh Afrikaner. It has fine, wand-like stems with a succession of cream flowers pencilled with grey veins. At night it develops a heavy, sweet scent like sweet peas or clove pinks.

Drought rating: very tough

Helianthemum

Origin

Helianthemums are the smaller cousins of the *Cistus*. They are sub-shrubs or woody-based perennials native to the Americas, Asia and especially the Mediterranean basin, where they grow in very dry, rocky places.

Season of interest

Helianthemums peak in late spring and summer, when the little bushes are completely engulfed in bright flowers.

Garden uses

Helianthemums are great edging around hot, dry paved areas (which approximates their

Helianthemums are miniature versions of *Cistus*. They come in a range of bright sunset colours.

Varieties

Most garden helianthemums are hybrids of *H. nummularium* and *H. apenninum*, forming miniature sub-shrubs 30 × 40 cm with masses of flowers 2.5 cm across. They are cheery little plants, sadly not widely grown in Australia, where they are usually sold simply by colour. They come in white, pinks, oranges, yellows and reds, and especially in electric sunset shades.

Drought rating: very tough

Limonium – sea lavender

Origin

A genus of woody-based perennials, mostly from the Mediterranean basin to central Asia.

Season of interest

Limoniums flower in spring, summer and autumn.

Garden uses

Limoniums are great plants for exposed sites, especially seaside gardens. They blend well with grasses and succulents and hummocky, coastal shrubs like curry bush. They are excellent for stabilising sandy banks.

natural habitat quite well). They can be used as ground covers in mixed plantings with other low, hummocky plants and grasses.

Cultivation

Helianthemums are plants of harsh, exposed positions in dry summer climates. They like full sun, plenty of airflow and perfect drainage. In such positions they are extremely tough. In close, humid conditions with overly moist soil, or when hemmed in too closely by other plants they tend to languish. They can be short lived even in positions where they are happy so every five years or so raise some cuttings to replace old plants.

Cultivation

Limoniums are suitable for the southern half of the continent. They don't like wet, humid summers. Limoniums need perfect drainage, ideally sandy or loamy soils. They need an open position in full sun. They don't like being hemmed in by other plants. *L. perezii* can be short lived – be prepared to replace it every couple of years.

Limonium peregrinum.

Liriope spicata.

Varieties

L. peregrinum (50 cm × 1 m) is a sprawling ground cover with many recumbent, woody stems growing slowly outwards from a central crown. The 6 cm leaves are matte apple green. The candy-pink, star-shaped, papery flowers appear on wiry, upright stems. This plant loves alkaline soils and performs very well by the sea.

L. perezii (60 × 50 cm) is more upright and bun-shaped than its cousin. It has larger, darker leaves and its papery flowers are lavender blue and white.

Drought rating: very tough

Liriope – lilyturf

Origin

Liriopes come from forests and shady scrub in China and Japan.

Season of interest

Lilyturf is evergreen and looks attractive throughout the year, with the autumn flowers a bonus at a time when not much else is in flower.

Garden uses

Liriope is a great ground cover for dry shade. Although it looks grassy, it actually has thick, succulent roots allowing it to compete well with the roots of trees.

Cultivation

Best suited to Mediterranean and subtropical climates, liriopes need a position in dappled shade to full shade in any soil type. They appreciate the addition of organic matter to the soil at planting and are more drought tolerant the more humusy the soil is.

Varieties

L. muscari (30 × 40 cm) has dark, glossy, grassy leaves and purple, grape-hyacinth-like flowers in autumn. A variegated variety is available.

L. spicata (30 cm × indefinite spread) looks similar to *L. muscari* but is finer in leaf and paler in flower. It spreads quickly to form a dense ground cover.

Drought rating: very tough

Narcissus – daffodils and jonquils
Origin
While we tend to associate daffodils with England and Holland, the overwhelming majority of narcissus species come from the Mediterranean basin – southern Europe, north Africa and the Middle East. The difference between a 'daffodil' and a 'jonquil' is a fairly blurry distinction.

Season of interest
Different varieties of narcissus flower from late autumn through until early summer, with early to mid spring being the peak season. They are completely dormant during the hottest part of the year.

Garden uses
The best use for narcissus is naturalised under deciduous trees, shrubs and perennials. Used in this way they receive light during their winter growth season.

Cultivation
Narcissus thrive in climates with frosty winters and dry summers – anywhere in

Narcissus bulbocodium.

inland or southern coastal Australia suits them. Sadly they do not perform well in climates with humid summers and mild winters like coastal NSW and Queensland. In mild coastal areas the multi-flowered jonquils (more correctly called 'tazetta' daffodils) tend to do better than classic single-flowered daffodils. Daffodils are planted as dormant bulbs during summer, most often by mail order. Resist the temptation to buy one of every variety listed in a bulb catalogue. For the passionate gardener this is easier said than done, of course, but it is better to buy large quantities of a single variety. Large drifts of a single variety, or small clumps of a single variety dotted throughout the garden look much classier than a mishmash of every possible colour and form. If you want to grow several different varieties, try to select ones which flower at different times so that the flowering season is extended.

All narcissus require full sun and moisture during their growth period but a dry rest period during summer. Narcissus are adapted to poor soils so their nutritional needs are modest. A little extra potassium can help

Paperwhites perform well in mild, coastal areas.

Narcissus cantabricus **subsp.** *foliosus*.

enhance flowering but excessive nitrogen encourages lots of floppy, leafy growth at the expense of flowers. When daffodils fail to flower year after year it is often the result of too much nitrogen, too little sunlight during the growing period or not enough winter chilling to initiate flowering.

Varieties

There are literally thousands of varieties of daffodils and jonquils to choose from. Many of the spectacular, large-flowered forms (such as the ever-popular King Alfred daffodil) have been bred as cut flowers for display in vases. They do not perform so well in a naturalised garden setting where their heavy, long-stemmed flowers tend to face-plant in the mud at the first sign of squally weather. The more modest, smaller-flowered forms of daffodils and jonquils are a better prospect for naturalising as they tend to be sturdier and look less fussy when planted *en masse*. Some good garden performers are 'Jetfire', 'Tête-à-tête' and 'Thalia'. Most of the exquisitely fragrant tazetta group of daffodils – those which Australians incorrectly refer to

as 'jonquils' – are excellent, including 'Geranium', 'Matador', 'Silver Chimes' and best of all the common 'jonquil' *N. tazetta italicus*. Paperwhites (*N. papyrifera*) perform well in milder areas, flowering as early as late autumn in some places. The golden hoop petticoat daffodil (*N. bulbocodium*) takes a couple of years to settle down and start flowering but mature clumps are magnificent. The pale yellow hoop petticoat *N. cantabricus* and its cream subspecies *N.c.* subsp. *foliosus* flower as early as late autumn. The pheasant's eye daffodil, *N. poeticus*, and its varieties flower in late spring after all other narcissus varieties have finished. They have white petals with a tiny, red-edged cup and are beautifully fragrant.

Drought rating: very tough

Nepeta – catmints
Origin
Nepeta is a large genus of perennials of the mint family. It includes the fabled catnip, *N. cataria*, a plant many people have heard of but few have actually seen. Many catmints come from hot dry, rocky slopes and dry grassland from southern Europe to central Asia, so are very tough and drought tolerant.

Season of interest
Catmints flower from mid-spring through until early autumn.

Garden uses
Catmints are extremely versatile. They are classic perennials for underplanting roses or flowering shrubs. They work well with other perennials and grasses in a flower border and

Nepeta 'Walker's Low' makes an excellent, long-flowering edging plant for paths and driveways.

they can be used as a ground cover. They look beautiful when used to edge paths and driveways but don't plant them too close to the edge as they tend to relax and invade the pathway as the flowering season progresses. Catmints can be used anywhere you would use lavender. In many ways they are superior to lavenders as their flowering season is so much longer (six months, as opposed to English lavender's one month).

Cultivation

Nepetas need full sun. They are tolerant of poor soils but abundantly repay any extra soil preparation and mulching you can give them. Nepetas can be cut back by two-thirds to tidy them up after their main flush of flowers is over in mid-summer. This will usually induce them to flower a second time. They need to be cut back hard in winter.

Varieties

Most garden catmints are derived from *Nepeta × faassenii*, *N. racemosa* and *N. grandiflora*. 'Six Hills Giant', 'Dropmore'

and 'Walker's Low' are very similar to one another, with mauve-blue flowers on long stems, growing to around 60 × 80 cm (slightly larger for 'Six Hills Giant'). 'Walker's Low' is the pick of the bunch as it is the most compact and self-supporting and it flowers over a very long period. 'Dawn to Dusk' has pale, dusky pink flowers and grows to 40 × 60 cm. 'Snowflake' (30 × 30 cm) has white flowers and is perhaps not as tough as mauve-flowered forms. Like all members of the mint family catmints have strongly scented foliage. There is a very small variety (20 × 20 cm) with grey, lemon-scented foliage and bright mauve flowers in Australia. It is usually labelled *N. cataria* 'Citriodora' but it does not resemble the upright, large-leaved *N. cataria* at all and is more likely a form of *N. × faassenii*.

Drought rating: very tough

Nerine

Origin

Nerines are native to South Africa in both winter- and summer-rainfall areas. Most garden varieties of nerine are derived from species from winter rainfall areas.

Season of interest

Different varieties of nerine flower from late summer through until late winter. They are dormant in summer.

Garden uses

Nerines are very useful because their flowers appear at a time when not much is happening in the garden. Although rarely seen used in such a way, nerines work beautifully when

Nerine sarniensis has given rise to many brightly coloured hybrids.

naturalised in large drifts, like daffodils, or planted in small groups under perennials and around the bases of shrubs in mixed plantings. They look great planted along the foot of a brick wall or other structure, or lining a path or driveway. Although their beauty is relatively fleeting, it is nevertheless spectacular and something to be looked forward to each year.

Nerine 'Rosea'.

Cultivation

Nerines require a spot which receives full sun during their growing season, in well-drained soil. Other than that there is not much else they need. Nerines are best transplanted in summer when they are dormant. Like many bulbs in the Amaryllis family they prefer to be planted with their necks poking above the soil. If in doubt plant them too shallow – the bulbs can pull themselves down to their preferred depth using special contractile roots. Also like other members of their family they resent being moved and take a couple of years to resume flowering after being transplanted. However, once they do, they get better and better each year, and in fact the best-flowering clumps are the most crowded and neglected ones.

Varieties

There are many hybrids and cultivars available, each growing to around 50 cm in height. They are mostly derived from the late summer flowering *N. sarniensis* which has orange-scarlet, gold-dusted flowers and the later flowering *N. bowdenii* which has ruffled, mallow pink flowers, white in *N. bowdenii* f. *alba*. 'Afterglow' has bright red flowers. 'Kenilworth' is an exquisite salmon-peach. 'Fothergillii Major' has large heads of orange-scarlet, gold-dusted flowers flowers. 'Coconut Ice' is white with a pink stripe on each petal.

Nerine 'Kenilworth'.

'Coral Queen' has hot, coral-pink flowers. 'Salmon Belle' is salmon as its name suggests. Despite *its* name, however, 'Rosea' is lurid hot pink.

Drought rating: very tough

Ophiopogon – mondo grass

Origin

Ophiopogons are creeping evergreen perennials from forests and shady scrub in China and Japan.

Season of interest

All year.

Ophiopogon japonicus **makes an excellent soft ground cover in dry shade.**

Ophiopogon jaburan 'Vittatus' has cool, cream-striped foliage.

Garden uses

Mondo grasses are excellent edging plants or ground covers for dry shade. They are super tough, despite their soft look. They have thick, succulent roots and compete well with tree roots.

Cultivation

Mondo grasses grow in Mediterranean and subtropical climates. They need a position in dappled to full shade in any soil type. The more humus you can add to the soil, the more drought they can endure. They grow well with their roots tucked under paving, edging or buildings, too.

Varieties

O. jaburan (30–60 cm × indefinite spread) has strap-shaped, dark green leaves and white flowers borne on arching stems in late summer. 'Vittatus' has cream-variegated foliage.

O. japonicus (5–20 cm × indefinite spread) is poetically called 'dragon's whiskers' by the Japanese. It has fine, dark green, grassy leaves but its flowers are inconsequential. A very tasteful plant which has enjoyed immense popularity in recent years.

Drought rating: very tough

Origanum – ornamental oreganos
Origin
Origanum is a small genus of herbaceous perennials of the mint family. Most species are native to the Mediterranean region, growing on rocky hillsides and in dry grassland. Several origanums are very well known to Australians thanks to their role in pizza and spaghetti bolognese – the culinary herbs oregano (*O. vulgare*) and the two marjorams (*O. onites* and *O. majorana*).

Season of interest
Origanums flower from late spring until late autumn.

Origanum 'Santa Cruz'.

Garden uses
The ornamental oreganos are wonderful plants, sadly underutilised in Australian gardens. They are perfect for underplanting roses or other shrubs and work beautifully with other herbaceous perennials and grasses. The smaller species have large, hanging flower heads and look best cascading over walls or the edges of raised beds.

Cultivation
Origanums need full sun and well-drained soil but are not at all fussy as to soil type. A small amount of organic matter in the soil helps get them established but too rich a living makes them floppy so don't overfeed them. Many are native to limestone soils so the addition of some lime or dolomite helps them along. Origanums need to be cut back to the ground in winter. They can become woody and lose vigour after several years so dividing them occasionally helps to keep them fresh.

Varieties
The larger varieties of origanum are derived from *O. laevigata*, the smaller from

Origanum 'Burnside Beauty'.

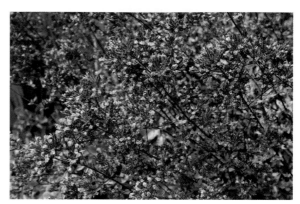

and wiry. This plant is a bit lax but looks good planted among grasses to hold it up and set off its flowers.

O. 'Kent Beauty' and 'Barbara Tingey' (10 × 20 cm) are very similar to one another. They have small, round leaves and relatively enormous flower heads which look like pearly pink hops. Tiny mauve-pink flowers emerge from the large bracts of the flower heads.

O. 'Santa Cruz' (30 × 40 cm) has airy flower heads which are a mass of wiry stems. Each stem ends in a cluster of pink bracts like a tiny ear of wheat. From these emerge the mauve pink flowers.

Origanum 'Kent Beauty' forms a mat of large, pink, hop-like bracts containing tiny, mauve flowers.

O. rotundifolium and *O. dictamnus*. The smaller origanums would have to be amongst the cutest xeriphytic perennials available to gardeners.

O. 'Burnside Beauty' (60 × 40 cm) is an excellent new Australian selection. It has rich pink flowers opening from burgundy buds atop thin burgundy stems. Every part of the plant is colour coordinated. It has a delicate, willowy habit but is not at all floppy.

O. 'Rosenkuppel' and 'Herrenhausen' (50 × 40 cm) are very similar to one another, with light pink flowers emerging from purple bracts, densely clothed in foliage.

O. 'Hopleys' (60 × 50 cm) has similar colourings but its flower heads are more open

Origanum 'Herrenhausen'.

Origanum 'Rosenkuppel'.

Pelargonium reniforme.

O. 'Buckland' (20 × 25 cm) has dusky pink, hop-like bracts with tubular, orchid pink flowers peeking out of them.

Drought rating: very tough

Pelargonium – 'geraniums'
Origin
Pelargonium is a genus of woody-based perennials and sub-shrubs mostly from South Africa.

Season of interest
Different pelargoniums flower throughout the year.

Pelargonium sidoides.

Garden uses
Pelargoniums are useful ground covers and filler shrubs. They are not star performers but make excellent support acts.

Cultivation
Best suited to subtropical and Mediterranean climates, pelargoniums want nothing more than a well-drained soil in full sun. They are best given a light haircut after flowering to keep them neat.

Varieties
P. graveolens (60 × 60 cm) is the scented geranium. Its leaves can be rose, lemon, mint, coconut or nutmeg-scented. It bears tiny pink flowers which hardly make any impact at all. A fairly unprepossessing little shrub, its beauty lies in the scent of its foliage and its indestructible temperament.

P. 'Dr Livingstone' (1.5 × 1 m) has very finely cut, almost ferny, bright green foliage.

P. sidoides (30 × 60 cm) is a stunning little plant which forms a mound of pewter, kidney-shaped leaves the size of a 10 cent piece, above which rise thin flower stalks bearing tiny flowers of the darkest, velvety red.

P. reniforme (30 × 60 cm) is similar to *P. sidoides* but bears hot pink flowers.

Drought rating: very tough to super tough

Perovskia – Russian sage
Origin
Neither Russian nor a sage, *Perovskia* is a small genus of woody-based perennials from Pakistan and Afghanistan. Like true *Salvias* they are members of the mint family.

Season of interest
Perovskias flower in summer but their flower bracts remain attractive into the autumn. Even after the plants shed their leaves in winter the stems stay bolt upright and ghostly white, looking particularly beautiful when rimed with frost.

Garden uses
This is a first-class, super-versatile plant which deserves to be in every inland and southern Australian garden. It combines very well with other perennials and grasses, roses, flowering shrubs or structural plants like agaves and yuccas. It can be used to line paths or driveways or anywhere you might traditionally use lavender. In many respects it is superior to lavender as it flowers over such a long period.

Cultivation
Perovskias will grow anywhere in full sun. They grow equally well in pure sand or pure clay (as long as it is not too wet over winter). They even tolerate salty soils. They are good

Russian sage is neither Russian nor sage! Photographs never do this gorgeous plant justice.

in exposed sites, including seaside gardens. Perovskias need to be cut back to a low framework of twigs in winter, 10–20 cm high, to keep them neat. Clipping them back by 10 cm in early summer before they flower helps to keep them compact and upright. This takes a fair bit of courage but it pays off later in the season.

Varieties
There are several cultivars of perovskia, all derived from *P. atriplicifolia* and *P. abrotanoides*. They vary from one another only subtly, all sharing lavender blue flowers and dainty silvery-grey foliage. Some varieties have quite ferny, cut leaves. 'Little Spire' (80 × 60 cm) is a compact, self-supporting form. 'Longin' (120 × 80 cm) is a tall but self-supporting form.

Drought rating: very tough to super tough

Plectranthus

Origin

Plectranthus are relatives of basil and coleus, native to Africa, Australia and South-East Asia.

Season of interest

Plectranthus are evergreen. Their flowers appear in summer or autumn. *P. ecklonii* flowers at a very useful time in late autumn when not much else is flowering in the garden.

Garden uses

Plectranthus make good ground covers or background shrubs for shade.

Cultivation

Plectranthus are easy to grow in any frost-free climate or in positions sheltered from frosts. They prefer partial to full shade and well-drained soil. In humid coastal areas they need no extra water but in inland areas they may require some summer irrigation. Plectranthus are very fast growing and great for filling gaps quickly. Propagation is as easy as sticking a cutting in the ground where you want a new plant to grow. Plectranthus can get leggy but pruning them back by two-thirds as growth commences in spring keeps them compact and tidy.

Varieties

P. argentatus (1 × 1 m) is native to the NSW–Queensland border. It is one of the best silver-leaved plants for dry shade. It has velvety silver leaves on purple stems and in summer bears thin wands of tiny lavender flowers.

P. ecklonii (2 × 2 m) is a fast growing sub-shrub from South Africa. It has mid-green foliage and large panicles of purple flowers in autumn. Pink and white varieties are also available.

Drought rating: very tough

Polygonatum – Solomon's seal

Origin

Solomon's seal is a genus of herbaceous perennials related to lily of the valley and aspidistra. They are native to woodlands of Europe, Asia and North America.

Season of interest

Solomon's seals are deciduous in winter. They are in leaf from early spring until autumn. Their tiny, hanging flowers appear in spring but they are really grown for their unusual nodding stems of satiny green foliage.

Garden uses

Solomon's seals are ground cover perennials for shaded areas. They are classic 'English' woodland garden plants so if you still yearn

Plectranthus argentatus.

Solomon's seal is surprisingly tough for an 'English woodland' plant.

for the English look in your garden, they are good plants to grow.

Cultivation

There are many species of Solomon's seal. Most of them need cool, moist conditions but a few species are much tougher than their 'woodlandy' appearance suggests. They grow anywhere which has at least a reasonably cool winter in partial to full shade. They prefer milder summers so they are better in coastal and mountain areas than in hot inland areas. In areas with very hot, dry summers, they tend to enter dormancy very early which defeats the purpose of growing them. Solomon's seals need leafy soil enriched with plenty of organic matter and autumn leaves. Under such conditions they are amazingly tough and low maintenance, needing only to be cut back in winter.

Varieties

P. × hybridum (often wrongly labelled *P. multiflorum*) is a robust plant growing to 1 m and spreading slowly to form large colonies. It has classic dull green foliage on arching stems and tiny, cream flowers. This is a very elegant plant.

P. odoratum 'Variegatum' (40 cm × 50 cm) has purple stems and leaves edged delicately in cream. A very subtle and beautiful plant.

If you like Solomon's seals you might also try the unrelated, but similar looking, Fairy Bells (*Disporum*) from Asia and North America. *D. smithii* from the west coast of North America is quite tough and *D. cantoniense* is remarkably tough considering its east Asian origins.

Drought rating: tough

Salvia – the sages
Origin

There are 900 species of *Salvia* from around the world (with just one species native to Australia). Salvias come from an enormous variety of habitat types including different kinds of dry climate. This is good news for gardeners as salvias are generally very colourful and generous plants in the garden. In addition to the 900 wild species there are hundreds more hybrid varieties of salvia. There are so many it is hard to know where to start.

Season of interest

You can easily have a salvia in flower in your garden on every single day of the year. The majority of species flower in summer and autumn, however. Many salvias are rather sloppy plants, somewhat lacking in form but this can be forgiven in light of their extreme generosity in the flower department. There

Salvia azurea.

are a few species which are statuesque enough to be grown for their form alone.

Garden uses

Salvias are great for introducing seasonal colour into the garden. The shrubby species

Salvia officinalis 'Berggarten'.

are useful gap fillers as they grow so quickly from a small cutting. The herbaceous species are magnificent in herbaceous or mixed borders, giving solid colour for weeks on end. The smaller shrubby species like *S. greggii* and *S. microphylla* make nice softeners when planted around big structural plants like agaves.

Cultivation

Most garden salvias seem to like similar garden conditions: a well-drained soil in full sun. However, their climatic requirements vary somewhat. The herbaceous species

Salvia chamaedryoides.

Salvia × sylvestris 'Blauhügel'.

Salvia × superba 'Superba'.

Salvia africana-lutea.

derived from *S. nemorosa* need a cold winter to give of their best. They are best suited to the inland and southern coastal areas. The subtropical shrubby species are only borderline frost tolerant and do better in frost-free conditions, especially in subtropical areas. The smaller shrubby species derived from *S. greggii* and *S. microphylla* seem to be happy just about anywhere. They are best cut

back *during their growing season* in spring and summer. Herbaceous salvias are best cut back to the ground in winter, shrubby species to a low framework of twigs 10 cm tall in early spring. Many salvias are short lived so have a few cuttings on hand as replacements.

Varieties

S. azurea (1.2 m × 60 cm), the so-called pitcher sage, is an herbaceous perennial from dry prairies and rocky, limestone areas in the southern and eastern USA. It has thin, willowy stems bearing a succession of sky-blue, large-lipped flowers in late summer and autumn.

Salvia nemorosa subsp. *tesquicola.*

Salvia leucantha.

Salvia nemorosa 'Ostfriesland'.

A truly wonderful plant which thrives on neglect; too much good living is guaranteed to make it floppy. **Drought rating: very tough**

S. chamaedryoides (50 × 80 cm) is a shrubby perennial from high altitude desert in Mexico. It has tiny silver leaves topped with thin racemes of bright ultramarine flowers from spring to autumn in flushes. When a flush has finished, give the plant a light haircut with hedge clippers to keep it tidy. **Drought rating: very tough**

S. greggii (50 × 60 cm) is a twiggy, shrubby perennial from deserts in Texas and Mexico.

Salvia microphylla comes in a range of colours.

The wild form has large-lipped red flowers (typical of hummingbird-pollinated desert plants) but there are many different coloured selections. 'Alba' is white. 'Bicolor' is soft pink and cream, 'Raspberry Royal' bright pink-red. *S. greggii* prefers sandy, or at least very well-drained, soils and tends to be short lived. Clipping it back by half after flowering helps keep it neat. **Drought rating: very tough**

S. canariensis (1.5 × 1.5 m) comes from the Canary Islands, as its name suggests. It forms a stout shrub with square stems covered in woolly, white hairs and large, arrowhead-shaped leaves which are sage green on top and white-woolly beneath. In early summer it bears masses of lavender-pink flowers from

Salvia canariensis.

Salvia greggii 'Bicolor'.

Salvia 'Anthony Parker'.

ruby-purple bracts which remain beautiful after the flowers have finished. This is a great plant for sandy soils and seaside positions but sadly it is not very frost hardy. **Drought rating: very tough**

S. africana-lutea (syn. *S. aurea*) (1.5 × 1.5 m) is a neat, bun-shaped shrub from coastal sand dunes in South Africa. It has small, sage-green leaves and large (for a salvia), copper-orange flowers which emerge from very large copper-brown bracts in spring and summer. This is a very useful plant for seaside gardens but also grows well in inland gardens in any soil type. It is very fast growing and a great plant for plugging gaps in the garden. **Drought rating: very tough to super tough**

S. guaranitica (syn. *S. ambigens*) (1.5 × 1.5 m) is a tall, upright perennial with azure flowers over apple-green foliage. 'Argentine Skies' is a form with sky blue flowers. 'Black and Blue' has black calyces. This is one subtropical salvia that does well in frosty areas due to its tuberous root system. On the downside it can be invasive. **Drought rating: very tough**

S. leucantha (1 × 1 m), commonly called Mexican bush sage, has long, dark green leaves

and white, felted stems. From summer until the end of autumn it produces white flowers from downy, lavender calyces. A very giving, reliable plant but sadly it is not very frost hardy. Pink and white varieties are available occasionally. **Drought rating: very tough**

S. microphylla (1 × 1 m) is very similar to *S. greggii* in habit and flowers. 'Iced Lemon' has pale yellow flowers. 'Sensation' has peachy-salmon flowers which contrast with the brown calyces. **Drought rating: very tough**

S. officinalis (60 × 60 cm) is the original herb sage from the dry maquis scrub of the Mediterranean. It forms a small shrub with, unsurprisingly, sage-green foliage and pretty pale purple flowers briefly in spring. 'Berggarten' (50 × 60 cm) is an excellent selection with very large, rounded leaves. You can use it just as you would normal sage in the kitchen. There are varieties with purple and variegated foliage commonly available but they are very prone to disfiguring powdery mildew and are not recommended. **Drought rating: very tough**

S. nemorosa (1 m × 60 cm) is native to dry grasslands and rocky slopes from central

Salvia 'Waverly'.

Salvia guaranitica.

Europe to central Asia. It is a rather gaunt perennial with pale lilac or pink flowers with purple bracts borne on long racemes in early summer. From a garden point of view this species is better represented by the subspecies *S. nemorosa* subsp. *tesquicola* (80 × 80 cm), which is more compact, more intensely coloured with bright purple bracts and blue flowers, and much longer flowering. 'Ostfriesland' (also known as 'East Friesland') (40 × 60 cm) is a very compact selection with intense lavender flowers and very dark purple bracts. 'Kate Glenn' (80 × 60 cm) is a new Australian selection with deep violet flowers. **Drought rating: tough**

S. × *sylvestris* is a hybrid of *S. nemorosa* and *S. pratensis*. *S. sylvestris* has also been back-crossed with *S. nemorosa* to form the hybrid *S.* × *superba*. These two hybrids have given rise to some of the best herbaceous perennial salvias. Varieties of *S.* × *sylvestris* and *S.* × *superba* include 'Superba' (90 × 60 cm) which is very intensely coloured with glowing blue flowers and royal purple bracts, 'Blauhügel' (also known as 'Blue Hills') (30 × 30 cm) which is probably the bluest of all the group with matching cornflower-blue flowers and bracts, 'Mainacht' (80 × 60 cm) has dark indigo-violet flowers, 'Lambley Dumble' (60 × 50 cm), is a new Australian selection with small, dark violet flowers on black stems. **Drought rating: tough**

S. 'Anthony Parker' (1.5 × 1.5 m) is a hybrid of *S. leucantha*. It forms a very neat shrub with inky blue flowers borne on self-coloured stems in autumn. An excellent new variety but sadly not especially frost tolerant. **Drought rating: very tough**

S. 'Waverly' (1.8 × 1.8 m) is a shrubby hybrid variety with pinky-white flowers emerging from fluffy purple calyces. Very long flowering and reliable for frost-free climates. Less so in frosty areas. **Drought rating: very tough**

Sedum – stonecrops or ice plants
Origin

Sedums are a genus of succulents of the Crassulaceae family from the northern hemisphere. Two kinds of sedums are grown – evergreen varieties which are treated like

True sedums grow wild in rocky places.

Sedum 'Autumn Joy'.

other succulents and deciduous varieties which are treated as herbaceous perennials, strictly speaking, members of the genus *Hylotelephium*. The succulent sedums are mostly too small and dainty to be of much use in the garden but the herbaceous species are large and robust and make excellent garden plants.

Season of interest

Herbaceous sedums flower in late summer and autumn, looking good all year round thanks to their neat, succulent foliage. Even when the flowers have died and the leaves have fallen their dry stems remain upright and decorative. The flowering season proper is very short – just a few days – but the flower heads remain highly coloured for months, just as if they were still in flower.

Garden uses

These are top-class perennials for planting in large swathes or in mixed borders with shrubs and grasses. Honeybees and especially native bees love sedums. They swarm all over their fragrant flowers during the short flowering season, sometimes in such numbers that their humming is audible from a distance away.

Sedum 'Matrona'.

Sedum stems look good even in death, lending structure to the winter garden.

Sedum 'Purple Emperor'.

Cultivation

Herbaceous sedums like a climate with a cool to cold winter. They languish in areas with warm winters. They need a well-drained but water-retentive soil in full sun. They do not perform well in shade and in overly fertile soil they flop.

Varieties

The herbaceous sedums are derived from *Hylotelephium telephium* and *H. spectabile* from Europe and Asia. The hylotelephiums are still placed in the genus *Sedum* by some authors and are still commonly referred to as 'sedums' by gardeners, but be prepared for a name change soon.

S. 'Autumn Joy' (syn. 'Herbstfreude') (1 m × 80 cm) is probably the best of all the

Sedum 'Vera Jameson'.

sedums. It is extremely neat and self-supporting, long flowering and its stems stay bolt upright over winter. It has pale pink flowers which quickly fade to dusty pink, over sage-green leaves.

S. 'Matrona' (1.2 × 1 m) has ice-pink flowers and sage-green leaves on purple stems. It fades to a chestnut-brown colour.

S. 'Vera Jameson' (20 × 40 cm) has purple leaves and stems with a plum-like bloom. Its flowers are dusty pink.

S. 'Bertram Anderson' (10 × 20 cm) is a pint-sized version of 'Vera Jameson', excellent for planting on retaining walls.

S. 'Purple Emperor' (80 × 60 cm) has dark wine-purple leaves and stems and dusty pink flowers.

Drought rating: very tough

Stipa gigantea – golden oat grass
Origin
Native to rocky slopes in Spain, Portugal and Morocco.

Season of interest

Golden oat grass looks its best from mid-spring to mid-autumn.

Garden uses

A magnificent grass to use in mixed plantings with shrubs, succulents and perennials. It gives incredible atmosphere to the garden as its airy, golden awns glimmer in the sunshine for months.

Cultivation

This plant likes climates with dry summers and cold winters – inland and southern parts of the country. It needs a very well-drained soil in full sun. The foliage tussocks die from the inside out after a few years and the plants benefit from being divided and replanted every four or five years. However, losses of new divisions are high so keep a few extras as an insurance policy. Although very easy to cultivate, *Stipa gigantea* is difficult to propagate as it sets very few viable seeds and resents division. This is why it is so rare in the nursery trade despite being such a fantastic garden plant.

Varieties

'Beth Chatto form' has recently become available. It is only slightly different to the more readily available wild species, with slightly wider leaf blades and larger flower heads. Both have tussocks 60 × 90 cm with flower heads growing to 1.8 m in height.

Drought rating: very tough to super tough

Verbena – vervains

Origin

A genus of herbaceous or woody-based perennials mostly from the Americas, with a few represented in Europe.

Season of interest

Verbenas flower in summer and autumn.

Garden uses

Verbenas are wonderful in perennial and mixed borders. They blend particularly well with grasses and look wonderful with old roses.

Cultivation

Verbenas are suited to Mediterranean and subtropical climate regions. They will grow in any soil in full sun or part shade. They

Stipa gigantea is one of the most atmospheric of all garden plants, here forming a golden haze behind *Lilium* 'Black Beauty'.

Verbena bonariensis.

should be cut back to near ground level after flowering.

Varieties

V. bonariensis (2 m × 50 cm) from Brazil and Argentina is commonly called purpletop. It is

Verbena rigida 'Polaris'.

a very beautiful ornamental plant. In wet summer areas it self-seeds vigorously and has become a weed of concern. In dry summer areas it is quite well behaved. It forms a very open, upright plant with a framework of thin, square stems topped with little blobs of purple flowers. Although tall it is completely transparent and may be planted in front of shorter plants which can then be viewed through it.

V. rigida (40 × 60 cm) is a suckering ground cover which produces masses of round heads of bright purple flowers. The variety 'Polaris' has flowers of palest silvery-lilac.

Drought rating: very tough

The top shelf – the crème de la crème of tough beauties for Mediterranean climates

Top perennials

Agastache 'Sweet Lili'

Anthemis 'Susanna Mitchell'

Calamagrostis 'Karl Foerster'

Gaillardia 'Burgunder'

Miscanthus transmorrisonensis

Nepeta 'Walker's Low'

Perovskia 'Little Spires'

Salvia azurea

Salvia nemorosa subsp. *tesquicola*

Sedum 'Autumn Joy'

Stipa gigantea

BULBS

A 'bulb' is an adaptation to surviving a tough season – either a hot, dry summer or a cold winter. Most bulbs are dependable garden plants in the right climate. Autumn, winter and spring flowering bulbs are mostly very tough (with a few exceptions) and summer flowering bulbs, from wet summer climates, can be surprisingly tough, too. Many lilies fall into this category.

Apart from the bulb genera mentioned individually, there are dozens of other less well-known genera worth growing. Some, like the foxtail lilies (*Eremurus*) and Madonna lilies (*Lilium candidum*) sound fiendishly difficult to grow in British gardening books, but that is only because they resent Britain's cool, wet summers. In dry inland parts of Australia they are no more difficult

than daffodils. All bulbs like a well-drained soil which is not too wet during their dormant season (be that winter or summer). As a rule, feeding

Iris reticulata 'Harmony'.

Moraea aristata.

Eremurus 'Romance'.

Cyrtanthus elatus.

Alstroemeria hybrid.

Crocus tommasinianus.

them too much nitrogen or planting them in too much shade is a recipe for lots of foliage and no flowers.

Bulbs for dry-summer climates

Acis autumnalis (syn. *Leucojum autumnale*)

Arum (true genus Arum, not Zantedeschia)

Asphodeline lutea

Brodiaea

Calochortus

Crocus

Cyrtanthus (syn. *Vallota*)

Eremurus

Erythronium

Freesia

Fritillaria

Galtonia

Gladiolus

Iris

Ixia

Scadoxus multiflorus subsp. *katherinae.*

Fritillaria meleagris.

Brodiaea elegans.

Lachenalia

Lilium (some species, such as *L. candidum,*
L. lancifolium and *L. regale,* and some
hybrids like *L.* 'Black Beauty' and the Aurelian
and Asiatic hybrids.)

Moraea

Muscari

Sparaxis

Spiloxene

Urginea

Zephyranthes

Crocus sativus.

Bulbs for wet-summer climates

Alstroemeria

Cyrtanthus

Eucomis

Gladiolus

Hippeastrum

Lachenalia

Scadoxus

Veltheimia

Zantedeschia

Zephyranthes

Brodiaea californica.

Fritillaria acmopetala.

Erythronium dens-canis.

Lachenalia aloides.

Muscari latifolium.

Fritillaria uva-vulpis.

Sparaxis hybrid.

Spiloxene capensis.

Ixia hybrid.

Lilium candidissimum.

Eucomis comosa Purple form.

Acis autumnalis.

Top shrubs

Cotinus 'Grace'

Echium 'Heronswood Blue'

Euphorbia rigida

Euphorbia × martinii

Lavatera 'Kew Rose'

Nerium oleander

Punica granatum

Rhaphiolepis cultivars

Rosa rugosa cultivars

Salvia africana-lutea

Top trees

Arbutus × andrachnoides

Brachychiton rupestris

Ceratonia siliqua

Lagerstroemia cultivars

Malus trilobata

Pistacia chinensis

Vitex agnus-castus

Top succulents

Aeonium 'Zwartkop'

Agave stricta

Beschorneria yuccoides

Hesperaloe parviflora

Yucca rostrata 'Sapphire Skies'

Plants for dry shade

Cyclamen hederifolium

Ruscus

Aspidistra elatior

Mahonia

Arthropodium cirratum

Helleborus foetidus

Francoa ramosa

Aucuba japonica

Fatsia japonica

Clivia

Hedera

Iris foetidissima, I. confusa and I. japonica

Rhaphiolepis

Pseudopanax

Anemanthele lessoniana

Epimedium 'Fröhnleiten'

Geranium maderense

Liriope

Ophiopogon

Plectranthus

Polygonatum

Trachelospermum

Plants for seaside gardens

Bupleurum fruticosum

Pittosporum tobira

Lavatera 'Kew Rose'

Cistus

Olea

Plumeria

Aeonium

Agave

Aloe

Alyogyne

Correa alba

Echium

Escallonia

Metrosideros

Myrtus

Nerium

Pseudopanax

Rhaphiolepis

Teucrium

Westringia

Salvia

Plants for the root zone of gum trees

Ceanothus

Cordyline

Correa

Dietes

Garrya

Hedera

Mahonia

Pittosporum

Rhaphiolepis

Pseudopanax

Ruscus

Agave

Yucca

Anemanthele lessoniana

Francoa ramosa

Liriope

Plectranthus

Plants for salty soils

Nerium

Pistacia

Perovskia

Artemisia

Tamarix

Brachychiton populneus

Cupressus arizonica

Olea

Vitex

Elaeagnus angustifolia

Eriogonum

Punica

Centranthus

FURTHER READING

There are dozens of wonderful books on dry gardening. This list is just the tip of the iceberg.

Blazey C (1996) *The Diggers Club Guide to Gardening Success*. Doubleday Books: Sydney.

Brenzel KN (Ed.) (2007) *Western Garden Book*. Sunset Publishing Corporation: Menlo Park, USA.

Burns JR (2008) *Australian Gardens for a Changing Climate*. Penguin Australia: Melbourne.

Chatto B (2000) *Beth Chatto's Gravel Garden*. Bloomings Books: Melbourne.

Cross R and Spencer R (2009) *Sustainable Gardens*. CSIRO Publishing: Melbourne.

Filippi O (2008) *The Dry Gardening Handbook*. Thames and Hudson: London.

Garner J (2007) *Dry Gardening Australia: Sustainable Drought-proof Gardening from the Soil Up*. Murdoch Books: Sydney.

Gildemeister H (1995) *Mediterranean Gardening: A Waterwise Approach*. Editorial Moll: Palma de Mallorca, Spain.

Handreck K (2001) *Gardening Down-under: A Guide to Healthier Soils and Plants*. Landlinks Press: Melbourne.

Handreck K (2008) *Good Gardens with Less Water*. CSIRO Publishing: Melbourne.

Irish M (2003) *Arizona Gardener's Guide*. Cool Springs Press: Nashville, USA.

Nankervis M (2009) *Plants for Australian Dry Gardens*. Murdoch Books: Sydney.

Nottle T (1996) *Gardens of the Sun*. Kangaroo Press: Sydney.

Nottle T (2004) *Plants for Mediterranean Climate Gardens*. Rosenberg Publishing: Sydney.

Parsons WT and Cuthbertson EG (2001) *Noxious Weeds of Australia*. CSIRO Publishing: Melbourne.

Peate N, MacDonald G and Talbot A (1997) *Grow What Where: Over 1000 Exotic and Australian Plants to Suit Every Garden Situation*. Lothian: Melbourne. [Author's note: later editions of this book have had all exotic plants expunged from their pages and now only contain Australian native plants. It is worth hunting down the excellent 1997 edition which is arguably much more useful to home gardeners.]

Taylor J (1998) *Plants for Dry Gardens: Beating the Drought*. Frances Lincoln: London.

Walsh K (2009) *Waterwise Gardening*. New Holland: Sydney.

INDEX